Walls

Also by Marcello Di Cintio

Harmattan: Wind Across West Africa

Poets and Pahlevans: A Journey Into the Heart of Iran

WALLS
Travels Along the Barricades

MARCELLO DI CINTIO

Edited by John Vigna.
Cover image: *El Muro* by Daniel Lobo, DaquellaManera.org
Cover and page design by Julie Scriver.
Printed in Canada.
10 9 8 7 6 5 4 3 2 1

Library and Archives Canada Cataloguing in Publication

Di Cintio, Marcello, 1973-
Walls: travels along the barricades / Marcello Di Cintio.

Issued also in electronic format.
ISBN 978-0-86492-663-0

1. Di Cintio, Marcello, 1973- —Travel. 2. Walls—Social aspects.
3. Barricades (Military Science)—Social aspects.
4. Human geography. I. Title.

NA493.D52 2012   355.4'4   C2012-902941-6

Goose Lane Editions acknowledges the generous support of the Canada Council for the Arts,
the Government of Canada through the Canada Book Fund (CBF), and the Government of
New Brunswick through the Department of Culture, Tourism, and Healthy Living.

Goose Lane Editions
500 Beaverbrook Court, Suite 330
Fredericton, New Brunswick
CANADA E3B 5X4
www.gooselane.com

MIX
Paper from
responsible sources
FSC® C016245
FSC
www.fsc.org

For Amedeo

Contents

9   **Introduction** The Wall Disease

16   **Drawing a Line in the Sand** The Western Sahara

52   **The Bogeyman is Coming** Ceuta and Melilla

73   **Zero People of No Man's Land** The Indo-Bangladesh Fence

100   **A Nakba of Olives** The West Bank Wall

130   **Walling Absurd** Nicosia/Lefkoşa

161   **Shun Thy Neighbour** The U.S.–Mexico Border

208   **The Mutilated City** Belfast

257   **The Great Wall of Montreal** The l'Acadie Fence

283   **Acknowledgements**

286   **Endnotes**

Introduction
The Wall Disease

The walk from Jerusalem to Bethlehem, on Christmas Eve, was less biblically epic than it sounds. Instead of a rocky path through shepherds' fields, the route followed paved sidewalks alongside a major highway. The entire "pilgrimage" took less than two hours. The air was cold — Jerusalem enjoyed a rare snowfall that winter — but visitors to Bethlehem felt more anxious than chilled. We were in the final week of 1999. Fears of millennial violence added a layer of tension to the Christmas festivities. In Bethlehem, television crews from around the world pushed microphones into the faces of tourists and asked why they didn't feel frightened. Palestinians spread the rumour that their leader, Yasser Arafat, refused to address the gathered crowd for fear of being assassinated. Nothing happened, of course, and looking back after more than a decade of intifada, war, terrorism, and economic collapse, one feels nostalgic for the phantom dangers of Y2K.

I recall little from the trek to Bethlehem aside from the noise of traffic and that I sniffed car exhaust instead of frankincense. I do remember, though, how the outskirts of Jerusalem and Bethlehem merged and blurred somewhere on Highway 60. I couldn't tell where one holy city ended and the other began.

When I returned to Jerusalem eight years later, a wall had erased any ambiguity between Here and There. High slabs of concrete now distinguished Bethlehem from Jerusalem. The actual existence of the Wall did not surprise me; the international media had derided the barrier ever since construction began in 2002. By the time I saw it, the West Bank Wall had already joined the Western Wall — Judaism's holiest site — and the ancient stone ramparts around the Old City to form the trinity of walls that travellers to Jerusalem visit and photograph. The Wall's impressive height, its concrete severity, and the clarity with which it drew its line astonished me. I was struck, too, by the huge banner hanging off the Israeli side, written in three languages and apparently without irony: PEACE BE WITH YOU.

Later that same trip, I visited Ramallah, another West Bank city edged by the Wall. It was a Friday during Ramadan. On the Ramallah side of the Wall, hundreds of Palestinians gathered to cross through the barrier for Friday prayers at Jerusalem's al-Aqsa Mosque. I'd read reports during the previous few days that soldiers with the IDF, the Israel Defense Forces, planned to forbid young men from passing through the Wall. Then I heard a rumour that men of any age would be barred — only women would be permitted into Jerusalem. Nobody knew exactly what would happen. As I passed the crowds, I noticed that the IDF had decided not to allow anyone at all through the checkpoint. Women and old men waited alongside the Wall, leaning against the cold concrete and hoping the IDF would change their mind again. I shared a taxi into central Ramallah with an aged Palestinian man. I couldn't understand his Arabic, but I knew what he meant when he shook his head and threw up his hands. He'd grown impatient at waiting to cross and decided to say his prayers at home. The man's return to his own house was his silent surrender to the Wall.

███

Human civilization has always been preoccupied with erecting walls. In the first century CE, the Roman emperor Hadrian built a 120-kilometre limestone wall across Roman Britain. Scholars still debate what Hadrian intended with his barrier. Some suggest he built the wall to exclude from his empire the savages he had failed to conquer, or to control trade and immigration. Others wonder if the Wall had any utility at all beyond a theatrical expression of imperial power — a spectacle. Plastered and whitewashed, the Wall would have shone for miles beneath the northern sun.

Hadrian's Wall continued to impress long after the plaster flaked off and the Roman Empire had given way to the British one. In 1754, English antiquarian William Stukely gushed that Hadrian's Wall was exceeded in its brick-and-mortar might only by the grand patriarch of human walls, the Great Wall of China. Stukely wrote, "[The] Chinese Wall makes a considerable figure upon the terrestrial globe, and may be discerned at the moon." One must admire the confidence of an eighteenth-century, earthbound scientist who describes the view from space. As it turns out, his claim was both bold and incorrect: the Great Wall of China cannot be seen from the moon. But the myth, like the Wall, endures.

So too does the impulse to build walls. In the 1800s, the Danish repurposed an ancient Viking Age wall as a military fortification in their war with the Prussians. In the 1870s, Argentina built a line of trenches and watchtowers called the Zanja de Alsina to protect Buenos Aires province from invasion by the indigenous Mapuche. At the beginning of World War II, France constructed a concrete barrier along its border with Germany to defend against a Nazi attack and called it the Maginot Line. The French fortified their line with artillery battlements, machine-gun installations, and anti-tank barricades, but it failed to impress Hitler's army, which simply marched around it. Later, East Germany built its own wall. The Berlin Wall went up in 1961, dividing East from West for almost thirty years.

Walls don't just divide us. They can make us ill. They can drive us mad. In 1973, East German psychiatrist Dietfried Müller-Hegemann observed that the Berlin Wall caused psychosis, schizophrenia, and phobias in the East Germans who lived in its shadow. They suffered rage, dejection, and alcoholism — and were more likely to kill themselves. The closer to the physical wall his patients lived, the more acute their disorders. Sometimes the emotional trauma expressed itself in the flesh; one of Müller-Hegemann's patients even suffered lockjaw. The doctor called the syndrome Mauerkrankheit — Wall Disease — and though he could not thoroughly research the syndrome for fear of prosecution by the East German authorities, Müller-Hegemann predicted that depression, despondency, and high suicide rates would persist in Berlin for as long as the Wall stood. The only cure for Wall Disease was to bring the Wall down. Sure enough, in 1990, another East German psychotherapist named Hans-Joachim Maaz described the "emotional liberation" felt on the November night the Wall finally fell. Thousands of jubilant Germans climbed the Wall, wept, and embraced each other atop the concrete, and proceeded to tear the Wall down with joyful abandon. "The wall's fall was the emotional climax of the unloading, the cathartic breaking-through of the unconscious," Maaz wrote. "The emotional blockage unclogged, the repressed came to the surface and the parts that had been split apart, united."[1]

The psychic pain inflicted by the Berlin Wall, and the humiliating failure of the Maginot Line years earlier, hardly dissuaded the world's wall builders. South Africa built a 120-kilometre electric fence, dubbed the Snake of Fire, along its border with Mozambique in 1975 to keep Mozambican civil war violence from spilling over the frontier. Until South Africa turned down the voltage in the 1990s, the Snake of Fire's 3,500-volt venom killed more people than the Berlin Wall ever did. Elephants have trampled down most of the fence since then, but the South African government is now considering re-erecting the barrier to keep Mozambican poachers from killing rhinos. The United States turned Baghdad into a labyrinth of vertical concrete and is currently building a wall along the Mexican frontier. India built fences along its borders with Pakistan and Bangladesh and through the disputed region of Kashmir. Walls separate North and South Korea and keep Zimbabweans out of Botswana. In addition to the barrier around the West Bank, Israel has nearly completed another wall along its Egyptian frontier to keep out potential terrorists and migrants from sub-Saharan Africa. Greece, though broke, is raising an expensive barrier along its border with Turkey. In spite of their fevered opposition to Israel's walls, nations of the Middle East are fortifying their own borders. Kuwait walls out Iraq. Saudi Arabia walls out Yemen. Iran walls out Pakistan.

Walls do not just rise on national borders. Italian officials in the city of Padua had grown weary of the drug trafficking, prostitution, and gang violence in Via Anelli, a run-down neighbourhood populated mainly by asylum seekers from Africa. In the middle of the night in August 2006, city contractors encircled Via Anelli with a steel wall three metres high. Padua relocated the residents to other parts of the city, then brought the wall down. In eastern Slovakia, a concrete wall rose in the village of Ostrovany on the edge of a Roma slum to keep "gypsies" from raiding their neighbours' vegetable gardens. Economic apartheid has replaced racial apartheid in Johannesburg, South Africa, where the wealthy, middle class, and poor alike enclose themselves within walled communities.

As news of these physical walls spread, they felt like a throwback to antiquity. Walls are supposed to be coming down. We speak of globalization, international markets, and global villages. Barriers to trade and travel keep falling, and we can communicate with anyone instantly from nearly anywhere in the world. Borders themselves seem to matter less and less. Our contemporary angels and demons — multinational corporations, climate change, global terror networks, Hollywood movies, bird flu, pollution, Katy Perry — are nationless and borderless and care nothing about the lines we draw on our maps and fortify with steel. And yet the walls continue to rise, parcelling the world into smaller, easily defensible cells that separate us from each other. Perhaps new walls are not anathema to our borderless world but the natural response to it. We are uncomfortable being so undefined. We need to put something, anything, under our control. So we counter economic and electronic entropy with simple geometries of bricks, barbed wire, and steel.

History has not been kind to the old walls. Almost all the historical walls inspired scorn and, when they failed, ridicule. Vancouver musician Geoff Berner sings bluntly about the Maginot Line:

> Maginot Line. Maginot Line.
> You thought you were so safe and strong.
> Maginot Line. Maginot Line.
> Stupid! Stupid! You were wrong.[2]

And no less a thinker than Dr. Seuss took on "the Wall." In *The Butter Battle Book*, Seuss's 1981 allegory of the Berlin Wall and the Cold War, an agent with the "Zook-Watching Border Patrol" brings his grandson to see the Wall on the "last day of summer, ten hours before fall." The Wall stands between the Yooks and the Zooks, and the grandfather explains the absurd necessity of the barrier to the boy:

> "It's high time that you knew
> of the terribly horrible thing that Zooks do.
> In every Zook house and in every Zook town
> *every Zook eats his bread*

with the butter side down
But we Yooks, as you know,
when we breakfast or sup,
spread our bread," Grandpa said,
"with the butter side *up*.
That's the right, honest way!"[3]

The very idea of a wall represents such negativity that their builders often reject the word *wall* altogether. The East German government prohibited East Berliners from using the term "Berlin Wall" and insisted they refer to the barrier as the "anti-fascist protection bulwark." (Wisely, Dr. Seuss did not try to rhyme this.) The new walls have inherited these semantics: only opponents of Israel's West Bank barrier and America's border fortifications call these structures *walls*. Supporters call them *fences*—a softer, kinder word. I decided early on to call all the barriers I would visit *walls*. Even when their physical structure more resembles a fence, the barriers still act as walls. They exclude and divide. The word *fence* suggests something built of white pickets where neighbours might lean over to exchange gossip and a cup of sugar, an image far too benign for the barriers I planned to see.

I understood why a nation might choose to erect a wall. Everyone can grasp ideas of political territory and national security and threats from outside. The Ming Dynasty feared the Mongols, the French feared the Nazis, and the Israelis fear terrorists from Palestine. East Germany wanted to keep their citizens inside, while America wants to keep undocumented Mexicans out. I wondered, though, about the individual souls who were forced into a strange intimacy with a wall. I could not comprehend being *personally* walled out. I come from Canada, a country bound only by oceans on three of its edges and the world's longest fenceless border on the fourth. We call this border undefended, and we mean it as a boast. My nationality grants me access anywhere. Nowhere in the world bars my entry. No place claims I am not wanted or not worthy. No one has ever built a wall for me.

What of those, like my Palestinian friend in Ramallah, who live alongside the new walls? What does the Wall mean for those in the borderlands between the United States and Mexico? Or India and Bangladesh? The Berlin Wall came down, but do the residents of divided Cyprus and Belfast suffer their own strains of Mauerkrankheit? I wondered what it meant to live a barricaded life. I wanted to discover what sort of societies created the walls. More than this, I wanted to know what societies the walls themselves created.

I suspected I would learn little from reading political pronouncements or staring at lines on a map. From a distance, the walls appear as territorial constructs, but for the people who live against them — those for whom the walls were built, to include or exclude — the walls stand as cold physical realities. I needed to be where the posts were pounded into the ground and where nations stake territory in bald concrete. I needed to be among those who butter their bread in the cool shadow of a wall. I wanted to understand why the walls exist, what they mean to those who live within them, and how they make us sick. So, in February 2008, because it seemed as good a place to start as any, I flew into the Sahara Desert.

Drawing a Line in the Sand
The Western Sahara

It was a time of no war and no peace. The ceasefire held, but cracks had started to show. The refugees were waiting, and though Malainin told me there was courage in patience, nearly forty years had already crawled by. More than a hundred thousand refugees had built a nation out of nothing on wretched, hard-packed sand. They were ready to cross over the Wall that separated them from home.

The "Wall of Shame" was built of sand and stone, but also of rumours, half-truths, and bluster. I had heard that Israelis designed the Wall and Americans provided the radar installations. I'd heard that the entire Moroccan army stood along its length and that the minefields lining the Wall were true catalogues of ordnance: three million mines of every brand and design. Someone told me the Wall was all that was keeping the Saharawi people from reclaiming their territory. Someone else told me it stretched for 2,700 kilometres, while another person said it was much less than that. I heard it was the longest wall in the world.

The Saharawi refugee camps lie on the eastern side of the Wall, near the city of Tindouf in the Algerian Sahara. The Algerian government granted the land to the refugees, but the Hamada du Draa is not much of a gift. The few hardy plants that survive here on the rocky limestone plateau grow armed with thorns. This land is far from imagined desert scenes. There are no sudden green oases here and no slow shift of curving dunes. Instead, there is pallor and gales that whip in winter.

Only the Saharawis themselves interrupt the paleness of the landscape.

16

The men walk through the camps in blue or white robes that crinkle like tissue, are embroidered with gold thread, and are scented by tea and tobacco smoke. The women swaddle their bodies in colours that don't exist in the natural desert. Bold reds. Tie-dyed blues and greens and purples. The colourful fabrics keep their skin cool and colourless. The women prize desert-pale skin. I found this vanity strange. But then again, here on the barren plain, any life at all perplexes.

Malainin Lakhal fetched me from the Protocol where foreign visitors are housed. He was tall and thin, wore glasses, and spoke in whispers that suited the vast silence of the desert where he lived. Malainin was the secretary-general of the Saharawi Journalists and Writers Union and spoke internationally at conferences about life in the refugee camps and the Saharawi struggle for independence.

Outside the peeling-paint exterior of the Protocol, the morning air remained cool, the sky sallow and overcast. Old shipping containers and wrecked cars lay on the sand. Wind moaned and tossed trash while Red Cross trucks sat idle. A half-dozen taxi drivers waited for fares inside their cars, but hardly anyone else was around. The sand blew into my eyes and burned. I tried to keep them open because it hurt less than closing them; each time I blinked, my eyelids dragged grains over my corneas and it stung.

I followed Malainin into a small shop that sold camp essentials: cooking oil, canned fish, detergent, tea, some wrinkled potatoes in a bin, and a few bolts of cotton on the counter. The cloth wraps into *lithams*, the long turbans the Saharawi men wear. "Choose a colour," Malainin said. I opted for olive green and the shopkeeper measured out a couple of metres. Malainin draped one end of the cloth over my head, pulled it tightly over my chin, and wrapped my head with the rest. "You can pull it over your mouth when the wind blows," he said. He bought a black *litham* for himself. "I am always losing my turbans."

Malainin and I left the shop and escaped the wind again in Restaurant Beirut near the highway. Malainin dribbled water from a plastic jug onto my hands over a basin. The chefs were offering spaghetti, camel with rice, and chicken. We both opted for the chicken, which we ate with our hands as a television in the corner showed Al Jazeera. Malainin asked me what I wanted to do in the camps.

"I want to see the Wall," I said.

The Moroccans built the Wall, but the story begins with the Spanish. In the late 1800s, Spain made a colony out of a bare patch of desert along the Atlantic coast south of Morocco, north of Mauritania, and west of Algeria. They dotted the coastline with trading posts and forts and called the region the Spanish Sahara. The Saharawi nomads who had driven their camels and built their tents on the land for centuries resented being annexed into a foreign protectorate. The Spanish, for their part, didn't have the stomach for aggressive colonization, at least not in the harsh Sahara. Aside from a few half-hearted forays into the desert to quell the loudest resisters, the Spanish generally left the Saharawis alone.

In 1936, Spain's Generalissimo Francisco Franco split the region into two territories, Río de Oro and Saguía el Hamra, and instituted full colonial rule. Even then, the Sahara hardly interested Franco until geologists found high-quality phosphate, used to make fertilizer and steel, near Bou Craa in the late 1930s. The Spanish built the city of El Aaiún near the Atlantic and linked the port to the phosphate mines with a conveyor belt nearly a hundred kilometres long.

Spain, like the rest of Europe, had little time left in Africa. By the 1960s, colonization had fallen out of favour and African nations were winning their independence. In 1966, the United Nations urged Franco to hold a referendum in the territory so the Saharawis could vote on sovereignty. Franco agreed, but he was in no hurry. At the same time, the Saharawis, who witnessed their neighbours in Morocco and Mauritania cast aside their colonial shackles, began to organize themselves as the Movement for the Liberation of the Sahara in 1967. The group marched in huge demonstrations that Franco brutally quashed. In one such incident, remembered by the Saharawis as the Zemla Intifada, the Spanish army fired on protesters armed only with stones. The soldiers killed eleven and wounded many others. Franco's heavy hand inspired the opposition to exchange peaceful demonstration for armed struggle. In 1973 a group of militants announced the formation of the Frente Popular de Liberación de Saguía el Hamra y Río de Oro: the Polisario Front.

As Franco's power and personal health begin to wane, another absolute leader, Morocco's King Hassan II, faced his own troubles. Moroccans had little faith in their "Commander of the Faithful." The king had barely caught his breath after surviving a bloody palace coup when members of his own air force attacked his private jet. Hassan escaped again, but he couldn't evade the growing anger of the populace. Moroccans rioted for bread and demonstrated for democratic reforms. Hassan needed to distract his subjects. He found an opportunity in the desert.

Armed with a dubious claim that the Sahara historically belonged to Greater Morocco, and buoyed by reports Franco was dying, Hassan marched 350,000 volunteers into the Western Sahara. The 1975 "Green March" claimed the region for Morocco, and Hassan quickly replaced his civilian marchers with Moroccan soldiers. Franco had neither the energy to resist nor anything left to lose. He defied the UN, pushed aside promises of a referendum, and signed a deathbed document dividing the Spanish Sahara territory between Morocco and Mauritania.

This outraged the Polisario. They had fought for the territory for decades and felt the Western Sahara belonged to them. In 1976, after the last Spanish troops left the region, the Polisario declared the independent state of the Saharawi Arab Democratic Republic, the SADR, and raised the Saharawi flag. Then they went to war with both Morocco and Mauritania. After three years of fighting, the Polisario soldiers pushed the Mauritanians back to their border in the south and forced them to declare Saharawi sovereignty over the territory. Then they focused on the Moroccans. Although the Moroccan troops outgunned and vastly outnumbered the Saharawi soldiers, Polisario troops encircled and destroyed the Moroccan units one by one in daring guerrilla operations. They captured Moroccan weapons and equipment and managed to knock the phosphate conveyor belt out of service.

The Moroccans, losing the war, changed their tactics. With the help of France, Israel, and the United States, Morocco devised a new strategy based on desert walls or berms. The first wall surrounded the "useful triangle" of the Western Sahara. This barrier secured the entire Atlantic coast and the phosphate deposits at Bou Craa. Each time the Moroccans gained a swath of territory on the eastern front, they built another wall to secure it. By the time the United Nations brokered a ceasefire in 1991, six walls had been built.

The walls extended eastward like ripples in a pond. Their combined length stretched to over 7,000 kilometres, longer than the Great Wall of China. The berm, apparently, can be seen from space.

Only the last wall, the longest, remains relevant. It was completed in 1987 and is still manned by Moroccan troops and watched over by UN peacekeepers. The Wall runs east-west along the border with Mauritania and north-south on the Algerian side, where it separates a narrow "Free Zone" from the rest of the Western Sahara that Morocco captured in the 1970s. Aside from Bir Lehlou, the SADR's interim capital, and another tiny settlement called Tifariti, the Free Zone is inhabited only by nomads, sand, and land mines. The berm, as the Wall is often called, is the longest and oldest still-functioning security barrier in the world. The Saharawis and their sympathizers call it the Wall of Shame.

▥▥

As we picked at our chicken, Malainin told his story about going over the Wall. On the night before he left his home in El Aaiún, he and his brother, Salama, met with their father. "Be a good man," his father told Malainin. "And follow the Milky Way. In the summer it will always lead you south. Remember, too, that we are Saharawi. It is better for us to die in the desert than in a Moroccan prison." He gave his sons two hunting knives in case they needed to kill someone.

Malainin was an agitator for Saharawi independence and known to Moroccan police in El Aaiún. He endured two months in prison there in 1992 and spent the next few years collecting information on the Moroccan abuses of the Saharawi people. In response to his activism, the Moroccans arrested and interrogated Malainin many times. They imprisoned and tortured him. The situation in the region intensified in the late nineties. The mass arrests and "disappearances" of known activists forced Malainin into hiding.

By the summer of 2000, after eleven months underground, Malainin reached breaking point. Any semblance of a normal life had been stolen from him. Malainin couldn't even visit his parents for fear of implicating them: activists stain everyone they touch with suspicion. He and his brother Salama, and another activist named Massoud, decided to escape to the Saharawi refugee camps in Algeria. They would be safe there, but they would have to go over the Wall. The three men chose to cross on the Mauritanian side. They'd heard there were fewer land mines buried in the south.

When they left El Aaiún, Massoud carried a teapot and some loose black tea while Malainin and his brother held the knives. They each brought along a single bottle of water and packed their *derahs*, the long slit-sided tunic of the Saharawis. Though they were all heavy smokers — Malainin smoked three packs a day — no one brought cigarettes; the journey would be arduous and the men did not want to be weighed down by anything inessential.

The men hired a smuggler to drive them within twenty kilometres of the berm. They would walk the rest of the way to the border, wait for dark, then take their chances crossing the minefield to climb the Wall. They planned to reach Nouadhibou, a city on the Mauritanian coast, before noon the following day. They could rest with friends there before making their way across the Algerian border and into the camps.

Malainin knew they could cover the twenty-kilometre distance in a little more than four hours. After five hours, though, they still had not reached the berm, and after eight hours they knew something was wrong. But they kept walking. The cadence of the men's footfalls on the sand and their turban-softened breath added the only sound to the silent desert. The sun set and replaced the day's swelter with a cool and clear desert night. Glancing upwards, the men followed the Milky Way south just as their father had instructed, but by the time the sun rose they still hadn't reached the Wall. They plodded forward through the morning into the heat of midday. Sweat dried into ragged rings of salt on their clothes. In spite of the scorch of the August desert, the men never drank their water. "We are Saharawi," Malainin said. "We save our water for tea."

The men would learn later that their smuggler was a poor judge of distance. He had dropped them over a hundred kilometres from the berm, and it wasn't until the evening of the second day that they spotted the barrier on the horizon. They had intended to save the tea until they crossed over the Wall; it was to be a sort of toast to their success. But reaching the Wall after their 36-hour march granted reason enough to rejoice. They hid behind a rock, squatted with aching legs, and brewed tea on a tiny, discreet fire.

The three men sat until night fell, waiting for the Moroccan army patrol truck to drive past. The truck dragged a sweeper behind it to erase its own tracks and make visible those of any jumpers. Once the truck had passed them, the men stood to cross the minefield and unwrapped their turbans. Each man held on to an end of the cloth so they were a turban's length apart – about three metres from end to end. If there was a problem, they could communicate by tugging on the fabric. And if one of them stepped on a mine, they reasoned, the other two would be far enough away to survive the blast. They moved forward knowing that this desert, which was their birthright, the very sand the Saharawis had struggled for, could erupt into sulphurous flame beneath their thin sandals. They had no path to follow. No way to be cautious. No way to be certain of their footfalls. They could only hold their breath and walk towards the Wall. They were not afraid, Malainin told me, because in that moment there was nothing else they could do.

When they were a few metres from the Wall, half of a soldier's face flashed into view in the spark of orange light from his cigarette lighter. The men froze. Then, linked by strips of black cotton and a dark resolve, Malainin and Salama quietly slid the knives from their sheaths. The brothers stepped quickly across the sand. There was no moonlight to glint off the blades and betray them. Ahead of them, somewhere in the blackness, the soldier continued to smoke. Better to die in the desert than in a Moroccan prison. Better to kill in the desert than to die at the Wall.

Malainin is a poet. He writes verses about jasmine buds, doves, and blushing, bleeding hearts:

> She came to me with memories of the feel of sand
> Of her beauty when we made the desert our bed.
> Do you remember the colour of my eyes when the moon is full?
> Do you remember the poems
> You sang for our parting on those sleepless nights?[4]

I couldn't imagine Malainin a murderer. Nor could I imagine the Moroccan prison cell where he was forced to stand for two days before being beaten and tortured with electric shocks for eighteen days more. I asked him if he really had been ready to kill.

"I was ready to walk across a minefield," he said.

By the time the men reached the spot where they had seen the lighter flash, the soldier had moved along in the darkness. The lingering scent of cigarette was too faint to follow. "We were both lucky," Malainin told me. "We didn't have to kill anyone, and he didn't have to die."

The first part of the berm is a metre-high sand wall lined with flat rocks designed to stop vehicles rather than people. The three men scrambled over it easily, but their sandals scratched against the stones as they climbed and Malainin feared the noise would alert the soldier. They paused and gripped the knives again, but no one came. They sprinted across a half-kilometre of no man's land until they reached a second wall, this one about three metres high. Once over this wall, they kept moving until they reached the railroad that links Mauritania's iron ore mines in the north to the port at Nouadhibou. They sat on the side of the tracks, put on their *derahs*, and brewed tea again, this time in true celebration.

After they drank their tea, the men found a transport truck mired in soft sand on the other side of a hill. The driver offered to take them to Nouadhibou if they helped him. The men spent two days unloading the truck, digging it out of the sand, and reloading it again. When they reached Nouadhibou, Malainin and his brother gave the driver the knives. "We didn't need them anymore," he told me.

███

Malainin and I took a taxi to Smara Camp, one of the six refugee camps on the *hamada*. Our driver clacked a cassette tape into the stereo, but the sound warbled and whined. He ejected the tape and banged it against the steering wheel a few times. When he stuffed it back in, a quartet of British-accented voices sang a weepy country song:

> Oh, I don't know why she's leaving,
> Or where she's gonna go,
> I guess she's got her reasons,
> But I just don't want to know,
> 'Cause for twenty-four years
> I've been living next door to Alice.

I turned to Malainin in the back seat. "What is this?"

"You don't know? It is Smokie. They are from England. You don't like them? They are very good."

"It's not what I expected," I said.

> Twenty-four years just waiting for a chance,
> To tell her how I feel, and maybe get a second glance,
> Now I've got to get used to not living next door to Alice.[5]

"The Saharawi love Smokie," Malainin said.

The main refugee camps are named after the towns in the Western Sahara where every refugee still has family living under Moroccan occupation. The naming is a kind of longing, the expression of an ache for home. Smara Camp was named after a town just a few kilometres west of the first wall Morocco built in the 1980s.

It was February 27, a holiday marking the date in 1976 when the Polisario declared the founding of the SADR. We arrived just before the parade began. Refugees marched on the highway as wind and sand blotted out the sky. Retired freedom fighters in blue *derahs* and black turbans held flags and marshalled the procession, but most of the marchers were children. Some young soccer players wore green and white jerseys and kicked a ball around. Plastic bats rested on the shoulders of young baseball players. I found the American pastime out of place here in the desert until someone informed me the equipment came from Cuban donors: Fidel Castro is an occasional supporter of the Polisario. The young players waved gloved hands at my camera, but I received no smiles from the female Koranic students who toted wooden planks covered in holy verses or from the women in traditional black and white dresses swinging small scythes in the air. Saharawi flags hung from the saddles on tall camels. Young girls trooped past in green camouflage fatigues and backpacks made to look like army transmitters. The boys carried rocket launchers and artillery shells fashioned out of cardboard. They sang patriotic songs and marched in place, as if rehearsing for a future, inevitable war.

I ducked in and out of a nearby community centre to rinse the dust out of my contact lenses and considered the rumours I'd heard about these camps. I read the Polisario held refugees here against their will and that some Saharawis practise slavery. While I saw no proof of these things, I knew that in the darkest days of the war the Polisario detained and tortured dissident refugees who spoke out against the Polisario's autocratic rule. Many refugees fled the abuses by crossing back over the Wall. The tortures ended in the 1990s after the camp security chief and main perpetrator of the abuses, Omar Hadrami, was sacked. He defected to Morocco and today enjoys a high position in the Moroccan interior ministry.

I'd heard another rumour that Algerian militants aligned with al Qaeda recruited suicidal foot soldiers from among the men in the camps. Malainin dismissed these claims as Moroccan propaganda meant to discredit the Polisario and all they had built here. He told me that the Saharawi people are disinclined to join militant religious groups because, as former nomads, they are used to praying alone. Until recently, there were no imams in the camps at all.

After the parade, Malainin showed me the traditional mosques: half-circle lines of stones, only two strides wide, that lay in the sand near the highway. The circles always curve east and there is always a small heap of stones midway along the arc. Since there is no water nearby, the devout use loose sand to perform their ablutions. They rub the sand over their hands and face and feet as a surrogate ritual wash. Then they step into the circle one penitent at a time and bend their prayers eastward; the piled stones are cairns that point in the direction of Mecca.

I've seen some of the grand mosques of the Islamic world. Istanbul's Süleymaniye Mosque and the al-Aqsa Mosque in Jerusalem. Iran's Sheikh Lotfallah Mosque and the shrine of Imam Reza. They stand as architectural treasures, some scented with rosewater and adorned with tiles and mosaics and gold. They speak to the artistic beauty that faith inspires, with prayer halls that hold multitudes. But no majestic mosques marked the Saharan caravan trails. No communities of believers and no Friday congregations. For the Saharawis, religion is divine intimacy. They don't need domed ceilings adorned with mosaics to inspire them; they have the Saharan sky. The Saharawis can touch God from within a simple curve of stones.

In Hassaniyya, the Saharawi language, the word for "tent" is the same word as "family." I stood on a hill overlooking February 27 Camp, named after the holiday that had just passed, and saw the tents rising between the houses like white sailboats on a sand sea. Abdulahe, a friend of Malainin, pointed to the tent where he was born. "You know, when I travel from here, I miss the tent," he said. "The tent makes me feel my roots. My nation. I was born in a tent. Grew up in a tent. You know, it means a lot to me."

Malainin had promised to arrange for me to see the Wall, but nothing happened quickly in the desert, and some days nothing happened at all. I spent much of my time in Abdulahe's care, moving from camp to camp, tent to tent, lying on foam mattresses. I learned what I could about life on this side of the Wall before I had a chance to see the berm itself. I became a reclining witness to the camps. Abdulahe often asked me, "Marcello, are you boring?" He meant to ask if I was bored, and though I didn't admit it, I often was. This frustrated me at first, but I soon surrendered to the camp's rhythm of slowness. The refugees had been waiting here for three decades for something to happen. I could wait a few days. There is courage in patience, after all.

February 27 Camp has a central mosque, a women's hospital, and a school for girls, but most of the buildings are family homes built of brick and slathered in mud stucco. Instead of digging foundations for these houses, the Saharawis lay rows of bricks directly on the sand and use stones to weigh down the flat, corrugated steel roofs lest the winds wrest them away. The homes are not meant to stand forever. The families would happily walk away from them if they were ever granted independence.

Abdulahe and I descended the hill and walked through the camp. I told him I liked the thin pipes the old men smoked, and he said he knew a *tienda* where I could buy one. Children called out "Hola" to me and demanded *caramelos*. I found it strange to hear so much Spanish in the middle of the Sahara, but as former colonists of Spain, nearly everyone can speak the language: children learn Spanish in school. Many Saharawis also study abroad in Spain and Cuba. I photographed a group of children sitting on aluminum water tanks. They cheered and waved two fingers at me in the victory sign.

We came across a group of men sitting cross-legged in front of a grid they'd drawn in the sand. They played a game with twigs and pebbles that looked something like checkers while their friends suggested strategies and applauded particularly clever moves. Long turbans enveloped their heads in grand folds I mimicked without success with my own olive green cloth. Orange sand, tossed about by the wind, got caught in the black fabric.

When Abdulahe was a boy, his parents sent him to a boarding school in Algeria's capital. "I remember my mother telling me I was a refugee, but I never knew what that meant until I went to Algiers," he said. "The Algerian students had money. They had sweets and toys and bicycles. The Saharawi students at the school had nothing. Not even a house to live in. When I came back to the camps in the summer, I asked my mother why the boys in Algiers had so many things that we did not have, and why they lived in houses and I lived in a tent. My mother told me, 'It is because you are a refugee. They have a country. You do not.'"

Although Abdulahe studied law in Algiers, he never worked as a lawyer. He drove a taxi for a while in Nouakchott, the capital of Mauritania, and worked on a fishing boat in the Atlantic. Now he worked with the camp youth. Abdulahe ran a weekly radio show and hoped to make documentary films about the life of young Saharawi refugees.

Abdulahe and I took lunch in the tent of one of his relatives. The tent was cool and spacious, with a few blankets piled in one corner and a sewing machine in another. A wire ran from a television to a solar battery outside. Two cellphones were strapped to the central tent pole, which doubled as an antenna and improved the reception. There were three young women inside, Abdulahe's cousins. One laid a blanket for me to sit on. Another dribbled lemon-scented perfume on my head by way of greeting. The third fetched a charcoal brazier, which she fanned with a flattened milk carton, and brewed tea. Abdulahe's mother came in, her face as round and inviting as ripe fruit. She asked me if I found the desert too hot. I replied that it was snowing in Canada and that I appreciated the heat. She pointed to the door flap of the tent where the midday light poured in and offered me a spot to sit in the sunbeam.

Abdulahe asked if I had any money to help pay for our lunch. I handed him a thousand Algerian dinars, about sixteen dollars. He passed it to his mother. The bill was the smallest I had but was, apparently, far more than we needed. In addition to the meal—lamb and squash couscous and a stack of curried camel kebabs—his mother gave me a handful of plastic jewellery and a bolt of yellow cloth imprinted with orange flowers. "Gifts for your wife," she said.

Some of the refugees run shops and restaurants, and a few draw pay by working for the NGOs that function in the camps, but most refugees survive on aid. They receive regular rations of food and tea. Camp officials deliver water every ten days or so, less frequently during the dry summer, from faraway wells. The provisions, however, are meagre, and most refugees rely on family members working abroad in Europe, Algeria, Libya, or Cuba to wire remittance money.

Abdulahe's uncle Mohammad joined us, and we all ate from the same platter. My hosts pushed the best morsels of lamb over to me. They filled my glass of apple Fanta before it was finished, and when I mentioned how much I liked the rich and gamey camel meat, they saved the rest of the kebabs for me.

Unlike the Wall that divides them from their homeland, nothing separates the visitor from the Saharawis. They quickly granted me their trust. Every family I visited was the same. I needed only to appear and they opened their world to me. The moment I sat, a glass of tea was placed before my knees. A pillow came for my head. Laughter was immediate. They invited me to rest, to eat, to sleep. There would be bread in the morning. Sterilized milk from a box. A can of berry jam. I too started to associate "tent" with "family." I knew, though, that their generosity was born of tradition rather than abundance. For the Saharawis, hosting visitors is an indigenous ritual. In the harsh desert, after all, an offered meal or glass of tea can mean the difference between living and dying.

After we ate, Abdulahe, Mohammad, and I stretched out on the blankets. One of Mohammad's daughters, Ama, brewed more tea in the corner. She held a blue teapot at arm's length and splattered tea into a tiny glass. Then she flicked open the teapot lid and poured the tea back into the pot with a deft twist of her wrist. Ama did this over and over again, and the glasses grew sticky from the splashing sweetness. The sounds—the spatter of the pour, the clicking teapot lid, the glasses against the metal tray—scored the desert afternoon.

Mohammad had fought against the Moroccans as a Polisario soldier in the 1970s when the war was most fierce. He once scaled the berm in the middle of the night to attack Moroccan soldiers sleeping on the other side. "I took two prisoners myself that night," he said. Eventually he too fled to the camps, but he'd been back to El Aaiún recently. After the 1991 ceasefire, the United Nations peacekeeping mission in the Western Sahara began flying Saharawis to and from the camps in an effort to build faith between Morocco and the Polisario. Mohammad visited his brother in El Aaiún. It was the first time they had seen each other since Mohammad fled to the camps thirty years earlier. I asked him about their reunion, but Mohammad wanted to talk about El Aaiún itself. "The old Saharawi neighbourhoods are crumbling," he told me. The only new homes belong to Moroccans from northern cities such as Marrakech and Fès. The Moroccan government lures these settlers to the Western Sahara with tax breaks and high wages in an effort to populate the disputed territories with non-Saharawis. He slid a glass of tea to me on a metal tray. "The Moroccans care only about the resources. They do not want to build a new Sahara."

I asked Mohammad about an offer the Moroccan government had made to give Saharawis limited autonomy in the Western Sahara rather than independence—an offer the Polisario had rejected. "I was seventeen years old when I came to the camps." He sat up and tugged on his sideburns. "Now I have grey hair. I would rather die here than accept integration into Morocco."

Ama was born in the camps. Now in her early twenties, she'd never seen the land her father fought for. "What do you think the Western Sahara is like?" I asked her.

She flicked the teapot lid closed, smiled, and turned her eyes upwards. "El Aaiún is very pretty. There are real streets and buildings. Lots of cars. The ocean is nearby, and it is a huge distance filled with water. You can swim in it, and there are fish. And it can rain there for days."

███

In the Saharawi tradition, tea is a trinity. The tea ceremony embraces three holy essentials, each beginning with the Arabic letter jim. *Jama'a* is the gathering. To drink tea alone is to waste it. *J'jar* means slowness. Proper tea cannot be brewed in haste. *Jmar* is the charcoal. Tea demands burning and boiling.

Abdulahe and I were at someone's house—I don't know whose—in Auserd Camp with Kamal and a cast of Abdulahe's relatives, who came in and out of the room at random. A considerable *jama'a*. Kamal splashed a stream of hot tea into a row of glasses. He told me how you could once buy a camel for a cup of dry tea leaves. Then he told me about Damaha, his mother, who had joined us in the tent. Damaha fought the Moroccans long before they built the Wall . She marched with the protesters in Tan-Tan who agitated against the Spanish in the years before the Green March. Damaha had little education, but the Polisario leaders tutored and inspired her towards resistance. By the time the Moroccans replaced the Spanish as the region's occupiers in 1975, Damaha had given birth to Kamal and divorced her husband. Her home became a Polisario safe house where Damaha hosted activists to discuss strategy and raise money. "Everybody gave what they could," Damaha told me. "I knew a woman who stole her husband's revolver to give to the soldiers."

One morning, in the winter of 1978, Damaha was hosting a monthly committee meeting in her home. An out-of-breath Polisario official rapped on the door. "There will be a battle today. Our soldiers are ready to attack Tan-Tan. Be ready to assist the men with whatever they need." At midday, the Polisario soldiers attacked Moroccan army positions. They held the town for four hours and released Saharawi prisoners from the jails. Soon, though, the Moroccan troops started to regain control of the town. In the early afternoon, three Land Rovers drove up to Damaha's house and a group of Polisario soldiers rushed out. They were frantic. "It is no longer safe here. We are collecting all the activists and bringing them to the refugee camps."

Damaha had always known this day would come; Saharawi activists in the Western Sahara may cling to hope but not to illusions. She already had a bag packed. Young Kamal, though, was not home. He had gone to play with his cousin that morning and had not returned. There was no time to look for him. She said a brief prayer that Kamal would find his way to his father's house, boarded one of the Land Rovers, and escaped to the camps. Almost a year passed before Damaha heard that Kamal was alive and safe. October 14 — the date hangs at the front of her memory. Twenty more years went by before Damaha actually saw her son again. They reunited in the camps in 2001.

I tried to ask her how she could leave her child behind in a city at war, but Abdulahe wouldn't translate the question for me. "You cannot ask her that," he said. "She is a mother."

Hamid, Abdulahe's uncle, had a similar story. He was born in Smara during the early days of the war. His grandmother cared for him during the day because his parents worked out of town. One evening, his parents returned home to a bombed city and an empty house. Hamid, who was eight months old at the time, was gone. So was his grandmother. His mother ran to her neighbour to see if he knew anything. "The Moroccans bombed the city today," he said. "The Polisario came to evacuate civilians. Your mother left with Hamid in a Polisario truck. They went to the camps." Twelve years went by before Hamid's mother received news that her son was alive. Twenty-six years passed before she saw him again.

In 2005, Hamid's mother arrived in a car filled with women who had come from the Western Sahara to visit their families in the camps. Hamid bent down and peered into the taxi window. He couldn't tell which of the women was his mother. Hamid said he wasn't nervous about their reunion, but when his mother hugged him, they both cried. She held on to him for most of the day and slept beside him that night. "She wanted me to feel like I was her son," he said. They stayed together for a month before his mother returned to Smara. "After so many years, she was just another woman to me."

I wanted to understand his typically Saharawi dispassion. I was tempted to attribute his stoicism to faith, the Muslim trust in the will of God. Who are we to question the life Allah grants us? But Hamid gave me another answer: there is always someone with a more tragic story. For every mother who has been separated from her son, there is a story of a son killed. For every man arrested, another disappears. The men and women who escape today have camps to shelter them, but a generation ago the displaced had to build the camps from nothing. Dwelling on your own misery dishonours those who have suffered more. "Mine is just one more story in the body of the Sahara," Hamid said.

Damaha and Kamal left the house just before lunch arrived. Abdulahe, Hamid, and I sat upright long enough to eat a large platter of stewed camel meat then lolled again on the thin foam mats that lined the room. Hamid's three daughters joined us for another round of tea. They were bright-eyed and pretty, their faces surprisingly freckled.

"What will you do to help the Saharawis?" Nabba, the oldest, bluntly asked.

I didn't know what to say. I told her I wasn't an activist, but I would write about their situation so people in North America might know what was happening here. My answer was embarrassing. It felt feeble and idealistic, but Nabba nodded and pointed a finger at me. "Write about the right things," she said. "Write about the reality of the camps. Even though food is plentiful and we are not starving here, we will never forget our aim. Remember, we are the last colony in Africa."

The sisters, and Abdulahe, are part of the first generation of Saharawis born in the camps. They are in their twenties now, and a second generation of refugees will be born in the next few years. The children might be sent to school in Europe. They will experience life outside the camps. I wondered if the idea of an independent Western Sahara, a place they may never see, will become an abstraction.

"We will teach them," Nabba said. "Our children will know who they are." Her eyes flashed when she spoke. For the first time, I saw the resolve the Moroccans had failed to tame. Instead, they enclosed it behind the Wall.

▓▓▓

Mustapha Said Bashir, a tall bear of a man, wore a ratty brown sweater that might've been inside out. Bashir was the brother of martyred Polisario fighter and national hero El-Ouali, the Saharawi Che Guevara, and the Polisario's deputy secretary-general. El-Ouali's portrait hung above Bashir's desk. I sat on a plastic-wrapped chair in his tidy office while he talked about the Wall.

"The entire Moroccan army is reliant on the berm," he said. Bashir spoke surprisingly good English. "The berm is their only strength. Without it, they could not resist our troops. Their courage depends on it. After their king, the berm means everything to the Moroccans."

"Do you really believe that the Polisario could defeat the Moroccan military?" I asked. "They have a huge army. They have modern equipment. And allies in Europe."

"We have done it before." He told me about the Polisario's arsenal of military hardware, mostly French- and American-made guns that Polisario guerrillas captured from Moroccan troops during the 1970s and 1980s. Bashir believed the decades-old weapons were all the Polisario needed.

I mentioned Kosovo to Bashir. He frowned, closed his eyes, and exhaled. The United States and most European powers were just then lining up to endorse Kosovo's declaration of independence and welcome the tiny Balkan republic into the community of sovereign states. Kosovo's path to self-determination took less than a year, while it had been forty-two years since the United Nations first called for a referendum on the future of the Sahara. The referendum has still not been held.

"International law is in the refrigerator," Bashir said. "We live in a lawless era." He believed the ceasefire would not hold for much longer, and that only armed conflict would earn the world's attention. "Frustration is gaining everyone. There will be a return to war."

"When?"

"Soon. In less than one year."

The organizers of the Sahara Marathon first conceived the event to encourage physical activity among the camps' children and to use the entry fees to fund sports-related projects. More than this, though, the annual race alerts an international audience to the Saharawi plight. Nearly four hundred runners, mostly thin Europeans, spend the days before and after the race living with refugee families. The more people know about their cause, the race organizers reason, the harder it will be to ignore.

I didn't come to the camps ready to race in the desert; I'd only realized my visit coincided with the marathon while en route to Tindouf. My plane was crowded with white men and women in track suits — not the crowd I expected on an Algerian flight into the desert. Still, I wanted to run. I had not been a competitive athlete for nearly a decade, and never a runner, but I wanted to be able to say I ran in the Sahara. I wanted the T-shirt. I knew I didn't have the stamina for the full distance, so I signed up for the ten-kilometre race.

Because I woke late, I missed breakfast and was the last runner to press into the bus to the starting line. The other participants looked far more prepared. I had only hiking shoes to run in, and my stomach felt tight. I hadn't had anything to eat or drink since the previous night's camel couscous and apple Fanta. I couldn't even fasten my official number to my shirt. Another runner noticed this, took pity on me, and gave me a couple of safety pins.

The bus turned off the highway onto the flat desert and got mired in a patch of loose sand about two hundred metres from where we needed to be.

Everyone stepped down and walked the rest of the way to a flagpole that marked the starting area. The start lines for the marathon and half-marathon stood somewhere far behind us, and those racers had already been running since before dawn. The fastest among them would eventually overtake the slowest of us. In the meantime, we waited for a starter's pistol or some indication that our race was to begin. I spotted the serious runners easily. They were invariably tall and lean and white and wore proper runner's bibs, little cloth caps, and nylon shorts cut high on their thighs. They strapped Lycra bandoliers with tiny plastic bottles around their waists. I imitated their stretches in the chilled morning air and tried to gather the nerve to ask one of them for a sip of water.

A few Saharawis were running as well, mostly teenagers in donated running shoes and loose jogging pants. The girls had scarves tied tightly around their heads. They didn't have any water either, but I watched them drink glasses of sweet tea in a nearby tent. Many of them looked as out of place amid the Europeans as I did, but for them the race was less an athletic event than an expression of existence. Morocco drew a line in the sand with the Wall. The Saharawis countered with the footprints of their youth.

An official appeared and spray-painted a crooked yellow line across the hard ground filling the air with a sudden aerosol stink. We all clustered behind the line. The real runners jostled their bony elbows near the front while the rest of us filled in behind. Someone blew a whistle and fifty runners trampled forward in the sand. The experienced athletes burst ahead in a smooth motion, their backs straight and their heels lifting little spurts of sand with each stride. The rest of us puffed along afterwards, giggling and apologizing in various languages as we collided into each other. Our initial cluster of runners divided like a cell, splitting into smaller and smaller groups, until I was trapped alongside a Saharawi girl who wouldn't let me pass her. Twice she sprinted ahead of me and each time she slowed to a walk, but as soon as I caught up she dashed off again.

Eventually I was alone. I jumped over a dry and flattened goat corpse and passed three women raking trash into piles for burning. The fragrance of smoke scented the otherwise odourless desert. The coolness of the morning melted into a thick liquid heat. February's Sahara, though, is no inferno. I'd gone for hotter jogs during Canadian summers. Blowing sand was a greater concern, but the wind was calm that day, the air dry but clean. A tall camel holding two turbaned riders in an ornamental saddle stood next to the water station at the three-kilometre mark. The men shouted "Bravo!" from their perch as a woman handed me a full two-litre bottle of tepid mineral water. Unrehearsed at drinking in motion, I ended up choking on more water than I actually swallowed and felt more embarrassed than refreshed. I grinned at the irony of nearly drowning myself in the Sahara and tossed the nearly full bottle onto the sand.

Truckloads of Saharawis rumbled up and down the route. The drivers pressed on the horns while their passengers leaned out of the windows to cheer on the runners and wave Saharawi flags. I lifted a weary hand to salute them. Once in a while I passed participants who had opted to walk, and occasionally faster runners swept past me. Most of the time, though, I had the desert to myself. Only the sound of the *hamada* under my too-heavy shoes crunched the silence. I sweated through my T-shirt. My thighs, not ready for such a morning, started to ache. My eyes stretched to the horizon over the flat sand on either side of me, and though I couldn't see it, I thought how alien the Wall must seem here in the otherwise boundless desert. How absurd that a man-made barrier striates such an expanse and renders any sense of freedom an illusion.

Near the finish line, the blanch of the desert gave way to walls of riotous colour. Hundreds of women, each wrapped in bright fabrics, flanked the final three hundred metres. Their desert saris, or *melhfes*, fluttered orange and yellow and blue. Swirls of purples. Splashes of black on green. One woman had pink pompoms on her veil. Despite the heat, many wore woven gloves to protect themselves from unwanted tans. For a few seconds, these women cheered for me. They ululated through their veils as I reached the final turn before the finish. Children held out their hands for me to touch.

I started to run faster. My eyes stung from the sweat that streamed into them. So much blood rushed to my head I could taste iron on the roof of my mouth. My knees hurt, but I sprinted the last few metres just to earn a shred of the ovation. Someone strung a souvenir medal made of recycled aluminum around my sweat-slimed neck, so light I could hardly feel it against my chest, and shouted out my official time. I couldn't hear it amid the shouts and the pulse in my head.

What started as an athletic boast became something more. Exhaustion stripped away my objectivity and replaced it with the loud spirit of the people. All I felt through my fatigue was their gratitude for my running under their flag. I was no longer the detached observer. In the middle of the desert, I was on their side of the Wall.

■■■

Salek wore a black leather jacket and carried his wallet on a chain. He had dark brown eyes and a shy smile and blushed when Malainin teased him for chasing girls. The Moroccan courts had found Salek guilty of assault, theft of state property, and distributing Polisario flags. A ten-year prison sentence waited for him on the other side of the Wall in Smara should he ever return home.

In the Western Sahara, Saharawi teenagers channel their natural tendency towards rebellion and misbehaviour into political protest. They tag public buildings with pro-Polisario graffiti and wave Saharawi flags. The Internet flickers with blurred video of Saharawi boys and girls, their faces hidden behind cloth, draping flags from power lines or spray-painting *Viva Polisario* onto buildings. They are the new foot soldiers in the battle for independence.

Two years before my visit to the camps, a nomad in the liberated zone lost track of his camel herd. One camel climbed over the berm and the rest, seventy animals in all, passively followed; intellect is not one of the camel's gifts. By some miracle, they didn't plod over any land mines. The camels passed a Moroccan army patrol and the soldiers herded them into a pen near their camp. The camels had been branded with Polisario markings and were, in a sense, spoils of war. The branding meant the soldiers could not bring the animals to market in Smara: no one would buy animals that were clearly stolen. To spite the Saharawis, the soldiers decided to starve the animals to death.

Rumours are perhaps the only things that travel fast in the desert, and soon everyone in Smara was whispering about the captured herd. Saharawis have a close relationship with camels. For centuries, camels have provided transport, meat, leather, and bone. The animal symbolizes Saharawi culture. The theft and abuse of the herd by Moroccan soldiers deeply offended their nomadic blood. Saharawis in Smara could only watch as the herd started to die off. After three months, those that remained were little more than skeletons.

Salek, seventeen years old at the time, assembled three friends for a mission of liberation. The boys watched the soldiers for a week to learn their routine. Then one night they sneaked out of Smara towards the camel pen. The boys jumped the Moroccan guardian and tied him to his chair with a length of rope they had brought with them. Salek gave the prisoner some water and placed a cloth below his head so he would be comfortable. "We told him his friends would untie him in the morning," Salek smirked. "We didn't want to hurt him."

They opened the gate. At first, the camels didn't move. The boys had to slap their haunches until the animals finally lumbered out of the pen. The boys split the camels into four groups of about a dozen. Each boy led his humped charges towards the valleys of Wad Seguria, and they agreed to meet later at a desert well they all knew. The boys reasoned that if the camels were divided, there was a chance at least some of them would remain free. A few might even cross back over the berm. Before they left, Salek took a wad of small Polisario flags out of his bag and scattered them in the pen as a final act of political mischief.

Each boy brought his camels into a different valley and set them free. Salek led his quarter herd to a spot where freak rains had washed away the berm and the land mines. He was the last to arrive at the well, and even in the darkness Salek could tell that his co-conspirators were smiling. The camels had all been freed. Exhausted, the boys slept beneath the lopsided desert stars and the reliable beauty of the Saharan sky.

The next morning, they started to return to Smara, but Salek had another idea. "Let's talk to Mustapha," he said. Mustapha, a nomad, lived in a tent near the main highway and was a reliable source of gossip. The boys wanted to know if news of their caper had spread. Mustapha invited the boys in for tea. Before the first pot of water had boiled, he said to them, "Do you remember those camels? Some Saharawis stole them from the Moroccans last night. They tied up the guard and threw Polisario flags all over. The Moroccans went crazy."

The boys grinned at each other from across the tent.

"The Moroccans know who did this," Mustapha continued. "Someone saw them. An informant. He recognized all of them. The Moroccans know all of their names and are waiting for the boys to return to Smara."

Salek and his friends knew they had no choice: they had to go over the Wall.

The boys had no water, no supplies, and no plan. Their families couldn't help them and they might never see them again. The boys only had each other, but Salek told me they were not afraid. They all knew people who had disappeared in Moroccan custody; all four would choose a land mine over a prison sentence. "Most important thing," Salek said, "is me feeling so close to my death."

It took the boys three days to reach the berm. They waited for dark before they climbed over the first wall and crossed through the strip of no man's land. The shortest boy was clumsy and slipped as his friends tried to boost him over the final barrier. Then their eyes filled with light. A soldier had heard the noise and caught them in his flashlight beam. For a moment the boys couldn't move, as if the light alone shackled them. They assumed the next light they saw would be a muzzle flash. Instead, the man turned to alert his fellow soldiers and the boys leapt over the Wall. Panic boosted them this time. They hit the sand on the other side and ran until their legs screamed. They found a nomad in a tent who led them to a Polisario military post. The next day they were delivered to the camps.

"I hate this story," Salek said. He meant he was tired of telling it. His parents still lived in Smara, and he hadn't seen them since the night he left to free the camels. "It was very important moment. To go. Go family. Go school. Everything change. Life change. Very important. I do not have the words."

███

After ten days in the camps, I was finally going to the Wall. By then, though, I wondered if I needed to see the berm at all. The refugees cannot see the Wall from their camps, and nothing compels them to drive out and view it. The physical structure does not matter to them as much as what the Wall represents: exclusion, the theft of their land, and the separation of families. The Wall cleaves the indivisible desert and separates a single people into those under occupation and those in exile. The berm is an unseen demon in the distance, standing between where the Saharawis live their half-lives and where they yearn to be. It doesn't matter what the Wall looks like as long as they are on the wrong side of it.

My driver remembered to stop for cigarettes, and he stopped for camel meat, which he bought out of a white van holding a butcher and two swinging carcasses. He also remembered his cigarette lighter. But he forgot to bring a functioning jack. When a tire blew out, he spent an hour digging a hole around the offending wheel to remove and replace it.

We drove to a Polisario border control post, where we picked up a soldier to act as our military escort. He wore army fatigues and plastic sandals but did not carry a gun. We stopped near some thorny bushes about three hundred metres from the berm, much closer than I'd anticipated. Malainin had sent his friend Salek to accompany me — not Salek the camel liberator, another Salek. He walked towards the Wall and waved at me to follow him. I didn't budge. "What about the land mines?" I asked.

"We are safe to walk a little further."

Many of the decades-old anti-personnel mines planted near the berm that continue to kill Saharawis and their livestock were made in the Soviet Union and Yugoslavia, countries that don't exist anymore because their composite states, like Kosovo, have since gained independence. It is a callous irony. I followed Salek, walking in his footsteps and staring at the ground in front of me. Salek laughed at me for being afraid. I couldn't see any mines, but I found the perforated end of a machine gun muzzle in the sand. Salek warned me not to touch it lest it was wired to explode.

Salek stopped about a hundred metres from the Wall. The Wall of Shame did not impress me. The berm stood about two metres high and was built with rocks and hard-packed sand. I expected some military majesty: towers and barbed wire and steel. Sharp edges and hardness. Instead, I saw a long hump of sand that snaked into the distance. The berm could have grown out of the *hamada* itself. It resembled a massive ripple of sand created by the desert wind. The Wall seemed more natural than sinister. Perhaps, after so long, the berm is an organic thing. Though they may dream of the sea, an entire generation of Saharawis knows no other boundary than this. The Wall has evolved from a military barrier into a symbol of Saharawi identity. The curved spine of a nation that doesn't exist.

Then again, this is all the barrier Morocco needs. Saharawi military tactics have always been based on lightning raids across open deserts. In ancient times, Saharawi soldiers rode camels; these days, Polisario troops drive jeeps. A heap of sand and rocks is enough to stop a charging Land Rover. This Wall might not inspire awe, but it does the job. Though I didn't know it at the time, this berm was the most effective barrier I would see on my travels, and the only wall that did what it claimed to do.

Through the zoom lens on my camera, I focused on two Moroccan soldiers who stood on top of the berm. Both wore drab army fatigues and were clean-shaven. One had an olive green cap on his head, the other a helmet. They smoked cigarettes and watched us. A radio stood between them in case we did anything worth reporting, and I imagined they were happy to see us. At least they had something to look at for a while besides the empty desert.

Salek and I walked back to the jeep. A small belt of rusted machine gun shells hung on a thorn bush nearby like a morbid Christmas decoration. Our driver snapped a few branches from the bush to build a fire and our soldier brewed tea. The driver hacked the camel meat apart with his knife and laid the slabs on the embers next to the teapot. Salek and I made tuna sandwiches and ate green olives while the camel roasted. We drank tea, waved away the flies attracted to the rich aroma of charring meat, and watched the Moroccans staring at us. Our driver stood and called out to them, sarcastically inviting them for tea.

Bashir told me that after independence, whenever it may come, the Saharawis will keep the Wall as a souvenir. But I wondered how quickly the desert could reclaim this land. Winter floods, like the one in 2006 that destroyed much of Smara Camp, could melt the berm away in a few seasons. Sandstorms will grind down what is left. The *hamada* will renew itself. The Saharawis will remember their history. They will remember their exile and their halved lives. But the desert will forget the Wall.

■■■

On most world maps, a dotted line marks the northern border of the Western Sahara. The territory is disputed: it is the Occupied Zone according to the Saharawi resistance and their supporters, the Southern Provinces according to the Moroccan king. On the highway, the only sign of the border was a trio of petrol stations selling cheap subsidized petrol and a tiny police post. Thousands of discarded plastic bags dotted the landscape, blowing in the wind and snagging on thorny bushes.

To get from the refugee camps to the Western Sahara required a convoluted journey and some paranoid preparation. Algeria's support for the Polisario strained relations with Morocco, and as I said goodbye to Malainin, he warned that the Moroccan authorities would deny me entry if they knew I had visited the Saharawi camps. So before I left Algeria, I sent my Sahara Marathon T-shirt, racing bib, and medal, along with a Saharawi flag I'd been given, home to Canada. I temporarily took down my blog. I also flipped through my pocket notebook and used a pen to change each appearance of *Saharawi* to *Babarawk*, a nonsense word I hoped nobody would ask me about. I considered disguising my journals, but since I could barely read my own writing, I didn't think there was much chance a Moroccan airport official could.

The land borders between Algeria and Morocco are closed — another consequence of their Western Sahara quarrel. To reach Morocco, I flew across the Mediterranean to Madrid, where I boarded a flight full of European vacationers back over the sea to Marrakech. My wife, Moonira, met me there the next day, and we spent two weeks in Morocco as tourists. With Moonira, I exchanged refugee tents for cool, clean hotels and rode camels instead of eating them. Moonira departed for home from Casablanca with a bag full of leather slippers while I made my way south, by bus, into the disputed territory of the Western Sahara.

In 1930, Michel Vieuchange, a Frenchman bored with France, became obsessed with Sheikh Ma al-Aynayn and the city he had built in the desert. Ma al-Aynayn was a nineteenth-century Saharawi warrior and Sufi sage who, along with his adherents, founded Smara in the Western Sahara. The city became both a centre of religious learning and a way station along the great caravan routes linking west Africa to Europe. Ma al-Aynayn resented the presence of Christian infidels in the Sahara, and his armies of Saharawi soldiers regularly attacked French army outposts on camelback. These guerrilla-like raids went on for years and would be echoed seven decades later in the tactics of the Polisario Front. The French eventually defeated Ma al-Aynayn's army and set fire to Smara, but the Polisario claim the Sheikh as their spiritual champion and the defender of Saharawi territory against foreign power.

Vieuchange wanted to find what remained of Ma al-Aynayn's holy capital. By the time he set out, Ma al-Aynayn was dead and the Spanish and French exercised control over the region. The Saharawi tribes, however, still posed a danger to Europeans. The Moors of the Western Sahara showed famous hostility towards foreigners, especially the hated French, and those who dared breach the sands risked both capture and murder.

The trip was agonizing for Vieuchange. For much of the voyage he disguised himself as a Berber woman — layered tunics, a suffocating veil, shaved legs — and as they neared Smara, his guides packed Vieuchange into a basket hanging from a camel. They arrived at Smara at noon on All Saints' Day in 1930. Vieuchange unpacked his camera gear and set out to photograph the city. His guides, nervous they would be caught with a French infidel in their care, allowed the explorer only three hours in Smara before stuffing him back into the camel basket. There was little left to see in Smara anyway. The city stood empty and half ruined. Vieuchange wrote in his journals: "Except for the nights when the fires light up your walls, for the days when camels, goods and men are installed on your earth, how truly deserted you are — town of desert — how often your walls know only the sun." Vieuchange's Smara was dead. Soon, too, would be Vieuchange. He died of dysentery on his way out of the desert. The last, ghastly, words in his journal were, "Stools — and stools — watery."[6]

I travelled to Smara to see what the refugees had lost and what life was like for those who resided in the disputed zone among their Moroccan occupiers. My Smara, unlike Vieuchange's, was alive, especially during the Thursday market. I walked from my hotel to the souk where I took breakfast from an egg-and-tea man in a tent at the edge of the market grounds. The vendor sat on an empty evaporated milk tin and served meals off a table made of upturned wooden crates. He cracked a cold hard-boiled egg from a metal bowl and peeled away the shell. Then he sliced open a piece of bread with a paring knife and mashed the egg and its blue-green yolk inside, sprinkling it all with cumin and salt.

The market was given over to heaps of fresh produce, a strange abundance in a desert town. There were piles of fennel, fat white radishes, eggplants, and red onions. Women shoppers picked through heaps of potatoes and muskmelons, bananas and peaches and avocados, all grown far from this place, and each knew to pluck the green tops from the onions before weighing them. One vendor splashed water on mounds of fresh mint and parsley to keep them from wilting in the heat that, by late morning, had begun to peak. A man sold flushable toilets near the gate. Young boys wandered between the stalls selling blue plastic shopping bags to those who were unequipped. Other boys pushed two-wheeled carts for big buyers. They competed with each other for customers and jammed their carts at the intersections between the market stalls. Sometimes they argued with each other; sometimes they cried.

Aside from the men in *derahs* and the uniformed soldiers, I couldn't tell the Saharawis from the Moroccans. No one knows exactly how many Saharawis live in the Western Sahara. In the disputed territory, counting is controversy. When the United Nations called for a referendum in 1992 so the Saharawis could vote on independence, census takers found themselves up against a wall of paranoia: each side blamed the other for padding the election rolls. The Polisario Front accused the Moroccans of importing dubious Saharawis into the region who they knew would vote against independence; tens of thousands were housed in a squalid camp outside El Aaiún until Morocco bulldozed the area in 2008 and resettled the settlers. Morocco charged that the Polisario exaggerated the populations of the refugee camps. The Polisario still demands that the referendum be held, and is confident their side would win, but it remains clear that Morocco will not agree to participate in a vote if there is a chance they might lose.

By late afternoon, the only fruits remaining in the market were bruised and squished. All that was left of the onions was a heap of discarded green tops. Fugitive tomatoes were mashed underfoot. There was enough work for all the cart boys as they wheeled their cargo to the parking lot, where taxis, trucks, and donkey carts waited to be loaded.

The streets became lively as the sun burned itself out for the day. On Stadium Boulevard, I passed shops selling *derahs*, *lithams*, and beautiful Moroccan caftans for women alongside everyday items such as clay braziers, tajines, and couscous screens. An old man sat and clicked his prayer beads next to sacks of spices and traditional medicines. Twice I saw beggars lay scraps of cardboard on the ground, strain their weak bodies to bend, and plead for charity. Young women, always strolling in threes with their arms linked like demure chorus girls, whispered as they walked. Two men selling cigarettes pegged me as a foreigner and called out, "Viva la Saharawi!"

Across Hassan II Avenue, the paved street yielded to gravel and the banal housewares gave way to flesh. Here, a strip of butcher shops lined up under crimson awnings. Great slabs of meat glistened under bright lights and the air felt cool with the metallic stench of blood. Skinned testicles hung from the carcasses to reassure buyers that the meat was male: Islam prohibits eating animals that are still nursing their young, so some Arabs eat only male animals to be safe. It was a lurid scene, all red lights and rawness.

I thought of the other Smara, across a minefield, over the Wall, and five hundred desert kilometres away from this place. I thought of the frustrated gardeners I'd met who tried to wrestle a few tomatoes out of the useless sand. I remembered the bins of wrinkled potatoes and the skinny sheep in makeshift pens. The camel carcasses hanging in minivans. I thought of the solar panels that offered each family a day's brevity of electric light. Compared with its namesake camp across the Wall, Smara is Eden. I understood why some would rather endure occupation than live in squalor on the other side of the Wall. And I understood why the refugees, after thirty years of courageous patience, still breathe Smara's name in reverent tones. A generation may well live and die in the camps without ever seeing this place, but they will still fight as long as the stories of Smara's relative abundance drift eastward over the Wall.

■■■

The next day, I phoned a man named Nasiri whose number had been given to me by a Polisario representative in Washington. Nasiri met me at my hotel. He was short, bald, and slight, and when he shook my hand and realized how little French I spoke, he called someone else on his cellphone who could translate for us. We took a taxi to his house on the eastern edge of Smara. My translator, a twenty-year-old Saharawi named Omar, arrived at Nasiri's house just as we did. We went up the stairs into Nasiri's red-curtained salon and he immediately began to brew tea. I returned to the mechanics of Saharawi hospitality I'd enjoyed in the camps. The same tea ritual. The same bottles of apple Fanta. Only Nasiri had a proper house with running water and electric light.

Nasiri said little that I hadn't heard before. The Wall symbolized the struggle for Saharawis living in the Western Sahara as much as it did for the refugees, and the Saharawis had the same faith in the Polisario Front, at least those who spoke to me. "If the Polisario says intifada, then we start intifada," Nasiri said. "If they say open war, then we go to war."

"Mustapha Bashir told me that the war will begin in less than a year," I said.

Nasiri paused to raise his eyebrows. Then, in a quieter voice, he said, "If this is what the Polisario says, then we will do it."

Nasiri told me that the Moroccan government in the Western Sahara imports great numbers of settlers from the north in an effort to reduce the percentage of Saharawis in the region and replace Saharawi traditions with Moroccan culture. I mused that this sounded similar to the scenario with the Israeli settlers in the West Bank. He frowned just as Bashir had when I mentioned Kosovo. The Saharawis do not like being compared to the Palestinians, who've fought for sixty years and seem no closer to having an independent state. Nasiri would rather equate the Saharawi situation with the East Timorese in southeast Asia. At least they finished their marathon to sovereignty.

Nasiri's wife served us a huge slab of mutton for lunch. His daughter, four years old with a riot of curly hair, came and nibbled off her father's plate. Midway through the meal someone knocked on the door and Nasiri rose to check who it was. When he returned, he sat back on the floor and said, "That was my friend. He said there are three policemen on the street. The Moroccans know you are here."

I stopped eating, a greasy pinch of mutton frozen in front of my mouth. "Are you serious?"

"The Moroccans do not want foreigners meeting with activists."

"If that's true, why didn't they stop me from coming in here? Why don't they knock on the door right now and bring me out?"

Nasiri laughed. "Maybe they will." Nasiri doubted they would do anything, however. Since things were relatively calm in the occupied zone, the police likely wouldn't bother with me. But if it were a sensitive time — if demonstrations had just been held, or if there were negotiations ongoing with the Polisario — the Moroccans would have stopped me from meeting with Nasiri. They might not have let me enter the city at all. "Right now, they are on the street because they want me to know they are watching," Nasiri said.

"Should I be worried?"

"They will do nothing to you. I am more concerned about him." He nodded towards Omar.

Omar was not an activist. He was a university freshman studying English literature. When Nasiri had called Omar, he told him to go into the house before we arrived. That way, if the police were following Nasiri and me, they wouldn't know that Omar joined us. But Omar arrived late. We all entered the house at the same time, and the Moroccans might have seen all three of us together. Because Omar met with us, especially with me, officials might start monitoring him. Omar told me he wanted to be a translator and would enrol in a translation academy when he finished his degree, but if the Moroccan government thought he was in league with the Saharawi resistance, they could make things very difficult for him.

"You could get into trouble," I said. "You could have refused to translate for me. Nasiri would understand. And so would I."

Omar shrugged. "I could not morally say no."

After our interview, Nasiri walked me down the stairs and out of his house. He pointed to the horizon. "There is the Wall." I squinted and saw a tiny brown ridge in the distance. This was the first of the six walls the Moroccans built in the 1980s. The abandoned barricade seemed insignificant, but the effectiveness of this berm had led to the building of the rest and Morocco's eventual control of the Western Sahara. If the Walls were like ripples in a pond, this is where the pebble fell.

I turned to Nasiri. "Where are the policemen? The ones who followed us."

Nasiri looked down the empty street. "They have left."

I doubted they were ever there at all. I thought about the Berlin Wall Disease and wondered if the barrier had infected Nasiri with paranoia. I couldn't imagine why the Moroccans would be interested in me.

▓▓▓

I spent a couple of days in El Aaiún, the capital city of the Western Sahara and Malainin's hometown. A stunning new mosque boasted carved plaster and stained glass. The mosque sat on a city square in the centre of town made of spotless tile where, on Fridays, local families laid out their evening picnics. As they sipped tea, young boys flouted the rules against playing football on the square and kicked balls around until policemen chased them away. Elsewhere in town, gleaming white UN vehicles crowded the parking lots of chic hotels: the UN peacekeeping force maintains its headquarters in El Aaiún. A new soccer stadium grew real grass — a near miracle in the desert. The wealth was inorganic, built of Moroccan subsidies and tax breaks, but manufactured prosperity is still prosperity, and the citizens enjoyed a sort of boom in El Aaiún that didn't exist in the cities of the north.

El Aaiún's Saharawi neighbourhoods boasted none of this freshness. I visited the old Saharawi district of Souq ez Zaj. The houses were falling apart and the walls marked with cracks and lesions. The Plaza del Canarias had none of the lightness and songbird whimsy the name suggested, only broken stone benches, old garbage, and a few emaciated trees. There was no one in the streets. A government information office stood in the middle of the neighbourhood, displaying victims of Polisario torture — dissidents who spoke out against the Polisario's autocratic rule in the 1980s. The men and women in the posters had blotched red bodies and broken faces with black bars over their eyes. The photos were designed to persuade the local Saharawis that the Polisario is no saviour and that they are better off as Moroccans.

I remembered Mohammad's daughter, Ama, who'd never seen El Aaiún but was sure the place was *zeina*. Lovely. She envisioned an ocean full of fish and rain falling from the sky. Real houses instead of tents. In the imagination of a refugee, any place on the other side of the Wall, wherever it is, must be beautiful.

▓▓▓

I travelled to Tarfaya to meet Sadat, the great-grandson of Sheik Ma al-Aynayn. (The Sheik had no shortage of descendants. Though he had only four wives, historians claim he fathered 68 children with 26 different women.) Tarfaya is a tiny fishing village on the Atlantic Coast. Antoine de Saint-Exupéry, the French pilot and author of *The Little Prince*, lived here in the 1930s. A small museum dedicated to Saint-Exupéry and the Compagnie Générale Aéropostale he flew for stands near the beach. Tarfaya is just north of the dotted-line border of the Western Sahara and far from the Wall, but the town is important to the Saharawi story. Building materials for Ma al-Aynayn's Smara arrived at Tarfaya from the Canary Islands. Donald Mackenzie, the nineteenth-century Scottish trader who introduced tea to the Saharawis, built a trading fort here just off the talcum-soft beach. More recently, the Green March of 1975 assembled in Tarfaya before heading south and claiming the Western Sahara for Morocco.

Sadat was thirty years old and the youngest of twelve children, all of whom attended university and have become politicians, judges, and community leaders. He worked out of an office at Saint-Exupéry's museum as Tarfaya's cultural officer. Sadat's aim was to preserve Saharawi arts and traditions in the face of "Moroccanization," but he was not otherwise concerned with politics.

He told me about a friend who, after graduating from university, decided to go to the camps and join the Polisario cause. As soon as he arrived, he was jailed and tortured by Polisario troops who didn't trust his intentions and accused him of spying for Morocco. After his release at the 1991 ceasefire, the Polisario gave him a rifle and sent him to the front lines. The man fled the camps a year later and returned to Morocco; he travelled through Mauritania, not backwards over the Wall. Now he was living in El Aaiún. "The Polisario can claim no moral high ground," Sadat said. "Both sides have committed abuses."

Despite sharing the bloodline of Sheik Ma al-Aynayn, Sadat was no warrior for Saharawi independence. "It is time for the Polisario to stop talking about the mere idea of independence and start talking about the practicalities," he said. He mentioned a recent document by Peter Van Walsum, a UN envoy charged with overseeing talks between the Polisario and Morocco, who said that since there is no international pressure on Morocco to give up the territory, "an independent Western Sahara was not a realistic proposition."

"This has been a great blow for the cause of independence," Sadat said, although he agreed with the realism of the statement. He believed the best the Saharawi people can hope for now is some sort of limited autonomy within the Moroccan state. They should focus on keeping their culture alive, not on illusions of sovereignty, he said.

"But what about the refugees?" I asked. "They've been fighting for independence for more than thirty years. Some have given up everything for the cause. What would you say to them?"

"I would tell them to come here."

████

Saleh runs the ugliest café in Tarfaya. Torn plastic and filthy blue mats scarred with cigarette burns covered each of the four tables. The cracked plastic chairs had been white in the distant past. Peeling, pastel green paint covered the walls, and a few bare bulbs, furred by cobwebs and dust, hung from the ceiling. Flies hummed everywhere and all his tea glasses were chipped. I suspected Saleh never cleaned anything, but he proved me wrong one afternoon when I saw him wipe each tabletop with the edge of a cloth he licked.

Saleh's was the kind of place you love *for* its shabbiness, not in spite of it. And you loved it for Saleh himself. Sadat told me that Saleh fought for France in World War II, but the French forgot about him. Saleh had a grimace for a smile, a pepper-grinder voice, and a face like something you could win at a carnival by tossing balls at milk bottles. His white hair curled like lamb's wool. Saleh dragged his feet when he walked, which raised the dust on the floor, but he brewed the best mint tea in town.

I walked to Saleh's café for tea one afternoon, but he waved me away from the door. When I returned to the café with Sadat later that evening, he asked Saleh why he hadn't let me in. The old man was aghast. "I thought he was looking for you!" he said to Sadat, his hands held before him in a gesture of innocence. "When I shook my head, I meant that you were not here! I didn't know he wanted tea. He never said anything! I would have served him. Of course! All he had to do was ask. Even if he did this..." Saleh mimed drinking from a tea glass. "He can come in any time. He just has to ask!" He walked behind the counter, shaking his head.

Saleh returned with two cigarettes for Sadat and faced me. "Even if you don't drink anything, you can come here! You can sit for five hours! Six hours! Read a book—anything. You are at home here. Life is good." He pointed upwards, and for a moment I thought he was pointing out the peeling paint, the cobwebs, and the dusty light bulb, but he referred to something beyond the ceiling. "God is everywhere! God is taking care of us!"

When he returned to deliver our tea, Saleh held my glass in front of me. "What is this called in French?" he asked.

"Thé," I said.

"That's all you had to say! One word! I thought you were looking for Sadat! You didn't say anything." He walked away again.

"He is going to be talking about this all week," Sadat said.

███

The next night, Sadat found me eating grilled sardines on Tarfaya's main street. "I got some calls today," he said. "You are the centre of attention here. Let's go somewhere quiet." He brought me back to Saleh's. The old man wore a pink sweater over a dingy white collared shirt. He served us mint tea and cigarettes.

"Three different Moroccan security people called me to ask about you," Sadat said. "They have been following you and want to know what you are doing here. I told them you were a student, and if the king wants to boost tourism in this country, he should leave the tourists alone."

I sat back in my chair. Sadat took a drag of his cigarette. I noticed he was missing part of a finger on one hand. I hadn't seen this before.

"Then they told me that you met with a well-known activist in El Aaiún," Sadat said. He mentioned a man's name.

"I didn't meet anyone in El Aaiún. And I don't know who that is."

"Okay. So they were lying. They were trying to trick me. They do this."

"I met with an activist in Smara last week. Not in El Aaiún. His name was Nasiri."

"I know Nasiri. That is probably why they are following you."

"They followed me all the way from Smara?"

"Yes. This is what they do."

"Do they know I am a writer?"

"Probably not. But don't worry. This happens all the time. A thousand times. This is what you should do. The police know your hotel. They were waiting there for you today."

"They were at my hotel?"

"Yes. So tomorrow morning check out of the hotel and come stay at my place. I have an extra room. No one will bother you there. You can stay as long as you like, and…"

I stopped listening to Sadat and focused on the strange tightness that was growing in my chest. I imagined uniformed men in Smara, El Aaiún, and Tarfaya calling each other with my name on papers in front of them. Flipping through ledger books at police posts to see where I'd been and when. Knowing my hotel and my itinerary and the people with whom I'd spoken.

I thought of the Sahara Marathon and how my name appeared on a long list of runners who had trampled the sands in support of a cause. I remembered breathing hard and flashing victory signs and feeling I was a part of something. But in the occupied zone I found a different sort of solidarity. My name was scrawled into a less innocent ledger. I'd crossed over another kind of wall, the one that divides the watcher from those being watched. I didn't feel afraid. The worst the Moroccans could do was deport me. But I felt small. Too small for this place.

The next night, I boarded a bus heading north. I told Sadat I'd spent enough time in the Western Sahara, I'd learned enough, and there were other walls I needed to write about. As the bus pulled away, I felt like a fugitive making a getaway in the darkness.

The Bogeyman is Coming
Ceuta and Melilla

The Africans at the Wall don't speak the same language, but tonight they share a common belief: if we are many, they cannot stop us all.

They camped for weeks in the forest. They prayed for rainless nights and ate what they found in Moroccan rubbish bins. They hacked footholds out of thick tree branches to make crude ladders. Now they wrap their hands with torn fabric to protect themselves against the barbed wire and wait under the half moon until their cellphones ring the signal. Then a surge of five hundred bodies crashes into the Wall, but it is too dark to see their faces through the security cameras. The bravest lead the assault. They lean their ladders against the chain links and begin to climb. Others scramble up behind them. Soon, men in uniforms appear on both sides of the Wall—Moroccan here, Spanish there—with flashing lights and the sweet stink of tear gas. The night goes medieval. Soldiers tear Africans from the wire while the climbers kick and claw. The chain link shakes and rattles. Sweat-glazed skin gleams under floodlights. A rubber bullet the size of a tangerine rips a toe from one man's foot. There is a Babel of screams: Arabic, Wolof, Hausa, Spanish. And there are gunshots. The noise drowns out an infant's cries. Women and children climb the Wall here too. Everyone dreams of Europe.

When the melee ends, tattered clothes snagged on the razor wire flap in the breeze coming off the sea. A man hangs by his neck. There are five bodies in all: two on the Spanish side of the Wall, three in Morocco. They most likely fell from the top of the Wall and were crushed in the stampede, but later there is talk of Moroccan bullets in the corpses. Some say a baby was one of the dead. Nobody knows exactly what happened. And nobody knows how many made it over. Two hundred, some guess. Probably more. The Spanish government calls in the army. The police take the ladders home as souvenirs.

■■■

One might blame Hercules. For his tenth labour, the mythic hero travelled to the edge of the world to steal oxen from Geryon, the three-headed grandson of Medusa. When Hercules reached the mountain that divided the Atlantic Ocean from the Mediterranean, he chose to smash through it rather than climb over. The seismic grandstanding let the ocean spill into the sea and forever divided Europe from Africa.

Half of the demolished mountain stands as Gibraltar. The other "Pillar of Hercules" rises on Ceuta, a narrow strip of land that dangles off Morocco's Mediterranean shore. Ceuta and its sister enclave Melilla represent the last remaining Spanish possessions in North Africa. They are strange geopolitical anomalies — each an Iberian fragment of Catholic cathedrals, midday siestas, and *arte modernista* surrounded by Muslim Morocco. As Spanish cities, Ceuta and Melilla also define the southernmost reaches of the European Union. Their city limits are Europe's borders. The enclaves, then, attract illegal migrants from as far away as south Asia. Scaling the fences into these Spanish colonial souvenirs means reaching Europe without risking a Herculean sea voyage across the Mediterranean.

I first saw the Wall from the Moroccan side, in Beni Yunis, a tiny seaside village where pastel houses hang off the forested slopes like Christmas tree ornaments. I arrived early in the morning. The Mediterranean draped fog on the hills while a few quiet men sipped tea, smoked *kif*, and read the morning paper in the lone café. After a tea I walked past purple thistle and wandering goats towards the army barracks with the motto "God. Country. King." written above the door. The Wall stood beyond the barracks, but an off-duty policeman stopped me before I got too close. The man welcomed me to Beni Yunis and wanted to talk. "All this belongs to Morocco," he said, pointing at the houses at the other side of the Wall, in Spain. "It should be returned to us. The Spanish oppose the occupation of Gibraltar by the British, yet they occupy Ceuta."

I asked if African migrants still camped in the forests near the Wall. "Not since September 2005," he said, referring to the night the Africans stormed the barrier. "The army went in and cleared everyone out." He pressed his wrists together to mime handcuffs. Spain also refortified the Wall. What was a double fence became a triple barrier, and it doubled in height from three metres to six. Fat coils of concertina wire were laid along the foot of the Wall and additional barbed wire was strung along the top. Automated tear gas dispensers were planned but not yet installed.

From a distance, though, the Wall looked delicate. It reminded me of the silver filigree I'd seen in jewellers' souks elsewhere in Morocco. Something a bride might wear around her neck on her wedding day. Instead, it is Europe's iron collar. A ten-kilometre choker of barbed wire and steel.

▓▓▓

Jeffrey James was among the hundreds who stormed the Wall that night in 2005, but he didn't make it over. Moroccan border police handcuffed him, beat him with their fists, and dumped him in the no man's land between Morocco and Algeria's northeastern frontier. James slipped back into Morocco through the porous border and trekked nearly a hundred kilometres along a well-beaten migrant trail. He dodged the bandits who prowled the route for black men to rob and made it to the railway. James stowed away on a cargo train bound for Fès. From there he took a bus to Tangier, then walked to the migrant camps outside Ceuta, and returned to the Wall. He assured me the camps still exist, regardless of what the Moroccan border policeman told me. James was caught at the Wall again, dumped again, and returned again. The arrests could not lessen his desire to reach the other side. Twenty times he made the same journey from fence to detention, to the border and back. When he told me this, he grinned like a rebellious teenager.

Jeffrey James and his African comrades are willing to gamble on Europe. "We are black. We take risks," he explained. For him, each night in the forest outside Ceuta meant another assault on the Wall. Sometimes he and his fellow climbers were caught and exiled over the Algerian border. Sometimes they were just chased away. Other times they were beaten. The smooth raised gashes on his arms journal these nightly trials; these are the barbed wire's brutal accounting. They reminded me of the ceremonial cross-hatches and patterned slashes I'd seen on the faces of men from Africa. Those scars marked a boy's rite of passage to manhood. James's barbed wire scars marked a new ritual and a different kind of passage.

Despite his wounds and trials, things could have been much worse for James. About a week after the mass assault on Ceuta's fence in 2005, another group of Africans stormed the Wall at Melilla, Ceuta's sister enclave a few kilometres east along the shoreline. The Moroccan border police captured fifteen men, loaded them into trucks, and drove south into the Western Sahara across the berm. The soldiers gave each man two bottles of water, tinned sardines, and some bread. They pointed to a line of stones that marked a narrow path through the minefield. "Walk straight," they said. "Do not step left or right." And then they drove away.

The Africans, like Malainin and Salek, walked nervously across the minefield, each stepping into the footprints of the man in front of him. But unlike the Saharawis, the Africans were not desert men. Their bodies knew nothing of the dry scorch of the Sahara. Their eyes had never before felt the sting of blowing sand. Once past the mines, they wandered for days until their food and water ran out, then they drank their own urine. Some men withered and died. A Polisario patrol rescued those who survived and drove them to Bir Lehlou or Tifariti in the Saharawi Free Zone, where they discovered that dozens of migrants had been discarded the same way. A warehouse in Tifariti was home for forty Bangladeshis and Sri Lankans caught at the Wall. The Moroccan authorities deny this happens, but the desert is littered with the testimony of Moroccan-labelled sardine tins.

At the end of 2007, James spent a full month camping with other African migrants in the forest outside Ceuta. They slept beneath the trees, ate food they either begged for or stole, and watched for Moroccan soldiers. Finally, in December, James made it over the Wall. "I put on blue jeans because they are thick. And gloves," James told me. Then he put on every shirt he could find. He wrapped his hands in rags and ran to the Wall with five friends. The razor wire at the base of the first fence snagged his outer shirt. He slipped out of it and kept climbing. James lost three shirts before he made it over. They hung on the Wall like shredded flags.

I met Jeffrey James at the Plaza de los Reyes in central Ceuta when he asked me for money. I mentioned that his name sounded as if it belonged to a cowboy, and he said it was a "good English name." James said he was from Sudan. He stood tall and thin and told me he had witnessed his two younger sisters being raped and murdered by rebels. James lived in CETI, the Short Stay Detention Centre on the outskirts of Ceuta and not far from the Wall. He had been there for five months and was waiting for his visa application to be processed. He was relieved to be in Ceuta. Although this Spanish outpost is not the Europe he yearns for, at least he can walk freely here, and he says the people are kind.

Hundreds of migrants get past the Wall into Ceuta each year. Some, like James, take their chances climbing the barrier itself, but most cross the border hidden in or under vehicles or on overloaded boats. Once over the border, they go directly to a police station to register themselves on Spanish soil. The registration grants them an official status and Spanish authorities cannot legally deport them back to the other side of the Wall. The police issue the newly arrived a receipt that allows them entry into CETI. The centre provides food, housing, and some medical care. Residents play soccer or volleyball on the beach to pass the time. Some, like James, beg for money in the plazas. But mostly they wait to be either deported home or granted temporary visas to mainland Spain, the "Peninsula" as it is called here, on the other side of the sea. Those who make it to the Peninsula find whatever jobs they can—domestic workers, custodians, trinket salesmen—and send money back to their families. When their visa runs out, they disappear into legal limbo. This is their dream.

James was trying to learn Spanish. CETI offered language classes, but the words were not holding. "I think a lot. I think too many things," he said as his knees bounced and his voice stuttered. "I cannot put anything in my fucking brain right now."

"Do you miss anything about Sudan?" I asked.

He shook his head.

■■■

The refugees in Ceuta may not have homes or passports or jobs, but each has a cellphone and an email account. Every flaw in the immigration machine disseminates instantly through virtual space. Strategies are constantly devised and revised. Weaknesses exploited. Loopholes identified and leapt through. The migrant networks are intricate, sophisticated, and invisible.

That Europe aims to stop these travellers with barbed wire fences is a foolish irony. Contemporary migrants are hardly barbarians at the gates.

The migrants know the currency in a good lie. They don ethnicities, nationalities, and religions as needed, then shed them like thick shirts on barbed wire. Everyone discards their passports and documents before they arrive in Ceuta. Identity needs to be pliable. Since Spanish authorities will not send migrants back into wars or disaster zones, many claim to be from Iraq or Darfur. When cyclones ravaged Bangladesh, a large number of south Asians arriving in Ceuta alleged to be Bangladeshi. Spain signed a repatriation agreement with Nigeria that allows Spanish authorities to send Nigerians home. The Nigerians know this, so most claim to be from somewhere else. Migrants lie about being tortured. They lie about going over the Wall; the dangerous feat inspires both awe and sympathy in officials. They even lie about their sexual orientation. Days after one Nigerian was granted asylum because his homosexuality put him at risk of persecution in his home country, dozens of Africans showed up at CETI claiming to be gay. I wondered how much of Jeffrey James's story was true. Perhaps none of it.

Psychologist Javier Espinosa worked in CETI and tried to foil some of the liars. He evaluated migrants who insisted they had been tortured in their home countries and were seeking asylum in Europe. Dozens of such claims filled the thick blue binder on his desk labelled TORTURAS. Espinosa told me it is very difficult to lie about torture and that he could quickly determine who was telling the truth by asking a few questions. Actual torture victims reflect the sensory experience of their ordeal in far greater detail. They include mention of emotions and thoughts, not just pain. False accounts lack these details and, instead, adhere to overly strict chronologies. The liars believe their stories will sound more credible if told exactly the same way each time, with every invented detail in its invented place. Psychologists like Espinosa know that real memories are more fluid.

Beyond these interviews, however, Espinosa offered little therapy to the migrants. "Many residents are stressed to be here," he said, "and some have trouble sleeping, but in general their psychological problems are not serious." The key was to keep them occupied playing sports and learning new skills or languages that they could use if and when they ever made it across the sea.

I disappointed Espinosa. He spoke good French and assumed that I, as a Canadian, could do the same. It annoyed him that he had to talk to me in strained English. Espinosa toured me half-heartedly through CETI, where we met Dr. Sergio Gonzales, the staff medical doctor, who tended to residents with minor infections. He also treated the wounds migrants suffered as they crossed the border. Since the Wall had been strengthened, fewer migrants climbed over and injuries were rare. Outside his office, African women hung laundry on the fences near their dormitories, and about a half-dozen migrants queued at the cafeteria for lunch. Few of the four hundred residents chose to eat at the centre. Spanish institutional food tastes bland on the spice-fired tongues of Africans and south Asians. Most migrants preferred to cook their own meals on fires they built in the forest outside the centre.

CETI issues residents entry cards that allow them to come and go as they please. The card reader at the gate also reads their fingerprints to prevent them from selling the cards to non-residents. Some spend their days begging for change in the plazas or supermarket parking lots. Others relax on the beach at the bottom of the road, the European mainland tauntingly within sight when the sky is clear. On Sundays, the Christians among them attend Mass at one of the Catholic churches and pray for immigration miracles. At the port, Algerians don't have the patience to wait for God. Instead, they spend their Sabbath looking for chances to stow away on trucks boarding the ferry to Algeciras, Spain. They lean against the terminal buildings, and the soles of their shoes leave black marks on the terminal walls like the Wednesday ash on Catholic foreheads.

I asked Espinosa if the residents were happy in CETI. He laughed. "How can you be happy here? Your face is not like the others. Food is not like at home. Your family is not here. You are living with strangers."

Later, I met another CETI worker, who told me in confidence about the staff's apathy, their beer-drenched lunches, and the Byzantine bureaucracy. I heard that some of the African men, physically strong and intimidating, stole money from the meeker south Asians. I heard about a prostitution ring in the centre controlled by the Africans. Sex on flattened cardboard in the nearby forest cost five euros with a condom, ten without. Compared to the hell so many had endured to reach this place, CETI offered a sort of comfort, but nobody wanted to be here.

If Europe is a fortress, CETI is the dungeon.

▰▰▰

No one was speaking Spanish on the number 7 bus. Most of the passengers were day labourers from Morocco. Women in drab overcoats and head scarves filled the seats, laughing with each other in Arabic and drowning out the music from the bus driver's radio. Most of the men stood in the aisle, gripping the rail with one hand and buckets of paintbrushes or plumber's tools with the other. The bus interior smelled of grease and latex paint. Everyone was anxious to earn their day's worth of euros. Cross-border workdays began before dawn for these Moroccans. Ceuta synchronizes its clocks with mainland Spain, so it is two hours later on the Spanish side of the fence than it is on the Moroccan side. Stepping into Europe means leapfrogging through time.

I was staying on the Moroccan side of the border, in Fnideq, and joined the Moroccans on their daily commutes. For them, the border was more fluid than rigid. Most Moroccan workers had day permits to enter the enclaves and were obliged, according to law, to return to Morocco before nightfall. But unless there was trouble, nobody paid much attention. Some Moroccans stayed in the enclaves for weeks, if not more, living with family in the Muslim neighbourhoods. If they were caught, the Spanish authorities brought them to the border and led them over the line. But nothing prevented them from returning to Ceuta again. Spaniards in the enclaves welcomed their cheap labour.

The number 7 runs from the border post at the end of the Wall to Ceuta's central plaza. From here, I walked through the city squares with their statues of Spanish military heroes and shops selling duty-free electronics to day trippers from mainland Spain. I walked past the Museo de Ceuta built out of Francisco Franco's former home. Franco earned his military reputation fighting Muslims along these shores, and while he bequeathed the Spanish Sahara to the Moroccans on his deathbed, he never let the enclaves go. I walked between the pastel churches of Our Lady of Africa and Our Lady of the Assumption. The two Santa Marias face each other across the Plaza de Africa beside a neo-Gothic monument to the heroes of the nineteenth-century Hispano-Moroccan war, a brief conflict sparked by a Moroccan attack on Ceuta's borders.

I continued past the house of the Franciscan Brothers of the White Cross and the café-bars where men and women enhanced their morning coffees with brandy. I passed Playa Benitez and its tidy pebble beach. This road led to CETI, but instead I climbed the steep Calle de Barriada Postigo where homes were made of brick and had names like Villa Ana and Villa Márquez. At the top of the hill was the local SPCA and behind the stink and yap of the dog kennels stood the forest where the men from India lived.

They were making breakfast on a vacant lot littered with broken bricks. One man minced ginger and garlic on a glass shelf cannibalized from a discarded refrigerator. When he finished, he slid his chopping into a pot warming over a fire. Nearby, two men mixed flour and water in a plastic tub and rolled the dough into chapatis with an empty vodka bottle. Another man cooked the chapatis on the hood of an abandoned car propped over a fire. He waited until each chapati began to blister, lifted the edge with a spoon, and flipped it with his fingers. When the chapati was finished, he added it to a stack of warm bread wrapped in yesterday's *El Pueblo de Ceuta*, the town's daily newspaper. As I watched the cooking, a boy just out of his teens handed me a plastic cup of chai. "Very hot," he warned. Shards of fresh ginger and rough-crushed cardamom floated over my lips.

Few of the Indians spoke any English. Those who did grew excited when I told them I came from Canada. They asked if I knew any of the bhangra musicians who lived in British Columbia and insisted I listen to the music through the wires dangling from their cellphones. One boy had heard a rumour that so many Indians lived in Canada that the street signs were written in Hindi. He didn't believe me when I told him this wasn't true. When I said I planned on travelling to India, the men insisted I visit the Punjab, where most of them were from. "Do you know Amritsar? There are too many beautiful things."

I had learned about the Indians the previous day from Rocky Ghotra, a nineteen-year-old Punjabi I met walking along the playa. He told me that seventy-two Indians, all illegal migrants, had left CETI to camp on the mountain directly across from the centre. He invited me to visit, and I waited until he walked sleepy-eyed into the clearing. Rocky led me to a spot on the edge of the lot away from the other men and laid a flattened carton on the ground. He slipped off his shoes before he sat as if we were on a proper rug instead of a discarded box on a snarl of weeds.

Rocky told me his life in India was modest but not destitute. His family were Sikhs from Haryana province who owned their home and had some land to farm. They couldn't afford much but had enough to send Rocky to school in New Delhi. By the time he was seventeen, he'd completed two years of a commerce degree and was enrolled in a program that would send him to Canada or Australia to continue his studies. Rocky was a fine student and the hope for his family's future.

He was also impatient. When an "agent" offered to transport Rocky to Spain, where he could study on a student visa, Rocky accepted and left his university. One of his professors warned him he was making a mistake, but Rocky's family trusted his instincts. Their son was intelligent and had never let them down. They sold their home and land to pay the agent. The euros Rocky would send home from Spain would be more than enough to live on, they reasoned. "When I remember that day, I feel..." Rocky began to say but never finished his sentence. Instead, he turned away.

The agent took Rocky's money and his identity papers and put him on a ship. Rocky spent fifteen weeks at sea but didn't know the route the boat took. Each time it docked, Rocky's smugglers blindfolded him. At the end of the voyage, the men pushed Rocky ashore and told him he was in Spain. "I found out afterwards that I was in Tangier. I didn't even have any shoes." Rocky persuaded a Moroccan vegetable vendor to stuff him under the seat of his car and drive him past the Wall and over the border into Ceuta. He climbed the hill and checked into CETI.

The average stay for a migrant in CETI is three months. In that time, Spanish officials either grant migrants temporary visas or send them home. Rocky waited almost two years, and some of the other Indians even longer, but nothing happened. The Indians blame the Pakistanis for this. According to Rocky, migrants from Pakistan realized they were more likely to gain entry into an increasingly Islamophobic Europe if they were Sikhs or Hindus from India rather than Pakistani Muslims. So they all claimed to be Indian.

Spanish immigration officials discovered the ploy and rejected every south Asian application outright. Eventually, Pakistan's ambassador to Spain helped identify which south Asians were actually Pakistani nationals, and all two hundred were deported back to Pakistan. Meanwhile, Rocky and the other Indians continued to wait.

During his stay in CETI, Rocky learned enough Spanish to read the local newspapers. One morning he read that the Spanish authorities planned to deport all the Indians living in the centre. Rocky gathered his countrymen together in the soccer field and translated the newspaper for them. The men knew what would happen — they'd seen it before. Armed policemen would surround the centre at night, heave them from their beds, and truck them to the airport, where a plane would be waiting to fly them back to India. The men asked Rocky what they should do. He told them to hand in their CETI entry cards. Then he led them out the gate and into the forest.

Their self-exile from CETI was meant to be strategic. The men knew the Spanish authorities would only bother to deport the Indians if they could deport them all; flying only a handful of men back to India is hardly cost-efficient. Dividing themselves among several camps in the middle of the forest made it impossible for the Spanish police to round them all up. In the case of a raid, the men would scatter. In the meantime, the migrants would appeal to city government officials, the media, and, if necessary, immigration lawyers for temporary visas. This was their plan, but the men had been in the forest for six weeks already, and no one was paying them much attention.

Rocky's skills in Spanish made him the de facto leader of the group. But Rocky was young and the burden was heavy. "My age is like a child," he said. "The men told me, 'Rocky, you have to do something.' I have to be active. I am doing what I can. It is very difficult for me, but I have to do it. There is no option for me."

We rose from the cardboard and Rocky led me into the forest to the camps the men had made. There were eight in all, each housing around eight migrants. Some had real tents, but the Indians constructed most of the dwellings from scavenged bits and scraps. Stones tied to cloth strips weighed down plastic tarps. An old door became a tent wall. Wooden pallets supported beds and blankets. Each camp had a small stove built of stones where the men cooked curries and brewed chai. They lodged toothbrushes and toothpaste between branches next to *bidóns* of water. A woman living in one of the Spanish villas on the hill allowed the men to use her garden house. Church and community groups donated sacks of food.

The men made some money by helping Spaniards carry their groceries out of the huge duty-free supermarkets. "It is begging," Rocky said flatly. He used the few euros he saved to call his family in Delhi. They thought he was already in Europe, and he refused to tell them otherwise. "If I told them where I was, it would be a big problem." After selling their property to pay for Rocky's voyage, his parents now worked on someone else's land. They struggled to feed themselves. Rocky's dream of a European education was stillborn in the surf on that Tangier beach. Now he needed to find real work so he could send money back to his family, who wondered what was taking Rocky so long.

"If I stayed in India, I would be working in a bank right now." Rocky placed his hand on his chest. "For my heart, I have done a big mistake. Two years in this fucking place. Without money. Without work. Without nothing."

The men had finished their breakfast and were playing cricket with a tennis ball and a bat carved from a plank. A chunk of Styrofoam propped up in an abandoned toilet bowl stood in the place of proper wickets. They invited me to play; one insisted on wearing my backpack as I stood to bat so the bag didn't have to touch the ground. I swung miserably at a few balls and returned the bat to abler hands. The men continued with their game while the dogs in the nearby kennel, sensing a ball being tossed around, barked themselves into a frenzy.

The migrants' good spirits surprised me. They laughed and joked and seemed more like boys at summer camp than homeless refugees. Rocky told me most of them suffered so much on their journey to Ceuta that they were content to camp in the forest. Most had travelled overland from India. Some stopped along the way to find work in places like Dubai and earn enough for passage over the sea to Africa. From there, they crossed the Sahara on foot. Many watched their friends die.

"They passed through the jaws of death," Rocky said. He had known one man, a Pakistani, who lashed himself beneath a truck he thought was boarding an Algeciras-bound ferry. When his friends shouted at him from the side of the road that the truck was heading to Morocco instead, the man frantically cut himself loose. He hit the pavement just as the truck rolled forward. His friends watched as the tire crushed his skull into the asphalt. The sight haunted and silenced the men. They rarely spoke at all anymore.

I doubted Rocky and the Indians, or most migrants in CETI, ever thought about the Wall. The barrier, after all, had not stopped them. Aside from a few daring Africans like Jeffrey James, migrants find other ways into the enclave. They bribe border guards. They pay smugglers to float them to Ceuta on boats or, like Rocky, pay to be stowed away in a car and driven over the border. The new and improved fence hasn't made entry into the enclaves any more difficult for them, only more expensive. Migrants pay up to 4,000 euros to smugglers for passage across the border. The refugees still arrive en masse and the Short Stay Centre is jammed full. The only difference now is that the smugglers have never been so rich. The Wall, for all its steely strength, has failed.

Instead of being held at bay on the other side of the Wall, migrants are now trapped inside and wait for something to happen. Mainland Europe is only a few kilometres from the beach. On a clear day, the Indians can see Gibraltar from their mountain. But these men are as far away from the Europe they seek as they have ever been. They have no papers. No money. No way to cross the water. If anything, the Wall is a symbol of incarceration rather than exclusion. It didn't keep them out, but it reminds them they are caged within.

Before I left, I told Rocky I would return to visit them again. "What can I bring you? Is there anything you need?"

"Nothing," he said. "Just pray for us."

∎∎∎∎

On the first night of the massacre, a Rifian tribesman dreamed an ant had swallowed the sea. His fellow fighters thought it a good omen.

In the summer of 1921, Spain controlled much of the wilds of northeast Morocco, known as Er Rif. The Spaniards had spent twelve years extending their protectorate west from Melilla, striking deals with some Rifian tribesmen and killing others. The Spaniards set crops on fire and stole cattle where they deemed it necessary. The Spanish commander, a hawkish general named

Fernández Silvestre, aimed to link Ceuta and Melilla with a continuous swath of Spanish-held territory. The mission was proceeding smoothly. The tribesmen submitted so readily to his power that Silvestre couldn't be bothered to disarm them. In the glow of his military success, Silvestre didn't notice how thinly he'd spread his ill-equipped and poorly fed soldiers across Er Rif.

Abdel Krim noticed. He'd been waiting for this moment for a long time. Muhammad Ibn 'Abd al-Karim al-Khattabi was the son of a Rifian tribal leader. He attended Spanish schools as a boy, then transferred to the famous *Medersa el Attarin* in Fès, where he studied horsemanship, musketry, and the Koran. Abdel Krim learned to resent the corruption of his European colonizers during his time as a journalist and translator in Melilla and began to write newspaper articles against the occupation. The Spanish grew weary of Abdel Krim and eventually jailed him. He escaped once but broke his leg in the attempt, and the police quickly recaptured him.

After serving his prison sentence, Abdel Krim hid for years in the northern mountains and dreamed of founding an independent nation in Er Rif. He cobbled together an army of a few thousand men from tribes that had only ever fought each other. He armed them with stolen Spanish Mauser pistols and rifles smuggled from the French and inspired them with an audacity and courage they had never seen. Then Abdel Krim waited for an opportunity to strike.

On the morning of July 17, 1921, three Spanish lines of about a thousand soldiers each marched out of their base at Anoual, along with a smaller party from Ighriben, to continue their press west. Krim's forces waited for them to descend into a gorge. Krim allowed the Spanish troops to get within two hundred metres before firing on them. They were so close that the rebels' rifle shells tore through several men at once. Abdel Krim said that the bullets flew like grain.

The Spanish force consisted mostly of twenty-year-old conscripts who had never faced such an ambush. They panicked and ran into the barrels and blades of their attackers. Silvestre sent in a relief column from Anoual but withdrew it after losing over 150 men in two hours. Krim's troops took the base at Ighriben and hacked the soldiers inside to pieces. Only twenty-five men made it back to Anoual; sixteen of these later died of injuries and exhaustion. Silvestre pleaded for reinforcements and support from Spain's navy and air force. His superiors ignored him at first; they didn't believe Silvestre could be having such trouble with bands of savages.

The slaughter continued for days. With their supply lines cut, the Spanish could not deliver water overland to the soldiers baking under the Moroccan sun. Spanish planes from Melilla dropped food and ice but missed their marks. Besieged soldiers watched as the Rifians harvested the Spanish provisions and carried them back to their camps. Instead, the Spaniards had to drink juice from pepper and tomato tins. Then bottles of vinegar, cologne, and ink. When they had drained these, the soldiers sweetened their urine with sugar and drank that. Finally they sliced open their arms with their bayonets and drank their own blood. Meanwhile, Abdel Krim's troops were observing the Ramadan fast. During daylight hours, they ate and drank nothing at all.

On July 22, Silvestre stood on the wall at Anoual and shouted, "Run! Run! The bogeyman is coming!" Soldiers dropped their rifles and, along with every Spaniard left in the protectorate, fled east towards Melilla. The bogeymen pursued and butchered. They stabbed or throttled to death any Spanish civilian they came across, not wanting to waste precious bullets on such weak targets. They nailed women to walls. Hacked off arms and legs and genitals. Tied victims' wrists together with their own bowels. By the time Abdel Krim and his army reached the outskirts of Melilla three weeks later, as many as nineteen thousand Spanish corpses lay hot and rotting behind him. Abdel Krim decided not to sack Melilla. The Rifians were bored with slicing throats.

Abdel Krim made the cover of that week's *Time* magazine, and the tribesman's omen came to pass. The ant had swallowed the sea.

■■■

I left Ceuta and followed Abdel Krim's route east through the Rif Valley to Bni Ansar, the town that runs into the border wall at Melilla. I have never seen an uglier place than the frontier at Bni Ansar. Wind off the sea kept the trash, especially the black plastic bags, in continual drift. Garbage piled everywhere. Pools of filth and slugs of spit greased the ground. Moroccan workers were rebuilding the border post, but I saw only demolition. The middle of the road was dug out into a trench. Walls were half standing. Rebars protruded from broken concrete like compound fractures. A man burned a heap of trash next to an aloe vera cactus, blackening the only truly living thing on the street besides the broken dogs and teenage runaways. The rough boys gathered behind my hotel at night to huff solvents from sodden rags.

The hotel was named, delusionally, the Four Seasons, and I could see the border post from my window. All day long, I watched caravans of illegal traders cross the border on foot loaded with duty-free Spanish goods, mostly clothing and banal household items such as toilet paper and detergent. To call them smugglers suggests something furtive and hidden, but there was nothing secret about what was happening. Moroccans, mostly women because they were less likely to be searched, crossed back and forth across the border many times every day. Their hands pulled taut the ropes that lashed the huge cubes of cargo onto their bent backs, their necks strained upwards, and shadows of sweat darkened their head scarves. Once past the Moroccan border post, each woman trudged to a parking lot and unloaded her contraband into a waiting car. Then she crossed back into Spain. The women reminded me of worker ants treading single file into and out of their nest in the service of a demanding but unseen queen.

The end of the immigration line reigned as the most lucrative post in all Morocco for border police. Thousands of Moroccans passed this point every day, and the guards demanded a few coins from nearly every one of them. The daily take was enormous. Police so covet the posting that officers assigned here often lease out the spot to their subordinates. Then they can spend the rest of the day drinking tea in the cafés while their underlings stand in the sun and harvest bribes.

The Moroccans queued up to have their work permits checked by Spanish border officials. Just like at Ceuta, the lines were long in the morning — thousands of day labourers passed each day — and the crossers pressed tight together. Impatient men climbed over the gates, braving the iron spikes to slip by the sluggish Moroccan border police. Just inside the Spanish passport control, in Europe, was the park where the smuggler women tied layers of new clothing beneath their coats, then strapped bundles of shoes and housewares to their backs. The park was a packaging apocalypse of empty cartons, shrink wrap, and twine.

I walked quickly through all of this. My Canadian passport allowed me to avoid the cattle chutes the Moroccans were subjected to. All I needed to do was dodge the spike-belts strewn lazily over the road to stop vehicles and avoid the touts who tried to sell me visa forms I knew were free at the immigration counter. I felt a twinge of guilt at the ease of my crossing. At my white man's privilege. The walls here and elsewhere may be tall and strong and steel, but they are not meant for everyone.

▪▪▪

The name Melilla comes from the Latin for honey, and the town centre is all sweetness. My bus dropped me at the polished Plaza España, where City Hall, the casino, and the Banco de España stand as monuments of *arte modernista*. Nearby, the old bull ring looked as if it were fashioned from fondant icing. Spaniards drank chilled Rioja at the tapas bar behind the Plaza de Toros where bartenders sliced serrano ham from salted haunches behind the bar. Midday drunks drained beer cans and napped beneath the hibiscus in Parque Hernández, and I, with nowhere else to go during the long siesta, found my own bench to lie on. The highest concentration of art nouveau buildings in the world rose above me. Confections of stucco cherubs and roses sugared the balconies and windowsills. Pastel facades resembled the honeyed interiors of summer fruits.

Sweet, too, were the spent vials of intravenous glucose strewn on the pavement where the hunger strikers lay. Twelve Algerians and six Kashmiris wilted on scraps of cardboard across from City Hall. When I first saw them, three paramedics knelt beside a Kashmiri man. A medic with rubber gloves injected glucose into his arm. One of the Algerians spoke good English. He wouldn't give his name, but he said the men had eaten nothing for six days. The skin beneath his eyes was dark and his cheeks sagged. He told me they had lingered in Melilla's Short Stay Centre for almost two years. Like Rocky in exile on the mountain in Ceuta, these men hoped their strike would draw attention to their stranding. "We will not eat until we find a solution, and the only solution is Peninsula," he said. "We can die here." He said paramedics had already delivered eight hunger strikers to the hospital, and they'd plucked another from the sea after he tried to drown himself.

The strikers were just the newest fraternity of hungry young men to be trapped in Melilla. In the days of the Spanish protectorate, Melilla was a garrison town populated by the unluckiest of Spanish conscripts. The soldiers assigned to Melilla were poorly equipped and undernourished. Officers and their wives exchanged guns for vegetables in the Rifian markets, and a popular joke claimed the lice growing in the soldiers' armpits were Melilla's only cattle. Hoping to be evacuated back to the Peninsula, soldiers rubbed stinging nettle into minor cuts, ate tobacco to appear jaundiced, and chased venereal infections in the town's brothels. Nearly a century before today's migrants arrived clinging to leaky rafts and strategic lies, men in the enclaves tried anything to get back across the sea.

The paramedics loaded the Kashmiri into the back of a yellow ambulance, and I thought of the tribesmen of Anoual who fasted for Allah while the Spanish soldiers starved under siege. Now new men were wasting away in the city of honey.

███

Melilla's most repeated boast is that of *las cuatro culturas*, the peaceful blending of Christians, Muslims, Jews, and Hindus. Melilla's Christian majority, about 50,000 souls, shares the city with about half as many Muslims. An active community of 3,000 Jews centres around Or Zoruah synagogue, an art deco masterpiece of arched windows and moulded plaster, and a few hundred Indian Hindus are scattered among them all.

But while the four cultures get along, they rarely get together. The relationship between the Christians and Muslims is especially strained. Although nearly every one of Melilla's citizens now holds Spanish nationality, only the white *cristianos* are routinely referred to as Spanish. Muslims are referred to as Rifians, *marroquíes*, or, disparagingly, *moros*. The Muslims rarely identify themselves as Spanish, regardless of their actual citizenship, but as *musulmánes*. Occasionally, tensions between Melilla's Christians and Muslims have flared into violence. In 1975, Muslims bombed a posh bar in support of Morocco's Green March into the Western Sahara. In response, bands of unhinged legionnaires thrashed Muslims on the streets until the military ordered them to stop.

Even now, during peaceful times, the segregation in Melilla is acute. Muslims earn much less than Christians, and few hold any of the enclave's lucrative government jobs. The tapas bars and swish villas are not for them. Instead, many live in the Cañada de la Muerte, the Ravine of Death. Moroccan mercenaries, employed by Franco to help regain Spain's losses in Er Rif, first settled the Cañada in the years after Anoual. While many Spaniards, especially Franco, sought to avenge the massacre, few saw the need to cling to empire in Africa. Even fewer wanted to wage war for it. So Franco hired Rifians to fight their own countrymen, and he built barracks for them on the Cañada. Today, the Cañada is the largest Muslim slum in Melilla.

A bloody 1893 battle between Spanish soldiers and Rifian tribesmen in the ravine gave the Cañada de la Muerte its name, but its reputation darkened further during the 1980s. In an attempt to rid Spain of drug dealers, Basque terrorists, and other undesirables ahead of Spain's inclusion in the European Community, the Spanish government passed a law to evict illegal immigrants. The Aliens' Law of 1986 bestowed legal Spanish residency on Spanish citizens, most former colonials in South and Central America, and some Sephardic Jews. The Muslims of Melilla and Ceuta were not on the list. Most did not have Spanish citizenship at the time, not even those born in Melilla and whose families had lived there for generations. The Muslims feared expulsion and protesters poured out of the Cañada. They staged hunger strikes on the Plaza España. Peaceful demonstrations, both for and against the law, degraded to riots. There was tear gas and rubber bullets. Placards accused the Spanish government of slavery and racism. Cars were overturned and burned. Eventually the government calmed tempers by offering citizenship to anyone born in Melilla and any long-time resident, but the damage was already done. The conflict left residual bitterness and distrust among Cañada residents. For the Christian *Melillanese*, the race riots were another reason to fear the *moros* and the Cañada itself.

I walked through the Cañada on one of my last afternoons in Melilla. The houses were square and sharp-angled, like a box of children's blocks upended on the hillside. The same pastels coloured the buildings as in Melilla's centre, but there were no *modernista* flourishes in the Cañada. The neighbourhood was built without any central plan. Houses went up wherever there was room, and when horizontal space was gone, they built upwards. Homes huddled close to each other as if for protection. The neighbourhood was tight and secretive, yet cheerful and clean. Women in pink djellabas, ravines of wrinkles and blue Berber tattoos colouring their faces, swept dust from the sidewalks. Potted flowers hung on windowsills. I passed a playground next to a café. Children ran in the park while men drank mint tea and smoked *kif*. This was the only place in Melilla where men openly smoked cannabis. They knew the police wouldn't come here.

You can see the border wall from the Cañada. I descended the ravine to walk along it. The multi-layer barrier begins on the Moroccan side with a briar patch of concertina wire. Behind it rises the first of three fences, six metres tall and leaning slightly into Morocco, as if bracing itself for an assault. Horizontal hinged panels on the top of this first fence are designed to collapse under the weight of whoever tries to climb. On the ground beyond the first fence is a web of steel cables meant to entangle anyone who makes it over. International human rights groups claim that these cables are razor sharp. This is an exaggeration, the cables are not that cruel, but they are strung taut enough to injure anyone who falls onto them from the top of the fence. The second fence is shorter than the first, but topped with the same collapsing grills. There is a narrow path for border police vehicles and then a third fence, six metres high, built of steel links as dense as the chain mail on a medieval knight. The links are so tight that the Moroccan village of Bni Ansar appeared blurry through the fence. The Wall was ferocious. Majestic. I couldn't help but admire it.

Local laws prohibit anyone from approaching the Wall, but no one protested as I walked beside the barrier and dragged my fingers along its chain links. The heat from the sun, the same heat that melted the Spaniards at Anoual, made the wire hot to touch. For all its steel intensity, I found moments of unexpected lightness there. Olive groves flanked the Wall on both sides, and drab green uniforms of the Moroccan border police were hung to dry on the barbed wire. Songbirds sang from their perches atop the fences. A vine of wildflowers broke through the wire, stretched across the nest of cables, and bloomed into pink blossoms. The flowers reminded me that this fence, just like the one at Ceuta, has not stopped the migrants from reaching the enclaves. Regardless of the Wall's ferocity, it could not spook to death their beautiful dreams of Europe.

I looked behind me, back up at the Cañada, and realized I had missed the point. The new barriers might fail at security, but like Hadrian's Wall, they succeed as theatre. The actual effectiveness of the walls is secondary to the illusion they create: one of exclusion and difference.

Mainland Europeans don't think much of Ceuta and Melilla. They see the enclaves as places to make money — civil servants earn double wages here — not as places to live. They dismiss the citizens of Ceuta and Melilla as uncultured hicks. Even fascists. Worst of all, they consider the enclaves more Moroccan than European. In 1987, an under-16 European Cup football match between Spain and Germany was to be played in Melilla, but the Germans insisted that Melilla was not in Europe and demanded a venue change. I met a teacher in Melilla whose school once hosted a class from the Peninsula. When the students returned home, they assembled a corkboard display of their visit to Melilla titled "Our Moroccan Adventure." The display infuriated the *Melillanese* teachers. To confuse the Spanish with the *moros* was a great insult.

For the Spanish who live in the enclaves, the walls demonstrate in hard steel the difference between Us and Them. The fences stand less as physical barriers than as emotional ones. They demarcate a line between perceived European Christian civility and Silvestre's bogeymen. The *Melillanese* are not preoccupied by the blacks and browns of Africa and south Asia — the migrants that the fences aim, but fail, to deter. In fact, they'll even toss them a euro coin to wash their BMWs. Just as long as everyone understands that the *melillanese* are not Muslims, not Arabs, and not Africans. In Ceuta and Melilla, the fortified line underscores identity. The Wall does not defend: it defines.

The Wall eventually passes Melilla's Short Stay Centre. I observed three African women coming out through the turnstiles that guarded the front door. One had long, slender braids and pushed a bicycle. Her friends followed. They watched from the side of the road as she mounted the bicycle and pedalled hard up the road that ran beside the Wall. When she reached the crest of the hill, she turned and soared back down. She lifted both hands from the handlebars and raised them into the air, her braids bouncing against her back. Her friends laughed and applauded and whistled. At the bottom, the woman turned and climbed again. Then she glided down again, her hands high in the air, reaching into the immense canvas of the African sky. Flying past the Wall of barbed wire and steel.

Zero People of No Man's Land
The Indo-Bangladesh Fence

Cyril John Radcliffe dragged his pen across a map of India, a place he'd never seen, and cleaved two countries from one.

After the dissolution of the British Raj in 1947, the Indian Independence Act called for the division of British India into two sovereign nations, the Dominion of India and the Dominion of Pakistan. The borders of the new countries were to follow religious lines: India would be for Hindus, Pakistan for Muslims. Mahatma Gandhi, hero of Indian independence, said: "My whole soul rebels against the idea that Hinduism and Islam represent two antagonistic cultures and doctrines. To assent to such a doctrine is for me a denial of God. For I believe the God of the Koran is also the God of the Gita, and we are all, no matter by what name designated, children of the same God."[7] Despite the rebellion of Gandhi's soul and the objections of secular politicians, the Hindu and Muslim nationalists who demanded religious homelands prevailed.

The British parliament assigned Radcliffe, a nearsighted Oxford-educated lawyer, the task of drawing the new frontiers. Radcliffe didn't want the job. No one did. The project involved separating 80 million people and divvying up more than 450,000 square kilometres of land to carve a bisected Pakistan—a West Pakistan and an East Pakistan—from India's flanks. (In 1971, East Pakistan won independence from the West and emerged as Bangladesh.) Radcliffe begrudgingly took the assignment with the understanding he would have six months to complete the gargantuan task. But when he arrived in Delhi in July 1947, sweating through his Englishman's suit, Radcliffe's superiors told him he had to finish in thirty-six days. He didn't even have time to send for more suitable clothes. W.H. Auden described Radcliffe's ordeal in his poem "Partition":

> …Shut up in a lonely mansion, with police night and day
> Patrolling the gardens to keep the assassins away,
> He got down to work, to the task of settling the fate
> Of millions. The maps at his disposal were out of date
> And the Census Returns almost certainly incorrect,
> But there was no time to check them, no time to inspect
> Contested areas. The weather was frightfully hot,
> And a bout of dysentery kept him constantly on the trot,
> But in seven weeks it was done, the frontiers decided,
> A continent for better or worse divided.[8]

The resulting borderline testifies to both Radcliffe's haste and his utter ignorance of India. The "Radcliffe Line" often sliced through the middle of villages. Sometimes the line split individual homes in two, leaving kitchens in India and salons in Pakistan. In some areas, the border ran through erratic-flowing rivers, so properties on the shoreline ended up on the opposite side of the border each time the river changed course. The borderline showed a misunderstanding of, or an indifference to, religious politics: Muslims and Hindus in many border areas found themselves on the wrong side of the line from their spiritual kin. Radcliffe knew his slapdash border was a mess. As soon as he submitted the maps, he fled India, fearing for his life. In a letter to his stepson, Radcliffe wrote: "There will be roughly 80-million people with a grievance who will begin looking for me. I don't want them to find me."[9] He insisted British soldiers search the plane bringing him home to England for bombs and assassins. He never returned to India.

Partition resulted in the mass migration of 12 million people, who flowed back and forth across the new border — the largest movement of people in human history and likely the bloodiest. Somewhere between 500,000 and a million people died in the violence that exploded during the weeks following partition. Hundreds of thousands of women and girls were abducted and raped. Radcliffe read about the horrors he helped create from the safety of his home in England, where, the next year, the Order of the British Empire rewarded his efforts with a knighthood.

India, for all its anger and indignation over Radcliffe's sloppy line, never corrected the border. Instead, the citizens of the new Dominion started to cast the frontier in barbed wire and steel.

■■■

India engulfs Bangladesh in an amoebic embrace. Aside from a short shared border with Burma and the shoreline where the mouths of the Ganges yawn green over the Bay of Bengal, Bangladesh is surrounded by its big Indian brother. The two nations have been reasonably familial since partition. India backed Bangladesh's final struggle for independence from Pakistan in 1971 and granted citizenship to four million Bangladeshi immigrants to India following the war. Neighbourly relations, though, quickly started to strain. As the population of illegal migrants from Bangladesh swelled to over 10 million, the welcome faded. In the early 1980s, a few years before she was assassinated, Indian prime minister Indira Gandhi recommended building a barrier along the entire 4,000-kilometre Indo-Bangla border to keep the migrants out.

The government launched the fencing project in 1986, and immediately critics doubted that a $4-billion barbed wire barrier would do anything to deter unwanted Bangladeshis from crossing the "zero line." (They were right—it hasn't.) But these critics did not understand the value of the Wall as a work of theatre the way Indian economist Jagdish Baghwati did. He wrote:

> While I believe that the late Prime Minister Indira Gandhi's decision to construct a fence along the enormous India–Bangladesh border in the state of Assam was an ineffective policy, I believe that it was nevertheless a splendid policy. For, to be seen to be doing nothing at all, even though one could not really close the border, would have been politically explosive since it would be read as indifference or indecisiveness. And building the fence was the least disruptive way of doing nothing while appearing to do something![10]

The Indo-Bangla Wall, like Hadrian's Wall, was valued more for its facade than its function. If the appearance of Hadrian's shining limestone was meant to impress his imperial subjects, the Indo-Bangla barrier served as an illusion to soothe an anxious nation. I suspected, however, that the Wall meant more than nothing to the villagers who lived against it. I wanted to visit the Bangladeshi border to see just how "splendid" a policy the Wall really was.

■■■

A 31-hour train journey from Mumbai's Chhatrapati Shivaji station brought me to Kolkata, capital of West Bengal province. The province shares a 2,200-kilometre border with Bangladesh, half of the total Indo-Bangla line. West Bengal opposed the idea of the Wall when the Indian government first proposed the plan in the 1980s. Bengalis on both sides of Radcliffe's Line possessed the same culture, faith, and language long before there was any sort of border at all. They share an appreciation for the mystic songs of the wandering Bauls, an adoration for the poetry of Rabindranath Tagore, and a taste for fish simmered in mustard gravy. Bengalis, east and west of the border, regard Kolkata — formerly Calcutta — as their cultural and spiritual centre. No doubt they even butter their bread on the same side. A physical barrier dividing these people, especially one along a borderline drawn by a myopic British lawyer, made no sense in light of these emotional bonds. Bengalis did not want to be apart, and the West Bengal government resisted the construction. By 2000, only 5 percent of the West Bengal–Bangladesh border fence had been completed.

Two years later, though, fears of Muslim bogeymen blackened the cross-border kinship. Indian observers regarded the rise of Islamic political parties in Bangladesh as evidence of growing religious extremism on the other side of the line. Reports surfaced of Pakistani terror groups operating in Bangladesh near the border. Officials accused *madrassahs* on the Bangladeshi side of the line of encouraging and planning terrorist attacks against Indian targets. Distrust of men in turbans and beards bloomed in the fertile dread of fallen towers. Indians associated Bangladeshis with Islam, and Islam with terror. The government of West Bengal relaxed its resistance to the Wall, and by the time I arrived there the fencing was nearly complete.

In Kolkata, I boarded another train east to the Bangladeshi frontier. The nearby border crossing at Petrapole, India's primary gateway to Bangladesh, is Asia's busiest land port, handling 80 percent of all trade between the two countries. All legal trade, anyway. Smuggling along the border is commonplace and tolerated, if not officially condoned. The local economies rely on informal passing of goods across the border — everything from fruit to heroin to Bengali prostitutes — and the smugglers do twice the business of the legitimate traders. The Indian border village of Jayantipur interested me more than the actual checkpoint, however. I'd read the village now stood between the border and the new wall, the barrier effectively excising Jayantipur from India.

The sunrise departure from Kolkata exhausted me, and I quickly fell asleep against the rattling hulk of the train. I woke, though, to music. A man on a nearby seat was singing in a sweet and smooth voice. His seatmates drummed along with their fingertips atop bags and boxes and on the wall of the train car. The singer stopped after a few short melodies and returned to the quiet banalities of his commute. The others did the same. The music lent colour to the passengers' voyage. A brief interlude of sweetness. I fell back to sleep.

When the train stopped, the passengers gushed out of the car onto the platform. The surge lifted me off my feet. I worried for a moment that I might lose my footing and be trampled, but the crowd pressed so tight together there was no room even to fall. I rode the wave of flesh out of the train and out of the station, where I hired a bicycle rickshaw to take me to Jayantipur. We sat stuck in a jam of rickshaws for the first half kilometre. Each driver honked his or her old-fashioned squeeze-bulb bicycle horn, turning the street into a riot of rubber ducks. The traffic eased once we reached the main road. Patties of fresh cow dung spotted the trees lining the route. The bottom of every tree trunk was encircled in a coat of these grassy black-brown discs, and each patty bore the handprint of whoever had splatted it onto the bark to dry. We passed a green jungle and ponds of clear water where women bathed and boys swam. The air was cool and clean. It was my first experience of rural India.

My rickshaw wallah told me that if I wanted to see the border fence I would have to seek permission from the Border Security Forces, the branch of India's military responsible for protecting the nation's boundaries. He dropped me off at the local BSF headquarters, just a few hundred metres from the border itself. A smiling official welcomed me into his office and sent for tea after I sat. He laughed when I asked to see the Wall. "It is not allowed. Not possible." He shook his head and chuckled through his moustache as if my request was the most ridiculous thing he'd heard in a long time.

I told him I didn't want to cross the Wall, or even touch the Wall, I just wanted to see it. "I am interested in borders and fences," I said. "I've visited many around the world. That is why I've come to India."

"Have you seen the Palestinian wall?" he asked.

"Yes."

"That is where we got the idea. From the Israelis."

I asked the officer about Jayantipur. He said I'd been misinformed. The Wall did not separate the village from India, but some of the village farmland was on the Bangla side of the barrier. Only the landowners were permitted to pass through the Wall to work the exiled fields. "You can go to Jayantipur," he said. "The village is right across the road. But you cannot see the fence."

I shook his hand, crossed the road, and walked into Jayantipur. Once I was out of sight of the BSF post, I turned east towards the border. I couldn't imagine the harm in my simply glancing at the Wall. Surely the official was being overcautious. At worst, someone in a uniform would consider me a foolish, lost foreigner and shoo me away. I hadn't gone far, though, before a teenager on a bicycle sped past and called out, "Salaam aleikum." When I shouted "Hello" back to him, he stopped his bike, circled back, and asked me in faltering English where I was going.

"I am going for a walk," I said.

"No. That way Bangladesh. No man's land. Soldiers." He mimed someone firing a rifle. "AK-47." He placed his hand on my shoulder and, with genuine concern, turned me back towards the main road. I was ready to disregard a government official but not quite willing to ignore the sincere warnings of a local boy. When we reached the road, the boy patted the bike seat behind him by way of invitation. I looked back one last time to where the Wall might be, then climbed onto the seat. The boy pushed the bicycle forward, stood on the pedals, and rattled me back to the train station. Each time he passed someone he knew, he jerked a thumb back at me and shouted, "Foreigner!"

■■■

The bombs bloomed into marigolds of flame and blasted the colour from Gauhati's Ganeshguri market as easily as human flesh from bones. The explosions negated the red of chilies, green of okra, orange of oranges, reducing all to a uniform grey and black. Only flames and blood stood out from the monochrome. It is a marvel how blood thickens when mixed with ash. And how it brightens.

Six motorcycles and Maruti cars loaded with RDX explosive erupted within five minutes of each other. The blasts scorched bodies and flung limbs aside, and by the time the police and firefighters arrived, the battered survivors needed someone to blame. The mobs overturned the police cruisers and set fire to the fire trucks. They smashed whatever windows the blasts had spared. No one could tell which fires were started by the bombs and which by the rioters. Terror and anger and frustration united in the thick black smoke.

There were explosions in villages outside Gauhati too. Thirteen bombs in all. The serial blasts killed 55 people. Or 73. Or 84. No one knew for sure. Some bodies were charred to the bone, their faces burned off. Horror-struck families, not willing to wait for DNA tests, claimed their dead based on height and build or the familiar shape of a faceless head. Sometimes they argued amongst each other over the gory remains and who got to take home the black bones. Four-year-old Moroni Sarma was the youngest to die. She was holding her father's hand when the bombs went off. The last to die was a man named Isaac Newton. His burns took eighteen days to kill him.

The papers and television speculated on who was responsible — Pakistani groups, Indian jihadists, or more local liberation movements such as ULFA, HuJI, and NDFB: northeast India's terror fraternities. What everyone agreed on was that, regardless of the acronyms of blame, whoever did this must have slipped past the Wall.

I arrived in Gauhati, the capital of Assam, just as the bombs exploded. I didn't hear the blasts over the radio in my airport taxi and knew nothing until I showed up at Paltan Bazaar looking for a hotel and found everyone watching the carnage on television. Some of the bombs had exploded only a kilometre away. No one wanted to rent me a room. I tried to call a contact I had in the city, but the blasts had knocked out the phone lines. I didn't know what to do, but I knew I didn't have the stomach for this kind of violence.

I found a seat in one of the last cars to get out of Gauhati before the army barricaded the highway.

India's far northeast is divided from the rest of India, not by a wall or fence, but by Radcliffe's clumsy pen, which nearly severed the northeast from "mainland" India. Only a tiny strip of territory, twenty-one kilometres across at its narrowest point, keeps the northeast from being pinched off altogether. Indians call the corridor the Chicken's Neck. The northeast's seven states — Meghalaya, Tripura, Assam, Nagaland, Mizoram, Manipur, and Arunachal Pradesh — felt different from the rest of India, especially as my car fled the smoke and chaos of the Gauhati bombings and crossed south out of Assam into Meghalaya. Villagers looked more east Asian than Indian, built hillside homes on pillars, and carried loads in long conical baskets strapped to their foreheads. Shacks sold whiskey and wine and fatty pork brains on rice. As we neared Shillong, Meghalaya's capital, checkered smocks replaced saris on the women. Bible verses appeared on bumper stickers and roadside signs. Blue Krishnas gave way to pale white Christs.

The Khasis, the major ethnic group in the region, were not always Christian. In the beginning — in their beginning — God created sixteen families along with the heavens and the earth. The families lived with him in the celestial paradise but were free to travel to earth via a golden ladder that stretched from heaven to Mount Sohpetbneng, the "Navel of Heaven." The holy mountain stands outside Shillong; I could see it from the Gauhati-Shillong road. Seven of the sixteen families became enamoured of the earth and asked God if they could stay there forever. God obliged and removed the golden ladder. The Khasis are the descendants of the seven families who opted out of paradise.

Welsh missionaries introduced the Khasis to an alternative god in the 1870s and coaxed them out of their sacred woods onto wooden pews. Most Khasis are now enthusiastically Christian. Old stone churches, Christian graveyards, and plaster crucifixes stand everywhere on the Khasi Hills. In Shillong, Sunday Masses overflow into the streets. Penitents sweat in their suits and stand along the street to listen to the services being broadcast from speakers on telephone poles.

Still, ancient traditions have yet to dislodge. Though the priests may scowl, Khasis still divine the future by breaking eggs or eviscerating chickens to reveal the prophecies contained within their wet guts. The Khasis remain one of the world's few matrilineal societies. Women own the land, the husband lives in his mother-in-law's home, and property passes from mother to youngest daughter. Recently, Khasi men have waved their Bibles and demanded an end to matrilineal inheritance, claiming the practice is an affront to their adopted god. Besides causing snickers among Western sociologists, these "Men's Liberation" movements have only made Khasi traditionalists more rigid. The ultimate hope of most Khasis remains the same: to eventually rejoin the nine families in heaven.

Shillong was close enough to Gauhati to be concerned with the blasts. By the time I arrived, soldiers filled the streets and every television was tuned to news of the attacks. At ten o'clock that night, six police officers knocked on my hotel room door. In light of the day's horrors, the authorities in Shillong wanted to know who all the strangers were and where they'd come from. Since I'd just arrived from the bomb smoke of Gauhati, I aroused their suspicions. One officer flipped through my passport while the others glanced around my room with wide, nervous eyes. Satisfied I wasn't a terrorist, the leader offered me a cold, tense handshake and bid me a good night. I recalled being tailed by the authorities in Western Sahara. There, I was afraid of the police; here, the police were afraid of me.

In the morning, I sought breakfast at Police Bazaar, Shillong's central square. It was early, and the city was only just rousing. Vendors assembled their breakfast stalls. They dropped balls of dough into sizzling pans of oil to make puri or rolled chapatis like the Indians on the mountain in Ceuta. Smoke from the oil merged with steam from tea kettles. I exchanged some ragged rupees for two hot puffs of puri, a scoop of spicy vegetable curry, and a dab of chutney served on a sheet of yesterday's *Shillong Times*. I sat in a stairwell with other men beneath a sign that said NO SITTING. The puri man handed me a second sheet of newspaper so I didn't have to sit on the bare cement. Then he passed me some chai. The tea was so hot it softened the thin plastic cup and I could barely hold it.

Around me, drivers of taxis and minibuses pressed on their horns and called out their destinations. Women sold cigarettes and halves of fresh betel nut on paan leaves. A single beggar, too tall and dark-skinned to be Khasi, pleaded for coins. Trucks loaded and unloaded, and a drift of discarded plastic cups, greasy newsprint, and green orange peels gave work to the sweeper man and his tiny broom. Water carriers panted under the strain of the water tins hanging on poles over their shoulders.

After my tea and puri, I bought the *Telegraph*, a Kolkata newspaper, from a vendor still assembling the inserts. I read that India would soon land a probe on the moon and that the biggest threat to the Indian nation came from Bangladesh. Forty-six points along the Indo-Bangla line are vulnerable to terrorists, the paper said.

█▌█

I hired a guide to take me to the villages along Meghalaya's border with Bangladesh. James Perry is Canadian but was born in Shillong to Christian missionaries. He returned to Canada to attend high school and university, and his tall, lithe frame testifies to his collegiate career as a distance runner. James, though, has lived most of his life in Meghalaya. He is married to a local woman, speaks flawless Khasi, and his English has a strange and lilting Khasi accent. James runs a tour company that guides visitors through northeast India. The region does not figure on many tourist itineraries — the crown jewels of Indian tourism are south and west of Meghalaya — and most of James's clients come for journalistic or anthropological pursuits, especially to study or write about the Khasis' cultural quirk of matrilineage. I was the first who'd come looking for fences.

Before we left Shillong, James arranged a meeting with the governor of Meghalaya, Mr. Ranjit Shekhar Mooshahary. The governor had once been the director general of the Border Security Force, so he knew the frontier. We sat with Mooshahary at his residence in the centre of Shillong surrounded by sculpted lawns, fountains, and flower beds. In his office, a white-jacketed servant brought us tea, dishes of cashews, and sticky *gulab jamun*. "The border fence is formidable," Mooshahary said. From across a huge wooden desk, he boasted about the fence's three layers of barbed wire, concrete pillars, and rolls of concertina. "The United States should copy our fence for their border with Mexico." No wall is built without bluster.

Still, Mooshahary admitted a problem with the Wall. India signed an agreement with Bangladesh after 1971 forbidding either nation from building a "defensive structure" within 150 metres of the actual border or "zero line."

For most of its route, the Wall respects the agreement. In some areas, however, natural topography such as rivers and cliffs makes this official buffer zone impossible to adhere to, and the Wall runs inside the 150 metres. This infuriates the Bangladeshis, who considered the construction of the Wall an act of aggression. The Bangla border soldiers, the Bangladeshi Rifles, have fired on wall builders who crossed into the legislated no man's land. Mooshahary defended India's border infractions with suspect semantics. "We can build within the buffer zone because a fence is not a 'defensive structure,'" he told me. "It is a preventative structure."

I told Mooshahary that I wanted to tour the borderlands. "You should not have too much trouble reaching the villages," he said, "but if you want to see the fence, you require permission from Delhi. I cannot give it to you." The idea of wading through the muck of Indian military bureaucracy made me shudder, but as we left the office, James told me that travelling to the Wall and feigning ignorance would prove a more efficient tactic.

The next morning, we sputtered out of town on James's motorcycle, past poinsettia trees that hung white and red blossoms over fences and lent Shillong an unexpected feel of Christmas. After a couple of hours we paused for a lunch of cheap noodles in the clifftop town of Cherrapunji, which lays claim to the record for the world's greatest annual rainfall. In an average year, nearly twelve metres of rain falls on Cherrapunji. During the monsoons, moisture from the Bay of Bengal collides with these cliffs, rises above them, and rages down. Indian tourists stand on the precipice in the dry season and imagine the downpour they've read about in their schoolbooks. Guinness World Records, however, betrayed Cherrapunji recently by granting the nearby village of Mawsynram the "official" rainfall title. The faithful in Cherrapunji dismiss this, insisting that the measuring cup in rival Mawsynram was bought at the local market and is hardly scientific.

Northeast India obsesses over world records. The world's hottest chili pepper, the Bhut Jolokia "Ghost Chili," grows here, and in 2009 a Gauhati woman ate fifty-one of them in two minutes to sear her way into the record books. I read about a man in Assam who was collecting poisonous spiders for his bid to eat a thousand of them in a day. I witnessed the mass frying of the world's largest *jalebi* — a deep-fried, syrup-soaked Indian pastry — the night before I left Shillong. Recently, the city broke records for the largest drum circle and the largest guitar ensemble. Considering the Khasis' self-exile from heaven, perhaps their guitarists' choice of song, "Knocking on Heaven's Door," signalled a change of heart. The constant striving for exceptionality was a strange compulsion. I wondered if the people on India's forgotten edges needed to shout to be noticed. And I wondered too whether the Indo-Bangladeshi fence, if it is ever completed, would claim the crown as the world's longest.

After lunch, James and I crisscrossed down the cliff face to the lowlands. He wore a helmet but I had none, and I could feel the wind grow warmer and wetter against my face as we descended from the cool air of the highlands to the damp air below. The autumn betel harvest had just ended, and the tall baskets used to soak the nuts lay in heaps like pillars of a fallen acropolis. Farther along, tiny women in checked aprons squatted at the roadside to collect pebbles for roadworks. James stopped the bike at the top of some stone steps, and we walked down into the village of Lyngkhat, where a soccer field straddled the border. One pair of goalposts stood in India, the other in Bangladesh, but only Indians are permitted to play here, each shot at the net a sort of benign invasion.

Lyngkhat is considered one of the 150 "adverse possessions" along the Indo-Bangladesh border, another troublesome quirk of India's dysfunctional partition. After 1947, villages along the new border found themselves on the wrong side of the line from where they felt they belonged. The disputed territories encompass more than five thousand acres of borderlands, and governments in Delhi and Dhaka have been unwilling to surrender any of this land to the other side. The legal status of those living in the adverse possessions is tenuous. Indians refer to these villagers as "nowhere people." No one knows on which side of the borderline they should be. Now that line was being reinforced by the Wall.

In Lyngkhat, a handful of Border Security Forces personnel from around India sweated in their tan polyester uniforms and ensured the Indian sanctity of the soccer field and of the village itself. Our arrival interrupted their boredom and seemed to make them nervous. A BSF soldier from Chennai insisted on holding our passports and my camera, but a superior officer scolded him to just leave us alone.

Lyngkhat was made of tidy wooden houses, each with a small veranda and a dirt yard for the dogs, chickens, and children. In the market, betel nuts, oranges, lychees, and fruits I'd never seen before lay on great stone slabs. A man, eyes glassed from drinking rice wine, passed us on his way towards the border. "I am going to defend my country," he joked and stumbled down the path. Another man invited us onto his veranda. He kicked off his sandals and sat on them while his son offered James and me plastic chairs. James spoke to the man in fluent Khasi. This must have surprised the man — not even the BSF soldiers spoke Khasi — but he betrayed no amazement. "The Khasis have excellent poker faces," James told me later.

We ate rice cakes wrapped in banana leaf while BSF soldiers drank in the adjacent café and pretended not to watch us. "There is no fence yet, but it is coming," the man said. "It will go behind my house." He pointed to a black stone pillar that marked the actual border. The marker was nearly invisible in the tall grass. Army engineers had already measured out the Wall's route and would soon drive posts into the ground. Because of the 150-metre agreement, most of the farmer's property will lie in no man's land, on the other side of the Wall. The BSF engineers planned to install a pair of gates in the Wall, but the man didn't know where they would be or when they would be opened. He worried too about how he would protect his fruit from Bangladeshi thieves if a fence stood between him and his fields.

The man was most concerned, though, about the potential loss of cross-border trade. Indians will not buy bruised fruit, but Bangladeshis will, and farmers sell their second-rate produce across the line. The trade is illegal, but the BSF are bribed easily and cheaply and will allow farmers to cross with a load of blemished oranges or a sack of cracked lychees. This happens daily in Lyngkhat. The Wall might not make the soft-fruit smuggling impossible — "We will always find a way," our host said — but it will certainly be more difficult and, if the required bribes increase, more expensive.

He was pleased that the Wall would help keep Bangladeshi thieves out of the village, but the BSF were already doing this. "Were it not for the BSF, the Bangladeshis would overrun Lyngkhat. They are poor and have nothing."

I asked him if he felt as if he was living next to an enemy.

"Things used to be better. The world was more honest," he said.

We left Lyngkhat and continued to Shella, another border village. There was no fence here yet either, but everyone knew it was coming. We hoped to spend the night in the Inspection Bureau, a sort of hostel for civil workers, but in spite of James's persistence, the caretaker would not take us in without official permission. Instead, a kind old woman in the house next door invited us to stay. Kwerilla Mawa loved to talk, sometimes uncrossing her arms from beneath her checkered Khasi apron to wave them at her story.

"When I was a girl, I used to cross into East Pakistan without even thinking about it. My family crossed to buy fish and eggs and dishes from China," she told us. "When East Pakistan became Bangladesh, it became harder to cross. Now, with the fence, it will be impossible." Mawa's family owned orchards of pineapple and betel and oranges. Like the farmer in Lyngkhat, they plied their bruised fruit across the border to the Bangladeshis. Nowadays, fearing cross-border terror, the BSF were more vigilant and harder to bribe. Mawa's oranges were rotting on the ground. And it would only get worse when the Wall came. The Shella village council protested the building of the Wall, and villagers had marched into the fields to stand in the way of the builders. They delayed the construction, but Mawa knew it would begin again soon.

"Do you know why the government wants a wall?" I asked.

"To stop us from going back and forth. I don't know. We are ignorant people. We don't understand much."

But Mawa understood power. She laughed like a young girl when I asked if she feared the Banglas across the line. "They are not all bad people. They are good people and we are good people. But India has strength, so we close them off. Whoever has strength can do this. You came to my house tonight and I could have told you to go away because it is my house and I have the strength."

She showed us to our room. I took the wood-plank bed while James spread a sleeping bag on the floor. In the morning, I pressed some rupees into Mawa's palm as I shook her hand goodbye. The gesture jarred her for a moment. But then she laughed again and the bills disappeared with her hands behind her apron.

James revved the motorcycle up the main highway from Shella to the top of the Khasi Hills. We passed back through Cherrapunji then descended the hills again a little farther east to another border village. Our route was inefficient. We covered very little lateral distance this way, but there was no other way to travel along the border. The only road that followed the frontier was a path flattened for the BSF, and we were forbidden to use it. So we rose and fell like a monsoon cloud against the hills. The road was rough. My back and legs stiffened on the motorcycle. I could tell James was also sore because we stopped more often at the roadside cafés that served tea from Assam. We both took it "red," without milk, and I realized I'd never drunk fresh tea before. Compared to this vegetal richness, the tea that emerges from the dry bags I soak in Canada tastes like iron filings.

The hills of the borderlands provide an economy of fruit and stone—lychee and orange for the farmers, pebbles for the road workers and, as we travelled east, limestone. We descended into Mahajai village beneath the overhead cable car that carried limestone from the quarries in the hills to the Lafarge plant in Bangladesh. There it would become cement, but on this side of the zero line, villagers cooked the limestone in enormous brick ovens to make edible lime. They smeared it on paan leaves, folded it around betel nuts, and munched it into a bitter-juiced mulch. The Khasis chew betel all day, and they hope to chew betel in heaven after they die. James taught me to remove most of the lime from the betel we bought—lime is bad for the teeth—but I left enough to numb my tongue on the side of the mouth I chewed on. The sensation was pleasant and warming, but the dental horrors of the Khasi men, their mouths abstractions of red smears and black holes, warned against making this a habit.

In Mahajai, I finally saw the Wall. Government officials were insisting to the newspapers that they'd nearly completed the Wall, but after three days travelling along the border this was the first time we saw any fencing at all. And here the barrier was only half built. We asked permission from the uniformed men in a police post to approach the Wall. An off-duty officer in a vest but no shirt guided us to the barrier. Taut strands of barbed wire linked two rows of fence posts. A two-metre-wide concrete path ran between the rows. Coiled concertina wire would eventually fill this space, while floodlights on towers would illuminate it by night. The entire structure was freshly painted, the black still sticky in the sweaty afternoon heat. This was hardly the formidable barrier His Excellency had boasted about in Shillong. Anyone with a pair of basic wire cutters would be able to defeat it. Most of the Wall was unfinished—a mere row of posts still bare of wire. Rather than a barrier, village women used the structure as a footpath to walk between their fields.

Despite its current weakness, the promise of the Wall worried the young village headman. We talked to him at one of the long wooden tables in a tea stall while the female proprietor sent us tea, cookies, and sliced apples. The headman's family home stood in what would become the no man's land between the Wall and the zero line. His house was set to be demolished. The government was promising to compensate him for his loss, but no one had named a sum. Even if the compensation turned out to be generous, there was no land nearby to purchase. He would have to move his family out of his ancestral village.

"I understand the fence is meant to protect the country," he said, "and I know it will come no matter what we say or do, but it will be a big loss for us. This is a poor place. The crops don't yield as high as they used to. We are not big landowners or businessmen. All we have is our homes. When we meet for tea, we ask each other, 'When the fence comes, what are we going to do?'"

"What will you do?" I asked.

"We will see what happens. We will deal with it then." He was a small man, but just like Mawa and the farmer in Lyngkhat, he seemed even smaller when he spoke of the Wall. There was something about the barrier that diminished the people who lived against it.

In a perverse way, the headman was lucky. Life would be even worse if he were to stay in the newly created no man's land. Elsewhere along the border, the walled-out homes were not destroyed, so compensation was not offered and villagers lived an excised life on the wrong side of the Wall. Estimates claimed 90,000 Indian citizens now resided between the border and the new fences. They had to show ID cards in order to enter their own country through black iron gates that opened for only a few hours a day. If a villager suffered a medical emergency when the gates were closed, he had to depend on the sympathies of the border guards to let him through. The barrier rendered all property beyond the Wall worthless. No one will buy a parcel of no man's land. And the marriage prospects for the village men grew dim. Women refused to marry men living on the wrong side of the Wall.

The Indians had fumed at Radcliffe's slapdash line, accusing the British of arrogance and sloppiness and lack of concern for the villagers along the border. Now, more than sixty years later, the Indian government was reinforcing the line with the same disregard for the same people. Big ideas of sovereignty and national security throw shadows over the concerns of the small farmer. "The fence is good for the nation," Governor Mooshahary had told me in Shillong. But the Wall disregards the citizens who live on the nation's edge. The government seems unconcerned that, for the villagers who live alongside the Wall, the barrier is not merely a geopolitical strategy but a material reality.

If the walls around Ceuta and Melilla stand against the Moorish bogeyman, along the Indo-Bangla border the bogeyman is the Wall itself. No one knows when it will come or, when it does, on what side of the wire their homes will stand. They don't know how they will be compensated, or when, or by whom. The people of the northeast already feel alienated from Mother India. Now the fencing cruelly defines their estrangement. Even the language of the Wall negates the border villagers. They are nowhere people living on the zero line, men dwelling in no man's land. Disowned by the Wall, I wondered if they felt Indian at all.

On the morning of her wedding, in January 2011, Felani Khatun's fifteen-year-old body hung upside down from the barbed wire fence. Her father, Nurul Islam, had arranged a marriage between Felani and her Bangladeshi cousin, who worked in a garment factory in Dhaka. He paid a pair of cattle smugglers three thousand rupees, about sixty dollars, to help him and Felani scale the fence into Bangladesh and to the village where the groom was waiting. Nurul climbed over the Wall with a bamboo ladder the smugglers provided, but when the barbs snagged Felani's blue skirt, the girl panicked and started to scream. The noise alerted the Indian BSF soldiers on patrol, who fired their rifles in the direction of Felani's screams. Nurul fled, but a bullet punched through Felani's chest and she sagged on the Wall. One witness said he heard Felani call out for water for half an hour before she finally bled out. Felani hung on the Wall for five hours, a memento mori pierced and fixed into place by the barbs, until sun burned away the fog and the BSF pulled her down. They tied her hands and feet to a bamboo pole and carried her away like a butchered animal on a spit.

Eventually the soldiers handed Felani's body over the borderline to her uncle. Nurul kept the gold and blue sequined dress Felani had planned to wear for the wedding, and Felani's little sister now uses her wedding sandals to play dress-up. But the modest jewellery Felani's mother gave her for the wedding — a pair of earrings, a nose ring, some gold bangles — disappeared. Felani's family believes the BSF stole the gold off the girl's body.

By 2006, Indian intelligence had realized that many of the terror attacks the country had suffered in the previous years were perpetrated by Bangladeshi militants working on behalf of agents in Pakistan. As a result, India amplified the military's efforts along the Indo-Bangladesh border to keep them out. The government added a second layer of barbed wire to the Wall, and doubled the number of BSF *jawans* assigned to protect it. Now, eighty thousand soldiers stand on the Indo-Bangla line. Military brass also granted the *jawans* authority to "deliver retaliatory fire" to anyone who breaches the border. The soldiers no longer needed permission from their superior officers. This was, in essence, a licence to kill. The BSF could now shoot on sight and shoot to kill with the military's blessing. India believed the harsh policy would deter crossers. Instead, the directive simply killed them. Between 2007 and 2010, the BSF shot dead over three hundred Bangladeshi nationals along the Wall. The deaths at the hands of trigger-happy border soldiers enraged officials in Bangladesh.

The BSF, though, showed little remorse. They claimed the border officers fired only in self-defence or when suspects evaded capture. The justifications convinced no one. India's own laws forbid the killing of suspects accused of crimes not punishable by a life sentence or the death penalty: smuggling and illegal migration hardly qualify. And most of those shot by the BSF in alleged self-defence were either "armed" with regular farming tools such as sickles and knives or unarmed altogether. Many were shot in the back.

Few Indians, especially those far from the border, mourn the deaths of smugglers and illegals along the Wall. They are nowhere people, after all. In a statement, the Indian government expressed official "sympathies and regrets" for Felani's killing and promised an investigation into her death. But they also asked their counterparts in Bangladesh to kindly keep their citizens away from the border at night.

My bus rumbled through the darkness towards Bhogdanga, a village on the Bangladeshi frontier that is completely surrounded by the Indian fencing. Assamese call Bhogdanga the "nowhere village." Another negation. It was fitting, I suppose, that I would not see Bhogdanga either.

I got as far as Dhuburi, the nearest town of any size to Bhogdanga. I planned to stay in Dhuburi for the night and travel the rest of the way to the border in the morning, but the only hotel in the town would not take me in because I was a foreigner. I needed permission from the local authorities, the manager said, and waved over a bicycle rickshaw. He told the rickshaw wallah to pedal me to the Circuit House, the town's police headquarters.

There, a dozen men in various uniforms swarmed me. I hoped one of them would scrawl a permission on a scrap of paper so that I could stay at the hotel, but the officials scoffed. They wanted to know who I was, what I was doing in Dhuburi, why I wanted to see Bhogdanga, and how I'd even heard of the place. "It is dangerous here," they repeated. "There is an insurgency." They summoned a magistrate of some sort and an intelligence officer. Then they made me fill out a line in a thick ledger and put me in a vacant room for the night, where I felt more their prisoner than their guest. I was surprised they didn't confiscate my passport.

In the morning, I met an official with the Indian secret service in his room. He was the ranking official in Dhuburi and still in his underwear. "You can go anywhere you want," he said, pulling up his trousers and threading a belt through the loops. "But you cannot go to Bhogdanga."

"Why not?"

"It is a trouble-prone area. Heaven for terrorists. You can go somewhere else."

"Somewhere else? I don't want to go anywhere else. If I can't go to Bhogdanga, I'll go back to Gauhati." I sounded like a child and was suddenly embarrassed, even though I was the only one in the room with his pants on properly.

"That is fine. There is only one bus to Gauhati. It leaves tonight. You must spend the day here in Dhuburi." He zipped up his fly like an exclamation point. Then he assigned two police officers with identical moustaches, red caps, and tan uniforms. I protested, but the official said, "They are for your own safety." Real barriers of barbed wire and steel guarded the border, but a second wall of paranoid bureaucracy kept me from seeing them.

The situation infuriated me. I walked out of Circuit House and onto the village streets while my two bodyguards followed, doubled up on a single motorcycle a few paces behind me. Soon it became clear the men were less interested in my personal safety than they were suspicious of my intentions. They stood behind me and listened over my shoulder when I called a friend in Gauhati. After I used an Internet café, they asked the proprietor, a seventeen-year-old boy, what websites I had visited. When I entered a bamboo shack for a haircut and shave — I had nothing better to do — the men sat outside and stared at me. After the shave, my barber rubbed my shoulders, slapped the top of my head, gripped a handful of hair, and snapped my head to the side. My neck made a sound like a cockroach being crunched under a boot. For all the warnings of insurgent terror, this spinal snap massage was the most peril I'd been in all day, yet my twin protectors never even twitched to my defence.

Afterwards, smooth of face and sore of neck, I made a game of losing my overseers. I walked slowly down the main street, ducked around a corner, sprinted down an alley, and listened for the motorcycle to rev in pursuit. I jumped onto bicycle rickshaws when I thought the twins weren't watching and waited for them to find me again. They remained stone-faced and unaffected by my insolence. When I grew bored with this, I tried to bore them. I walked slow laps around the same street, forcing them to circle over and over. I made them watch me take tea in four consecutive tea stalls, one right after the other. I couldn't tell if they were amused or angry. They never smiled or scowled. They reminded me of the Moroccan soldiers who had watched me from the top of the berm. Maybe these Indians were just as bored and didn't mind playing cat and mouse with a petulant foreigner.

Eventually I walked to the riverbank and watched the industry on the shores of the Brahmaputra. The river forms part of the border, and the Indian government had gone so far as to erect fences on some of the tiny sand islands, called *chars*, that speckle the river. Freshwater dolphins swim elsewhere in the Brahmaputra, but there was little peace for them in Dhuburi, where sun-blanched *bhot bhottis* sputtered and rattled back and forth across the water. Some boats shuttled bamboo from the far side and onions from the near, filling the hot air with their earthy aroma. Other boats carried the day's workforce from villages across the river. The passengers who could not fit in the shaded holds stood erect on the wooden roof decks and tried to keep their balance. Bracelets clinked on the wrists of the Hindu women while streaks of vermilion plunged from their foreheads into tightly parted hair. Long-bearded Muslim men came to barter for lambs. Their wives wore black hijabs and gold in their nostrils. Sikhs stepped off the boat decks onto the beach and rushed to pray at their white gurdwara. Bicycle rickshaw wallahs waited for them all and argued over fares. I wondered if any of these people, in the rush of their daily toil, had time to worry about the so-called insurgency that plagued the walled edges of the nation and, apparently, endangered me.

When the *bhot bhottis* emptied, barefoot men heaved netted sacks of onions and neatly bundled bamboo from overloaded two-wheel carts for return trips across the river. It was a quiet industry. The silent strain of bent backs. The soft thud of sacks piled on sacks. There were BSF *jawans* in Dhuburi too, and I watched them take milky tea and samosas in the tea stalls, their batons idle on the tabletops. Quiet too were the washerwomen who laid soap-smelling saris over the stones, the trash-nibbling goats, and the cows who lazed in the sunshine and dust.

The sacred bovines were safe from the butcher's block here among the Hindus who revered them, but they could hardly be smug lest they be smuggled. The illegal trade of Indian cattle into Bangladesh is a lucrative business on the borderlands, accounting for half of all illegal trade across the border. The scourge of "cattle lifting" gave the Indian government another reason to wall the border. India's Hindu majority refuses to allow cattle to be exported for slaughter, even though cows are routinely, and legally, butchered within the country by India's non-Hindu minorities. Muslim and Sikh chefs in India perform spicy miracles with beef. The absurd prohibition gives rise to a cross-border black market in Indian cattle. The bovines are worth far more as beef in Bangladesh than as idols in India; a single animal can fetch $900 in the Muslim meat markets. Herders and truckers co-operate to bring cattle to the border. At night, smugglers walk them across the zero line. Where there is fencing, they lift the animals over the barrier, sometimes with ingenious makeshift winches built of bamboo and barbed wire cannibalized from the

Wall itself. Once across the border, the cows are legal again and gleefully taxed by the Bangladeshi government. Perhaps Bangladesh's opposition to a fortified border has less to do with old partition agreements than with the potential loss of beef tax and the main ingredient in tikya kebab.

I stayed on the riverbank until the purple smear of dusk gave way to darkness. A full moon scattered light across the Brahmaputra like coarse salt spilled over a tabletop. Birds and bats rioted in the trees. I'd let my disappointment at not seeing Bhogdanga blind me to the beauty of this place. I fetched my bag from the Circuit House and a battalion of six policemen, one fragrantly drunk, walked me to the bus station. They all stared up at me in the window until the bus pulled out of town and safely away from the borderlands.

My time in Dhuburi wasn't a complete loss. Before I boarded the bus, I met a journalist at the restaurant where I ate dinner. He gave me the business card of a friend, a television news editor named Utpal, whom he thought would be willing to escort me to Bhogdanga using his press credentials. Eventually I met with Utpal in Gauhati, and we agreed to meet the following Friday for a trip to Bhogdanga.

▉▉▉

Then, 2,500 kilometres away from Assam, terrorists struck Mumbai. On the evening of November 26, 2008, ten men armed with grenades, bombs, and assault rifles stepped out of their speedboats and laid siege to the city. The attackers walked into Chhatrapati Shivaji Terminus, where I had caught my train to Kolkata, and sprayed bullets into 164 people waiting on the platform. Fifty-eight died. The terrorists killed ten more people at the Leopold Café and five more at Nariman House, a Jewish community centre. Reports later surfaced that the attackers tortured the Jews they found before executing them and that they believed killing a Jew was worth killing fifty non-Jews. The men blew up two taxicabs with time bombs, hijacked a police car, and shot at officers on the street. They tried to shoot patients at a hospital, but the staff locked up the wards and the gunmen moved on. Eventually the terrorists stormed two hotels, including the iconic Taj Mahal Palace, where they took and killed hostages, set fires, detonated grenades, and fended off

Indian armed forces for an astounding two and a half days. By the end of the attack, the terrorists had slaughtered 165 people and injured nearly 300 more.

I watched the assault, the rising death toll, and the confusion born of the siege on the television in my Gauhati hotel. I called my wife and family to reassure them I was about as far away from Mumbai as I could be without leaving India. (They hadn't heard about the Gauhati bombings a few weeks earlier; those blasts hardly made the news back home.) In truth, I felt no closer to the attacks sitting in Gauhati than I would've felt sitting at home in Canada. From the eastern edges of India, Mumbai might as well have been on a different planet. Those around me felt the same. The Assamese I met self-identified with Assam first, many not considering themselves Indian at all. On the distant edge of the country, the ethnic groups of the northeast feel ignored and alienated by mainland India. I met one man in a hotel bar who, after too much whiskey, told me the siege on Mumbai made him happy.

The attacks, in both Mumbai and Gauhati, proved the impotence of India's border fencing, at least in protecting against terrorism. The Wall standing along India's borders with Pakistan and Bangladesh was erected, in part, to prevent such violence. Yet in the span of a single month, two major attacks rattled the country, and authorities blamed both on perpetrators from the other side of the Wall. India would endure ten terrorist attacks in total during 2008, with a combined death toll of nearly four hundred people. The Wall succeeded in keeping poor farmers from their own fields and fruit sellers from the Bangla markets, but the splendid barbed wire did not deter men with guns and bombs.

I hesitated to call Utpal because I knew what he would tell me. Sure enough, when I finally called, he said that in the wake of the Mumbai siege the BSF would not permit anyone, least of all a foreigner, anywhere near a sensitive border area. The borders were shut tight and the BSF were nervous. Utpal had tried his best to plead my case to the authorities, but he could only apologize. I would not get to see the Wall at Bhogdanga.

■■■

I waited a week to allow the Mumbai-born anxiety to settle, then flew to Tripura, another of northeast India's border states. There, a journalist named

Debunker used his connections to secure permission from the BSF for us to see the frontier. We travelled on his motorcycle alongside the border fence to Lankamura, a mostly Hindu village two kilometres from Agartala, the capital. Lankamura was another tidy border settlement of clean, mud-stuccoed houses with corrugated roofs. Men in *dhotis* turned soil with short hoes while women watered bitter melon vines with metal vessels shaped like pomegranates. Other women, gold rings shining in their noses, led cows by tethers to nibble on dry rice stalks. The rice itself dried on the narrow border road. We etched lines across it with the motorcycle tires.

Debunker stopped in front of a small bridge where a gap in the Wall necessitated a BSF post. A soldier from Uttar Pradesh stood watch beneath a wooden canopy labelled with the BSF emblem and its misspelled motto: "Duty Un To Death." The soldier told us his posting was hardly an exciting one. "There are no hills here, so nowhere for militants to hide," he said. He told us the people who lived along the border were simple and poor and easily exploited by smugglers. He protected them and called them "God's own people."

Another man, a village farmer in a white shirt, rested in the shade the BSF post threw over the road. He told me his family was on the Bangladesh side of the international line. When he was a child, he used to cross the border and walk through the rice paddies to wave at the Bangla trains with his cousins. When they were older, they met to play cricket. "We could cross freely," he told me. "The BSF either ignored us or asked for a little money. Maybe ten rupees." As India started to fret about militancy along its borders, the BSF hardened. Crossing the zero line began to get difficult and, for the first time, felt like a crime.

Then the Wall rose. "I can visit my relatives only in the daylight, when the BSF opens the gates," the farmer said. Because his fields were on the other side of the Wall, he had to mind the gate schedule. He used to be able to harvest vegetables in the early dawn and sell them in the market the same day, but the BSF didn't open the gates early enough for him to do this anymore. Soldiers sleep later than farmers. They have little understanding of, or concern for, the farmer's agrarian needs. Now the man had to harvest his produce the day before and store everything overnight. His vegetables wilted and softened by morning, and by the time they reached the market they were worth much less.

"There are good things about the fence," the farmer conceded. In the days before the Wall, local men supplemented their farming income by bootlegging phensidyl cough syrup across the border. The Muslim government in Bangladesh prohibits alcohol, and addicts there drink the medicine, usually thinned with water, in place of whiskey. The Wall killed much of this trade outside Agartala, the man said, and former smugglers were now focusing their labour on farming. Also, the Wall reduced the number of Bangladeshi bandits who crossed the border at night to steal vegetables and lift cows. The farmer worried, though, for his family on the other side. "They are becoming more Bangladeshi than Indian," he said. This last comment fascinated me. I didn't understand what it meant to become more of one nationality than another. I wanted to know how a mere construction of wire and steel could cause identity to drift. I asked the man what he meant, but he only shrugged.

Debunker and I continued along the road to the regional BSF headquarters. A volleyball net hung over a swept courtyard, and the plastic chairs in the VIP kiosk where we sat were painted gold. An official joined us and said, "The fact that the terrorists who attacked Mumbai infiltrated the city by sea rather than land proves the border fencing is working." I doubted many Mumbaikars thought the deadly sixty-hour siege vindicated the military's border strategy, but the man contradicted himself before I could argue the point. "The design of the fence is a failure," he said. "It is difficult to maintain, especially through the paddy lands, and it can be crossed over easily when there is no soldier watching. The wires can be cut. It would be better if it were a concrete wall."

The officer arranged for a military jeep to escort us to one of the openings in the fence. There, a BSF guard unlocked and slid open the gate, and we stepped through the wire to the other side. I felt a strange thrill. Weeks earlier, when I had first inquired about the border in West Bengal, officials told me I was forbidden even to see the Wall. Now I was crossing through it, fingering its black barbs as I passed into the buffer zone between two uneasy neighbours. This was a false subversion, of course. The soldiers charged with protecting the Wall escorted me through it. I was no infiltrator. Still, I could feel my pulse quicken a little as I stepped past the cool steel into forbidden space.

My soldier brought me to a house in Jayangar, an Indian village on the wrong side of the Wall. As we arrived, women in hijabs sifted rice on a clay terrace while a solitary cow ate grass from a cement bowl. The women stood when they saw us and called into the house for Fasluhak. The old man emerged. A fabulous white beard tumbled out from the underside of his chin and he smiled at us through teeth black-striped and rotten from betel. His shirt was made of white mesh, his *dhoti* checkered and held up with a bit of rope from which dangled an iron key. Fasluhak called to one of his sons to bring us some chairs, but before we sat he asked our BSF escort if he could change the evening gate opening from six to seven-thirty. "My son works in the city," he said, "and he does not come home until after six, when the gate is already closed." The BSF official smirked and said he would look into it.

Fasluhak's family built the house forty years before there was any border here at all. Then, at the time of partition, black stone markers were laid that declared "India ends here." I spotted them from Fasluhak's courtyard. The end of the footpath leading from the house was in another country. However, the nomenclature meant nothing to Fasluhak's family and the other villagers who lived and worked in what was now, suddenly, borderland. Issues of nationality are not relevant to these rural lives. All that matters is one's family, one's faith, and the land's yield of rice and cauliflower. In 1971, East Pakistan became Bangladesh, and I wondered if Fasluhak's family even noticed. "We have seen three borders already," Fasluhak shrugged. "The British border, the princely border, and now the Indian border." Lines drawn on maps in faraway offices held no significance for Fasluhak.

The new fences, though, demanded allegiance. The barrier imposed a thin sense of nationality on men like Fasluhak, who had never considered such things before. Fasluhak and his family used to identify as Bengalis from Jayangar; after the Wall, they became Indians from the state of Tripura. In Meghalaya, the Wall disowned the border population; here, the Wall claimed them. For the first time, the villagers were deemed different from those across the line. More than this, the Wall insisted they were somehow better. "It would be best not to have relations with the Bangladeshis," Fasluhak said, as if the Wall suddenly made those on the other side dangerous and immoral. Just like the man in Lankamura, Fasluhak could not explain why he felt this way.

I thought of Ceuta and Melilla on Europe's edge, where the new fences embody old notions of identity. Those fences enforce Spanish anxiety with wire and steel. "We are different from the Moors," the Spaniards cry, and the walls prove this. They stand less as security barriers than as monuments to Spanish insecurity. But on India's frontier, the new walls play the opposite role. They impose a national identity, an "Indianness," where there was none before. The physical border meant nothing here. Villagers on both sides crossed back and forth freely. They spoke the same language and played cricket in the same fields. Married daughters on one side to sons on the other. They ignored political boundaries. My frustration at not being able to see the border in Jayantipur and Bhogdanga was foolish. For generations, these people never saw the border either.

The Wall screams for the mingling across the line to stop. The Wall christens the villagers Indians and warns them that those on the other side are not. Three strands of barbed wire obliterated all these people had in common — which was everything. The Wall says Bangladeshis cannot be trusted. Now men like Fasluhak want to avoid them, and the farmer at the guard post worries about his relations becoming more Bangladeshi — whatever that means.

A Nakba of Olives
The West Bank Wall

"We don't have flower sellers in Jayyous because the fields are full of flowers," Mohammad Othman told me as he knelt to photograph a gathering of wild camomile blossoms.

Together we climbed the southern hills of the village through orderly rows of olive trees whose leaves shone silver in the Palestinian sunshine. Such sunny days had been rare that February, and Mohammad took advantage of the brightness to snap photos. He planned to send the pictures to his girlfriend, Rose, who lived in America and loved to dance. "If I remind her that Jayyous is beautiful, maybe she will come and visit me again," he said. He stopped again and aimed his lens at a red anemone growing alone in the tall grass.

This was Mohammad's favourite spot in Jayyous. From here he could see the whole village. Below us, cactus and weeds tangled in the shallow valley that funnelled the complaints of donkeys and the clatter of boys on bicycles. Most of Jayyous rose on the other side. Old homes were built of stone, new ones of bare cinder block. Rebars protruded like antennae from half-built pillars on unfinished top floors. We spotted workers climbing wooden ladders to cement pale white tiles over the grey brick of a new mosque. The old mosque, blue domed and modest, stood in the centre of the village. The pale minaret pointed into the sky where, more than a decade ago, the Jayyousi had watched Saddam Hussein's Scud missiles fizzle past on their way to missing their targets in Tel Aviv. You could see Tel Aviv from this hilltop too — it was only a few kilometres west — and on clear days you could see the Mediterranean.

Mohammad knew every inch of these hills. His family owned olive groves not far from here, and he used to camp beneath the trees with his brothers when they were all boys. When Mohammad was ten years old, his father assigned one olive sapling to his charge. He told Mohammad to mark the tree's growth with his own. "If you are growing faster than the tree, something is wrong," his father said. "It means you have to give it more water. Take care of it more." Both Mohammad and his tree reached adulthood in unison from Jayyous's fertile soil.

The olive trees of Jayyous heralded the coming of the Wall, and they would be its first victims. In the autumn of 2002, villagers found land acquisition orders from Israeli authorities pinned to the trees' grey trunks. The papers declared the land would be confiscated and the trees bearing the orders uprooted. There was no further explanation. When the Israel Defense Forces, the IDF, arrived with their guns and armoured bulldozers, villagers met them in the fields. They fought hand to hand with the soldiers but could not stop the trees from being wrenched from the ground. In all, more than four thousand trees fell in Jayyous during the early days of the Wall.

The preceding spring had been bloody in Israel. The Second Intifada raged and violence against Israeli civilians swelled. Terrorists blew themselves up in horrific explosions. They scattered bodies on the ground in nightclubs and restaurants and on the streets alongside charred public buses. More than 650 Israelis had been killed since the violence began two years earlier. The Israeli populace, terrified, demanded protection from their government. Increased checkpoints and armed incursions into the West Bank did not staunch the blood. The Israeli military needed a new strategy.

They adopted, instead, an ancient one. They decided to build a wall. The National Security Council had already approved in principle a year-old proposal to block Palestinians from crossing into Israel by foot. In 2002, the Israelis expanded the plan, designing a system of barriers that would stretch for more than seven hundred kilometres around, and into, the West Bank. For most of its route the Wall is a three-metre-high fence equipped with pyramid-stacked barbed wire, electronic sensors, and night-vision cameras. IDF patrols smooth the strips of sand next to the fence to better reveal the footprints of anyone who makes it over. Few do. Just touching the fence alerts soldiers in nearby command posts, who dispatch troops along the patrol roads that flank the fence in order to intercept the intruder. The border police can reach any part of the barrier within eight minutes. Red signs on the fence in Hebrew, Arabic, and English threaten "mortal danger" and warn "any person who passes or damages the fence endangers his life."

Alongside the larger Palestinian centres, and anywhere the IDF deems threatened by sniper fire, the Wall is a wall. Great grey slabs of concrete rise eight metres from the ground and are bound so tightly together as not to permit a thread of sunlight to creep through. Floodlights and security cameras mark the length on top of the Wall, and cylindrical watchtowers pose like vertical cannons along the route. I followed the graffiti-tagged Wall in Bethlehem and Ramallah. What I found most striking about the barrier was its nerve. Its concrete conviction. The Wall makes no pretences towards grace or sophistication. The Wall is blue-collar and proud. It is cold and rude and hard and stone.

The Wall is also illegal. In 2004, the International Court of Justice issued an "Advisory Opinion" on the Wall. The ICJ concluded that the barrier's route breached both humanitarian and human rights law. The court demanded Israel stop building the barrier, tear down what had already been built, and compensate those who had suffered from its construction. Palestinians saw victory in the ICJ decision, but the "Advisory Opinion" was about as binding as it sounds. Israel ignored it. The next year, the Israeli High Court of Justice countered the ICJ with its own ruling declaring the Wall legal under their interpretation of international law.

Most Israelis refer to the Wall as a separation barrier or an anti-terrorist fence. The barrier was built to save innocent lives, its proponents claim. Certainly a nation has the right to secure its borders and the duty to protect its populace. But the route of Israel's wall betrays other intentions. Only about 10 percent of the Wall follows the Green Line, the armistice boundary drawn in 1949 and internationally accepted as the border between Israel and the West Bank. Most of the Wall tracks east of the Line and inside Palestinian territory. In some areas, the Wall penetrates deep into the West Bank, swinging wide around Jewish settlements in order to keep them, and much of the land surrounding them, on the "Israeli" side. The Wall also divides Palestinian villages from both their farmland and neighbouring towns. In all, the route of the Wall annexes almost a tenth of Palestinian land to Israel. If the Wall can be admired at all, it must be for its audacity.

When the Wall rose in Jayyous, it carved away 70 percent of the village territory and separated farmers from their fields and greenhouses. Twelve thousand olive trees, twenty-five thousand fruit trees, and all six of Jayyous's groundwater wells were exiled beyond the barrier. The farmland remains accessible in theory, but the Israelis insist Jayyousi farmers apply for permission to reach their fields through a pair of yellow iron gates, one south of the village, the other to the north. The gates are not always open and permits are difficult to obtain.

I could see the Wall from my vantage point on the hill, and I could also see the holes in the Israeli argument. If Israel fears infiltration of terrorists from the Palestinian side of the barrier, as proponents of the Wall insist, it would have made more sense to leave Jayyous's farmland on the same side of the Wall as the men who cultivate it. This would have eliminated the need for the gates altogether, and a continuous barrier is more difficult to breach than a gated one. Furthermore, routing the fence between the village and the fields put the barrier right up against the houses of Jayyous, well within the range of the potential snipers Israel claims the barrier protects against.

But in Jayyous, the Wall has nothing to do with security and everything to do with Zufin. The Zufin settlement stands between Jayyous and its view of the sea. Lev Leviev, an Israeli diamond magnate, funds Zufin's construction and expansion. Leviev is Israel's richest man and is worth, some say, a half billion dollars. (Though Leviev had been a donor to UNICEF, the United Nations' children's fund couldn't stomach Leviev's settlement projects and so severed ties with him in 2008.) About a thousand settlers live in Zufin's houses, which loom west of Jayyous on a hilltop overlooking the farmland and olive groves annexed by the Wall. Palestinians fear this fertile land will be cleared and granted to Zufin for the settlement's expansion. Ancient trees, most now unreachable by the families that have always tended them, will be ripped from the earth. Hundreds of new homes for settlers will rise in their place.

It was a bad day for a protest. I stood in Mohammad's kitchen and looked out of the window at the rain pouring down.

Mohammad's second-floor apartment was only half finished, rarely cleaned, and smelled of new plaster and cigarette smoke. A week-old tub of yogurt sat on the countertop among spent Yellow Label tea bags and cigarette butts. Plastic soda bottles and falafel wrappers spilled onto the floor beneath the hole in the countertop where a sink should have been. The previous day's pita had hardened into leather. One of Mohammad's brothers brewed tea with water from the bathroom sink, the only running water in the place, for the small gathering of activists from overseas waiting in the salon. Julia, a German activist with the International Solidarity Movement, boasted about being blacklisted and strip-searched by the IDF. She advised me to remove my contacts. "The tear gas gets behind your lenses," she warned, tracing on her eyeliner.

There was supposed to be a demonstration against the Wall that day, but earlier in the week the IDF had raided Jayyous. Soldiers entered the village at night, seized about a hundred young men, and penned them in the school gymnasium. The IDF troops also occupied several village houses and spray-painted a Star of David over a pro-freedom mural on a school wall. They took about a dozen men with them when they left; the men were still in custody somewhere in Israel. I wondered if the night action by the IDF would intimidate the young men out of their weekly protest. I asked Mohammad if anything was going to happen. He replied that he didn't know. He said "the street will decide." I didn't believe him. His cellphone rang all morning. If anyone knew, Mohammad did.

All of Mohammad's beloved family fields and olive groves, and the tree he grew up alongside, were exiled to the other side of the Wall when the fence went up in Jayyous in 2002. The seizure of his family's land inspired Mohammad towards resistance. In 2006, he moved from Jayyous to Ramallah to work with Stop the Wall, a grassroots activist campaign that aims to stop and dismantle what most Palestinians term the Apartheid Wall. Since then, Mohammad has become a leading voice against the barrier. He is likeable and speaks eloquently in English—even though, as a schoolboy, English was Mohammad's most hated subject. He meets with journalists and activists from around the world, tours them around Palestine, and speaks internationally about life under Israeli occupation. He told me he had Jimmy Carter's cellphone number programmed into his phone.

Most of Mohammad's work, though, centred on Jayyous, where his family still lived and where he kept the bare apartment where we waited for something to happen. He was the "youth coordinator" for Stop the Wall and organized the weekly demonstrations. Each Friday, Mohammad accompanied a throng of protesters through his village to demonstrate at the south gate, not far from where the camomile and anemone grow. Since the protests began in November 2008, Jayyous had become a magnet for "internationals" wanting to express their solidarity with the Palestinian cause. A man in Jayyous told me that before the Wall, the only place he'd see a European was on television: now the Jayyousi were used to foreigners. When I had arrived from Ramallah the day before, old men in the village, assuming I was an activist, nodded welcomes from their storefronts where they peddled eggplants, cauliflowers, and peppers from plastic crates. Young boys rushed to shake my hand while their sisters, lacking the boys' bravado, waited until I passed before calling out "Hello" and "How are you?" and "Where are you from?" ·

From Mohammad's window we watched the road leading from the centre of the village to the Wall's south gate. At around noon, just as the group in the kitchen decided there would be no demonstration, we saw a half-dozen young men walking up the road. Another group followed them. They didn't have banners or flags or any other accoutrements of protest. "It is the shabaab," Mohammad said. The word is Arabic for "youth," but in the context of occupied Palestine *shabaab* refers to the bands of rebellious young Palestinian men, the stone throwers and troublemakers, who wage their miniature intifadas on the IDF. Mohammad pulled on a black coat with a fur-lined collar, pocketed his cellphone, and handed his camera to Aidan, a Canadian volunteer with Stop the Wall. Mohammad walked down the stairs and out the door. The rest of us followed him up the road.

We stopped at the edge of an olive orchard and watched the shabaab calmly lift stones from the road and hurl them over the trees. Aidan told me IDF soldiers were positioned on the other side of the grove. I could not see past the grey trunks and grey-green leaves, and the shabaab could not see where their stones landed. Eventually a clank of rock against metal signalled that someone had hit something. Probably an IDF jeep. The stone throwers turned to each other and grinned.

The response came quickly. A pop from behind the trees and a tear gas canister wheezed yellowish smoke overhead. I thought of Julia and feared for my contact lenses, but the wind whipped away the fumes. Then an explosion boomed so loud that my head vibrated. Everyone cowered. Sound grenades. I looked back and forth, suddenly breathing hard, wondering if and where I should run. I glanced over at Mohammad. He ducked from the noise and covered his ears with his hands. Like the others, he smiled nervously from his crouch. The shabaab laughed and reached for more stones to continue their assault on soldiers they could not yet see.

Someone yelled something in Arabic and the mood changed. The boys started running out of the groves. They still grinned but were obviously fleeing something. Aidan looked calm. I asked him what was happening. "The Israelis are coming," he said.

I heard the army jeep engines rumble. The shabaab began to roll small boulders into a line across the road to slow the IDF vehicles: their own wall, for what it was worth. Mohammad shouted at Aidan to help. He ran forward and rolled a rock into the line. He was the only international among the barricade builders, and Mohammad reminded him to wipe the dirt from his hands afterwards. "Otherwise the Israelis will know you helped us."

I envied Aidan. He was a Canadian like me but also, somehow, one of the shabaab. I wanted to join him. I believed in this cause. I wanted to be a part of this rebellion rather than a mere witness. The barrier these men fought against inspired me to write about walls in the first place. Cowardice, though, stopped me. I feared pain. The burn of tear gas. The red welts raised by a soldier's baton. I imagined being arrested, blacklisted, and deported. I chalked up my inaction to an observer's neutrality, but really I didn't have the nerve.

There was not much of a barrier built before the men abandoned it. The Israelis were too close. The protesters ran down the road and joined the boys, who again gathered stones to throw. I didn't want to run. I felt that running would implicate me somehow, but then another grenade exploded and rattled my head. I fled with the others up the road and around a corner where someone had written *Stop the Wall*. My muscles turned to stone and my legs shook. I cursed quietly to myself. Nothing in my experience had prepared me for this. I felt helpless and desperately wanted someone to guide me through, but I was no one's concern. All I could do was imitate the others and trust that they knew how to stay safe. So I ran when the shabaab ran and stopped when they stopped. I spotted Aidan and sprinted to his side. Then a new sound, a crack I didn't recognize. "Rubber bullets," Aidan warned. We ran again. I didn't look back. I was afraid to see how close the soldiers were.

A man opened the door to his house and waved us in. "You are welcome," he said. Mohammad, Aidan, and I followed him inside and up the stairs to a salon. My breathing slowed and my muscles relaxed. Our host sprinkled cologne from a flask onto a rag and held it out to us in case we had tear gas in our eyes. Then he led us to the roof. From there I could see the mixture of panic and pleasure on the street. The shabaab laughed and collected wet stones, smiling as they fled the jeeps. They retreated and advanced. They gathered into gangs, scattered, and then reassembled. Their protest had a sort of ease, an instinctual cadence, and the hurled stones clattering on the street sounded like colliding billiard balls.

I could see the soldiers for the first time. I watched them creep around the houses and through the village gardens. The soldiers were probably not much older than the shabaab, but their bulky fatigues and military training made their movements seem measured and mature. We spotted a pair of them advancing through a cluster of greenhouses in a bid to outflank a platoon of stone throwers. Mohammad called and warned someone with his cellphone. Aidan took pictures. I heard another pop, and a tear gas canister sailed over-head trailing a ribbon of sweet-smelling smoke. It was close enough that I could see the red ember burning on the fuse. I watched the canister just miss the roof where we stood and realized the soldiers were firing at us. We dashed back inside.

Our host set up some plastic chairs for us in his salon. He put a teapot over a flame and turned the television to an English-language movie channel. His banal hospitality calmed me. If this man felt secure enough to treat us like everyday guests, then we must be safe. We sipped tea and listened to the blasts and shouts outside while Napoleon Dynamite mumbled on the television. Then Mohammad received a call on his phone and left us. Aidan and I finished our tea and walked back into the rainy streets.

The melee had progressed farther into the village. We turned a corner, stepped over another row of boulders the shabaab had lined up across the road, and continued to a ledge overlooking the valley. Israeli soldiers assembled on the other side. I saw them ducking under the clotheslines on the rooftops and taking cover behind black water tanks. On the ledge, a half-dozen shabaab hurled stones at the IDF with homemade slings.

Mohammad told me that Palestinians are born knowing how to sling a stone. He joked that West Bank boys emerge from their mothers' wombs swinging their umbilical cords over their heads. I stood behind the shabaab, afraid of being hit by an errant rock, and watched as they co-opted King David's weapon against his own heirs. Some wrapped kaffiyehs around their heads to hide their faces, but most didn't bother. The rain slickened cheeks too young for beards and soaked through their blue jeans.

A boy in his late teens carried a sling made of denim and nylon cords. He threaded a finger through a loop on the end of one cord and gripped both ends with his right hand. He lifted a rock from the road, placed it in the cradle of denim, and held his arm straight out from the side of his slim body. The stone swung back and forth in its cradle as if being lulled to sleep. The boy bent his legs and turned to spot the soldiers over his shoulder. He paused for a moment in this taut, proud pose.

The boy swept the sling over his head and his hand spun on its wrist. The cords blurred and whistled as the stone strained against its cradle. He cocked his body back, twisted his face into a sneer, and snapped the rock into the air as his body lurched forward. When the sling released, it made a sound like a bird and, relieved of its turning force, fell slack at the boy's waist as the stone flew. But the boy did not watch to see it land. His eyes searched the ground. He lifted another stone and cradled it. The sling swung and whirled and whistled again. His movements possessed a furious, graceful beauty.

I didn't want to leave the boys. I couldn't resist their swagger, but I would've found no beauty if the rocks actually struck anyone. Mohammad told me about an older man in Jayyous—a veteran of the First Intifada—who was a sniper with a sling. He was not in action that day. I never saw any of these boys hit anyone. But this was not the point. For the shabaab, it was enough just to resist. To not cower. To fill a hard grey sky with hard grey stones.

The IDF insists the stone throwers trigger the army's reaction. The moment a rock gets thrown, the marchers become rioters and the protest an insurrection. Activists can hardly cling to claims of non-violence, the Israelis say, if the shabaab pelt soldiers with rocks. As much as I admired the shabaab's rebellion, I struggled to reconcile hurled stones with peaceful protest. A sling is inaccurate and archaic, almost as prehistoric a tactic as a fortified wall, yet it remains a weapon. A sling is designed to smash and crack. A slung stone can shatter a skull; dozens of soldiers have been wounded in this way. When I asked Mohammad about this, he told me rocks were all the Palestinians had. "Stones are the only way for us to show power. To show anger. To show togetherness." The sling boys were icons of resistance. Yet Mohammad insisted that "nobody in Jayyous is willing to kill another human being."

I believed him. Nothing about Mohammad or the boys on the ledge felt barbaric to me. The shabaab slung stones out of defiance not blood lust. Besides, the battle on the streets was hardly even. Far more Palestinians than Israelis have been injured in these weekly clashes. Mohammad himself took four rubber bullets in the back during one demonstration. The IDF has often been accused of using live ammunition against the protesters, and some Palestinians have been killed during demonstrations. One of these was 28-year-old Mustafa Tamimi. In 2011, an IDF soldier aimed a tear gas rifle out the door of a military jeep at Tamimi and, because he was chasing the jeep and throwing stones, shot him in the face. Tamimi died a few hours later. As I watched Israeli forces, clad in bulletproof vests and helmets, emerge from armoured jeeps to wage war on rock-throwing teenagers, the IDF claims of self-defence seemed absurd.

Just up the road from the stone slingers' ledge, Aidan and I entered a small community hall where a dozen men had gathered. They had built a fire in an indoor pit and a man offered us chairs so we could warm ourselves. Another man brought us hot coffee in tiny plastic cups and pointed to a table laid with pastries. "Welcome," he said.

I asked him why they had gathered.

"For funeral."

I felt I'd trespassed, but the man put his hands on my shoulders when I tried to stand. "Welcome," he said again, insisting I sit back down. Life goes on in the face of the IDF raid. So do the sacred rituals of death.

I finished my coffee and spent the rest of the afternoon in Mohammad's house, watching the siege from his rooftop. Eventually two IDF jeeps drove into the village with rotating blue lights and sirens. Soldiers on loudspeakers declared the entire village a "closed military area" and commanded the villagers not to leave their homes. A few hours later, the soldiers and the shabaab tired of their wet combat. The army jeeps left soon after the sun set.

Mohammad returned home. A few of the internationals arrived later. The house was damp with the cold, so he started a fire with dried olive branches in a brazier outside his front door, let the flames burn down to coals, and carried the brazier inside to warm the salon. After the curfew ended, Mohammad, Aidan, and I left to fetch food—fresh pita, hot falafel, plastic tubs of yogurt and hummus—while the others watched television and smoked cigarettes. The room smelled of burning tobacco and olive when we returned. Even though it was still cold, Mohammad left the salon window slightly ajar so the satellite receiver cord could curl out to the rooftop dish. We slapped at the mosquitoes that infiltrated the gap.

Julia said she wanted to fly kites over the Occupation and she wanted to watch *Chicago*. While the musical was not to anyone else's taste, the group relented. She and a few other internationals had spent most of the day's siege with Palestinian families, hoping to discourage arrests and home invasions by the IDF. They filmed the Israeli actions on hand-held cameras and posted the shaky video on YouTube. The film shows IDF jeeps driving into the village, soldiers firing tear gas and pushing foreign activists against a wall. It shows a Palestinian woman running after an IDF jeep holding her arrested son. It shows one soldier blowing pink bubbles with bubble gum and another scratching his ass through his drab fatigues. It does not show the stone throwers, nor does it show Mohammad.

■■■

"First the Israelis built a wall. Next they will build a roof," Basel Abbas told me, smiling at his joke. "Maybe they'll open it up a little during Ramadan so we can see the moon."

Basel knows barriers. He grew up in Nicosia, the capital of Cyprus, where barricades divide the city into a Greek south and Turkish north along what is also called the Green Line. The barricades went up in 1974, and an entire generation of Cypriots came of age without ever stepping past the barriers. Basel's parents worked for the PLO embassy in Nicosia. At the time, Cypriots from both sides of the barricades could not cross without special permission. But Basel and his family crossed all the time. They lived in the south and shopped in the north, where food and clothing cost less. They could go back and forth across the border because they were refugees. They had no nationality, and thus no national loyalties. They were not bound to the rules and prejudices of any country. On the divided island of Cyprus, the family's statelessness granted an ironic and perverse sort of freedom.

I was anxious to hear Basel's thoughts about living along two Green Lines, especially since a few days later I would head to Nicosia myself, but Basel had little to say about his time in Cyprus. He left the island when he was thirteen and hardly remembered anything apart from the blue helmets on the UN soldiers who stood along the barricades. "I didn't really understand the conflict," he told me. "Everywhere I've lived, something horrible had happened. Or will happen." He was born in the shadow of the barricades in Nicosia and moved to Palestine in 2000 just before the first blasts of the second intifada. When Basel travelled to Belgrade to study sound engineering, the Serbian prime minister was assassinated at the end of his street. Now he lives in Ramallah, not far from newer walls on an older Green Line, and is a founding member of a sound-and-image arts collective called Tashweesh.

Immediately after the Wall rose in Palestine, artists from around the world swarmed the West Bank armed with stencils and spray cans to colour the greyness. In the few years since its construction, the Wall has morphed into a renowned open-air museum of graffiti and spray-painted political messages. The most famous graffiti is in Bethlehem, where Banksy, a reclusive British street art star, painted ironic murals of the occupation on the Wall. A Kevlar-wearing peace dove. A little girl frisking a soldier for weapons. A rat with a slingshot. The graffiti gave birth to a cottage industry among taxi drivers who earn extra fares by offering "Banksy tours" of Bethlehem.

Basel has an affection for graffiti, and he told me that writing on walls forms part of the Palestinian narrative. During the First Intifada, beginning in the late 1980s and before mobile phones, Palestinians under IDF-imposed curfews communicated by writing on their homes' exterior walls. Spray-painted messages denounced Israeli incursions and announced demonstrations. The walls invited guests to weddings and mourners to funerals. Sometimes they threatened and called for revenge: "The PFLP will avenge the death of..."

Basel, though, distrusts the attention the Wall receives from artists from elsewhere. Though he understands the draw of the Wall, and concedes the barrier has inspired sympathy for the Palestinians, he fears the barrier is being commodified. "The Wall is not central to the Palestinian experience," he insists. The artists who come to paint the Wall don't always understand that everything the barrier represents – apartheid, injustice, racism – existed long before the Wall itself. "I've never been allowed to cross the Green Line into Jerusalem," Basel said. "Not before the Wall and not now." The Wall is a stark and sudden manifestation of the occupation. The barrier provides a potent symbol to rally around, a theatre for outsiders to stage their solidarity dramas, and a surface to both spray with paint and pound with fists. But only the physicality is new. "The Wall is not the point," he insisted. "It is not all about the Wall."

Basel ordered another coffee and I motioned for another Taybeh, the only beer brewed in Palestine. We were in Pronto's, an Italian restaurant in central Ramallah. Even as Basel and I spoke of war and walls, I felt far from the conflict in Ramallah. No prophet or saint – be they Christian, Muslim, or Jew – ever lingered long enough in Ramallah to gild it holy. This lack of blessedness is Ramallah's blessing. No one fights for this place. There was nothing sacred or ancient here to fight for. The city bills itself, instead, as the "new" Palestine. There are young people everywhere. They gather at the nightclubs and bars for cocktails and hookah pipes. Many study at Birzeit University up the hill, and few young women wear the headscarves of the devout. On the weekend, there are concerts, poetry readings, and performances by young Palestinian artists like Basel and his collective.

I liked Ramallah. I liked the city's creamy stone buildings. I liked that the streets always smell of fruity hookah smoke and that the coffee was always good. Still, something rang false about the place. I didn't understand why Palestinians, whose traditional cafés are such joys, decided to open a Starbucks knock-off called Stars and Bucks. I didn't know why a region filled with olive groves needs an Olive Garden restaurant or why a faux French café called Café de la Paix boasts about pastries "fresh from Tel Aviv." I didn't understand why kaffiyeh-wearing internationals who crowd the smoky bars feel the need to compete with each other for the attentions of Palestinian hipsters. Ramallah is the centre of something, but I didn't know what.

Basel knows. He calls it the Ramallah Syndrome. "People in Ramallah are disconnected from resistance," he told me. Ramallah boomed after the Wall. Men from rural communities who found themselves separated from their farmland drifted to Ramallah to find work. I heard a theory that the Palestinian Authority has not acted strongly against the Wall because farmers displaced by the barrier end up working for the PA in Ramallah. The city has become the playground for a new kind of upper middle-class Palestinian, one who is enamoured of images of American-style wealth beamed into his satellite dish, spends his money on clothes and in cafés, and buys homes on credit—a phenomenon that has no history in Palestinian culture.

Basel told me about Rawabi, a manufactured suburbia rising out of the Palestinian hills near Ramallah. "The first new Palestinian city in recent history," according to the Qatari real estate company behind the construction. When it is finished, and if Israel grants permission for an access road to be built, Rawabi will house forty thousand "New Palestinians." Basel considered the project a slap in the face to the refugees and the notion of "right of return." "They are saying 'Fuck you to your old towns—we'll make you a new one.'"

Rawabi was nearly complete. I'd heard the development described as "American-style," but an artist's rendering of its white stone high-rises reminded both Basel and me of something else. "It will look like a settlement," he said. "Israelis love it. We are becoming settlers just like them."

While they wait for their suburban paradise to be completed, the middle-class Ramallawi chase Western trappings, watch prices rise, and confuse wealth with peace. "It is an illusion," Basel said. "Just because there are new cafés and bars doesn't mean we have independence. Anything can happen at any time. We don't control our own borders. We use Israeli currency. We buy Israeli goods. We are not producing anything. The West Bank is the number one consumer of Israeli products. Economic peace is bullshit." Then he added, "These people forget that five minutes down the road there is a wall."

■■■

On the other side of the Wall, I rode a bus to Neve Daniel, a settlement near Jerusalem, with a bottle of kosher wine in my bag. It was Purim, and a man I met in a Jerusalem café, Avraham Bechar, had invited me to celebrate the holiday with his friends in Neve Daniel. I'd never visited a Jewish settlement before and was nervous. I didn't know what to expect. I'd only ever seen settlers on television waving Bibles and raging against anyone—Gentile or Jew—who dared suggest they did not belong on the land their god granted them. International law deems the settlements illegal, and even most Israelis believe the settlements stand as barriers to real peace. If the Islamic jihadists represented extremism on the Palestinian side of the struggle, then the settlers represented extremism on the Israeli side.

Avraham was in his early twenties, slim, and, like most of the settlers, born in America. He didn't seem an extremist. He suggested I bring a bottle of wine for the family that was hosting us, then he called me back to warn me of some potential awkwardness. "Since you are not Jewish, you will not be allowed to pour anyone's wine." He was afraid I would be offended by this prohibition. I found his concern charming. Avraham knew about my interest in the Wall and told me that the settlers too were against it. They didn't object to the route of the Wall, however, but to the notion that any of the West Bank—referred to by settlers by its biblical names, Judaea and Samaria—belonged to anyone but the Jews. For the settlers, Israel spans the land from the Jordan River to the sea and must not be divided. The Wall is a slur on their god.

Purim fascinated me. Jews dress in costume, sometimes as characters from the biblical story the holiday derives from but most often in disguises that would befit North American Halloween. They eat and drink to a reasonable excess. Drunkenness during Purim has a spiritual component: imbibing of wine inspires believers to express their joy and gratitude to God. The bus was filled with costumed young Israelis and American yeshiva students. I eavesdropped on their holiday plans and discussions of who was going to which party and with whom. I know little about Judaism, but I've always associated the faith with ancient and sombre devotion. I was surprised to see Judaism linked with glittered makeup, coloured wigs, and unabashed joy.

The Wall follows the highway to Neve Daniel. For the benefit of the settlers, I suppose, the Israelis have made the Wall pretty here. Some of it is built of textured stone in various shades of pinkish tan and ivory. The implications of the barrier—its effects on Palestinian life, its silent rejection of peace—are whitewashed by a pleasant, garden-wall aesthetic.

Avraham met me at the bus stop, and I followed him as he delivered holiday greetings to one of his neighbours, an English professor who invited us into her home. She stirred a spoonful of Nescafé into a mug of boiling water for me and listened as I told her about my time in the northern West Bank, about the Palestinian farmers who'd lost their land, and how the route of the barrier debunks any claims that Israel built the Wall for security. She nodded and conceded this "might" be true. Then she told me that, since some settlements find themselves east of the Wall and are excluded from Israel, "both sides are losing." Avraham added that Arabs have contributed nothing to the world since inventing algebra and that Israel has "the most moral army in the world," a bumper-sticker-worthy claim I heard repeated like a mantra by IDF apologists.

After my coffee, Avraham and I walked to the house where we would celebrate Purim. More than twenty people crowded around the table, most in costume, and at least half of them teenage girls. Rabbi Yitzchak Twersky and his wife Geula hosted us. Geula was a respected Israeli artist whose vivid paintings of religious and political scenes—Jews reading the Torah, Israeli paratroopers "liberating" the Western Wall—hung about the house. The Twerskys had ten children, the oldest a twenty-year-old woman, the youngest a three-month-old girl. The noise at the table was amazing. At times everyone talked at once, with one or two people singing Purim songs at one end of the table or the other. With all their guests and the happy racket, my hosts had little time to talk with me about my project. This relieved me. I feared such talk would lead to talk of politics, and I knew my views would be as repulsive to them as theirs were to me. I didn't want to get into an argument while a guest at their holiday table.

Regardless, things grew uncomfortable. First, I touched the wine bottle I had brought. I thought I was only prohibited from serving it, but Avraham whispered that I couldn't touch the bottle at all once it was opened. I'd defiled it. "It's all yours now," he said, smiling. I felt terrible but lucky that only Avraham witnessed my transgression and that he didn't seem offended by it.

Then the family sang "Home on the Range" for a Twersky boy dressed as a cowboy. When they finished, Geula announced she had another version of "Home on the Range" she had written when the family lived in New York. Rabbi Twersky shook his head. "Please don't sing that song," he said.

"Okay. I won't sing it, but I'll tell you the lyrics." She turned to me. "You have to remember that I am from the inner city." Then she recited:

"Oh give me a home,
Where the cockroaches roam,
And the mice come out at night to play.
Where seldom is heard,
An English word,
And the bodegas are open all day."

Geula beamed at me. I turned to Avraham, who said quietly, "That was bad, but funny." I didn't know how to react. I wanted to say I found the song offensive. That it fit exactly with my image of what settlers are like. I wanted to thank her for showing her true colours to me and vindicating my discomfort at accepting her generosity and at being here at all. But I didn't say anything. Instead, my cheeks burned. I quietly ate my Yemeni mushroom soup and tender brisket and felt like a fraud.

After the meal, one of the children, a four-year-old girl dressed as an angel but with her wings tied on upside down, climbed into my lap. While the post-meal prayer distracted the rest of the family, the little girl reached across the table, grabbed a handful of cucumber and kohlrabi sticks, and stacked them like building blocks.

"What are you making?" I whispered in her ear.

"A choo-choo train," she whispered back.

The girl reminded me a little of my niece, Olivia, whom I always miss when I am away. Her immediate trust of me, even though I was a stranger, was touching. For a moment, it sweetened my discomfort. But as we both played with our food, something occurred to me. If I had been asked, in that moment, whether or not I thought this little girl's home should be taken away from her, I would have said yes. I would have supported the bulldozing of her house, of her school, of the playground down the road where she climbed the monkey bars and swung on the swings. They don't belong here.

I had a hard time reconciling my opinion of the settlers as a group with the hospitality of this family and the tenderness of this one child. I did not change my mind about the settlements. The Wall annexes Palestinian land, displaces farmers, and uproots olive groves to make room for settlements like these. The settlements are immoral. But even certainties grow complicated when confronted by individual souls.

Weeks later, I wrote about my experience at Neve Daniel on my blog. I wrote about the racist song, the little girl dressed as an angel, and my struggle to juxtapose the Twerskys' hospitality with the immorality of the settlements in general. In response, Avraham accused me of having it "in for the Jews." Geula Twersky wrote that her inner-city song celebrated contentment, not prejudice, and accused me of stabbing her family in the back. Rabbi Twersky charged me with harbouring "baseless and highly prejudiced racism against Jews" and made reference both to my Muslim wife and what he termed the "so-called Palestinians." What better way to deny the existence of Palestinians, I thought, than to hide them behind a wall?

███

I walked to Ramallah's taxi park, took morning tea from a stall, and waited for a ride to Qalqilya from drivers who always seemed like bullies. According to the day's newspapers, Hillary Clinton was meeting with Mahmoud Abbas, the Palestinian Authority leader, somewhere in town. The men at the taxi park didn't seem to care. Neither did the young students who, with bags hanging off their backs and exercise books folded in their hands, waited for rides to campus. It was the first warm day in a week. The streets smelled of fresh baking and cigarettes.

Our car lined up at a checkpoint on the one main road leading into and out of the city. Soldiers just out of their teens checked the driver's documents and peered into the car. Qalqilya's share of the Wall extends from the right and left of the road and encircles the city on three sides with tall concrete slabs. The city is almost entirely surrounded. Since Qalqilya is the capital of the district and the only city of any size in the region, the checkpoint lines can be long. Villagers from places like Jayyous come to Qalqilya to visit the bank, to shop for housewares and furnishings, or to get their cars repaired. Sometimes, families come to visit the zoo. When a city enclosed by the Wall is also home to Palestine's only zoo, the metaphors come cheap.

The zoo was nearly empty that day. Only a couple of Palestinian families toured the cages. Leopards lazed in pens too small for them. A Syrian bear paced back and forth in a cage that reeked of urine. Baboons gripped the blue wire cages like convicts, and birds perched in enclosures with no space to fly. One row of cages housed a decidedly more domestic menagerie: rabbits, guinea pigs, and chickens. I wondered if the zoo purchased the latter at the poultry bazaar just up the street.

Despite the cramped and smelly cages, the bright colours and kitsch lent a cheerfulness to the zoo that was absent from the rest of my time along the Wall. Bill and Melinda Gates paid for the "safe playground" in the middle of the zoo. Women in hijabs with brown-eyed children wandered from cage to cage and ate ice cream at the painted picnic tables. The zoo's star occupant, a hippo named Dubi, reigned over the peacocks that shared his small concrete pit. A pipe continuously poured in water, and when Dubi opened his immense jaws to drink, the children cheered. They ran in terror, though, when he turned to fling his feces at them over the rail.

There used to be zebras and giraffes here, but they were killed in 2002 after boys at the neighbouring schools hurled stones at a passing Israeli army patrol. The soldiers responded by firing tear gas and rubber bullets. The smoking gas canisters missed their targets and clattered inside the zoo. The gas poisoned the zebras. And the pop of rubber bullets so panicked Brownie, a male giraffe, that he cracked his head against a door frame. Brownie fell down and died, and his pregnant mate miscarried a week later. It is cruelly apt that the zoo's veterinarian, Dr. Sami Kader, is also a taxidermist. He stuffs and mounts some of the animals he cannot save. A gassed zebra, a shrapnel-killed ostrich, and Brownie the giraffe and his stillborn calf are among Kader's glass-eyed dead.

After my time at the zoo, I found a café in the centre of town where I waited for Rafiq, a local activist. I sat at a dusty card table and ordered a hookah and Turkish coffee among the bearded men. Rafiq arrived late: he had been standing in front of bulldozers, demonstrating against the

Wall in a nearby village. Israel was rerouting the Wall to include a cluster of Palestinian villages to the east side of the barrier. Seventy percent of village land, however, would remain on the Israeli side, to be annexed by Israeli settlements, and hundreds of olive trees would be destroyed. Rafiq and the other demonstrators had gathered between the bulldozers and the olive trees. Eventually the bulldozers moved on.

It was a small victory and likely a temporary one. Rafiq harboured few illusions. He knew the groves would eventually fall. Trees that stood for centuries would be torn down in minutes to secure land for settlers who had been on the land for two years. Rafiq spread out a map of Qalqilya district, dragged his finger along the line that marked the Wall's planned route, and showed me what would be lost in its path. Once the land and trees were gone, families would have to buy olive oil for the first time in generations—a great indignity for growers of olives. More than this, though, the olive trees represented the Palestinians' enduring presence and stewardship of the land. The trees and the Palestinians shared the same roots. Ripping out the trees symbolized a spiritual expulsion. "This is a new Nakba," Rafiq said. It is a word meaning "catastrophe" that Palestinians use when they refer to Israel's founding in 1948.

I took a taxi to Jayyous to meet a man named Saleh. He invited me into his salon, served me sage tea and bread with za'atar, and told me that in Jayyous everyone is a farmer. "Everyone has land," he said. "Even teachers and shopkeepers own fields and greenhouses." Before the Wall, Jayyous was famous for its tomatoes, cucumbers, and eggplants. People used to come from all over the region, some from Israel, to buy directly from the farmers. Saleh himself built greenhouses and tended guava trees on the land he inherited from his father. He reached his fields at dawn, paused at midday for food and rest, then worked until darkness. His operation was modest but profitable. He could afford to hire three workers and add some olive and almond trees to the family holdings.

He saw the notices posted to his grove in 2002 and then watched as bulldozers uprooted fifty of his trees to build the Wall. Once the Israelis erected the barrier, Saleh and other farmers worried that IDF-imposed curfews would keep them off their land altogether. The farmers did not leave their fields for a month. They ate their own produce and whatever their families tossed to them over the Wall and slept on the floors of the greenhouses between rows of tomatoes.

Israel insisted the farmers apply for permission to pass through the IDF-controlled gates to their fields. The farmers boycotted the permits at first. They couldn't stomach applying for permission to work on fields that had always belonged to them. But as October approached and olives ripened on their branches across the fence, the men feared missing the most important harvest of the year. They relented and accepted the "permit and gate" scheme. Bestowing validity on the system by participating in it was an error. "This is our fault," Saleh said.

At first, Israel granted permits to almost everyone, even children and long-dead farmers whose descendants filled out the forms on their behalf. The Civil Administration issued 630 permits in all. Then the Israelis began to demand proof of ownership of the fields. In rural Palestine, where land passes informally from fathers to sons, there is rarely a record of transfer. Land titles often remain in the name of an original owner who may have long since died. The Israelis do not recognize this undocumented inheritance, so permit applications can be complicated and are likely to fail, even for long-held family plots. Palestinians may register land officially, but this process is both expensive and risky: the Civil Administration can confiscate land from owners who don't have all the required documents.

More and more permit applications were refused, even for farmers who'd been granted permits in the past. Before the Wall, about three thousand Palestinian farmers used to work the fields around Jayyous. Between January and May 2009, Israel granted permits to fewer than a hundred. Saleh had one, but he could not obtain permits for his family members or hired hands. Saleh couldn't work his land alone, so he managed one or two greenhouses by himself and rented out the rest. He raised chickens in a coop beside his house to earn a few shekels from their meat and eggs.

If there is comfort to be had under occupation, it is in the fields of Palestine. There is serenity beneath the silvery olive leaves and downy young almonds. For the men who till this soil, each morning begins with a pilgrimage from the village noise and the clamour of the family home to something like peace. "The fields are a place to smell the flowers. To smell the fresh air," Saleh said. The Wall soured this solace. Now Saleh started his day by facing uniformed soldiers and their guns at the gate. He would lift his shirt so a twenty-year-old conscript could see he wasn't wired to explode. Farming his inherited land was no longer Saleh's birthright but a fragile privilege that might be revoked three months from now. Or six months. He didn't know. "I am nervous all the time," he told me. The Wall infected Saleh with a Palestinian strain of the Wall Disease, one that manifests through humiliation, anxiety, and hopelessness. Many Palestinians believe the true intention of the barrier is to make life so difficult that they will eventually move away. They see the Wall as a silent notice of eviction.

The next day was Friday, and a good day for a protest. The sky was clear over Jayyous and the air warm, but some villagers were growing weary. An old man shouted at the passing protesters from his front door. "Go home! Stop causing trouble!" Earlier that day, inside the mosque, village elders had pleaded for a Friday without clashes. The village needs a break, they said. One family lost a coop of chickens to tear gas. But the shabaab would not be dissuaded. They ignored the angry man. His wife came out, placed her hand on his shoulder, and led him back into the house.

Once again, the shabaab launched their stones at the IDF beyond the south gate. And once again, the jeeps and soldiers rumbled in. I was starting to learn the rhythm of the siege. I learned I didn't need to run if I simply stood aside. A few soldiers took up positions at the top of a hill from where they could look out over most of the village. I stood a few paces behind them, leaning against a wall, and they didn't seem to care that I was there. After my previous Friday with the shabaab, it felt strange to watch the clashes from the other side, from over the IDF's shoulders. The shabaab danced and taunted from the ledge across the valley and slung stones that had no chance of hitting anything. In response, the IDF fired sound grenades and tear gas. One of the soldiers in front of me, a female recruit in ill-fitting blue fatigues, appeared new and clumsy. A senior officer helped her load her tear gas rifle. If the siege sometimes seemed like a game for the shabaab, for the IDF it was a training exercise.

The soldiers left their post on the hill and advanced down the street towards the shabaab. Sound grenades exploded. Slung stones rattled on the pavement like popcorn. Soldiers showed their middle fingers to the boys who laughed and shout "Jayyous!" each time a tear gas canister fell short, the white smoke billowing amid weeds. The pale minaret of the mosque stood behind them. On the rooftops, women watched the action on the streets while draping wet clothes over laundry lines. The normal duties of a regular afternoon punctuated by shouts and explosions and arrests that had also become commonplace.

▓▓▓▓

The fingers of Yusef Njim's right hand were sore and black. "Some spray cans are more finger-friendly," he said, and after spraying hundreds of messages on the Wall, he should know. Yusef found the neck of a broken bottle on the ground and discovered it fit perfectly on his spray finger. The ad hoc prosthetic eased the painting. At the same time, Yusef also found an unfired IDF rifle bullet. He tossed it to me. "A souvenir of Palestine." I thanked him and put the bullet into my pocket but dropped it on the ground when he looked away. I could not imagine what would happen at Ben Gurion airport if I tried to board a plane with live ammunition in my luggage.

Yusef returned to the Wall and peeled away a few flaking Palestinian campaign posters from long-ago elections. The paste behind them had dried into dust and powdered Yusef's long hair and denim jacket. He rattled his can and sprayed the next message on his list onto the grey concrete:

> *Zahour ma femme*
> *cherie, je t'aime*

The air smelled sweet with aerosol. Yusef moved half a concrete slab to his right, checked the paper in his hand, and wrote:

> *Hey Ruby, let's get married*

Yusef was a writer for Send A Message. The project allows people from anywhere in the world to relay a short note to a chosen receiver by having Yusef and his cohorts spray-paint it on the Wall. The sender pays thirty euros, and the recipient receives emailed photographs of the sprayed message. Money raised by the project funds a Palestinian youth centre in Ramallah. Send A Message was just over a year old when I met with the men, and already 1,200 messages had been sprayed onto the Wall, most of them by Yusef.

Many messages expressed a sort of long-distance solidarity with the Palestinian cause, but most didn't. This surprised me. According to Faris Arouri, a coordinator with the project, a full two-thirds of the messages they wrote were "silly." There were birthday messages, wedding announcements, and everyday pronouncements of love. There were also "ads" for personal blogs, radio stations, and the websites of favourite rock bands. Someone had a falafel recipe sprayed on the Wall, and Faris told me there had been at least a couple of marriage proposals in addition to the new plea for Ruby's hand.

Yusef and Faris would not spray anything racist, insulting, or obscene on the Wall. They also refused messages they disagreed with. Messages that referred to the Wall as a "Security Barrier" would not be written. Neither would overtly pro-Israel messages. I told Faris I'd seen *This wall saves lives* painted on the Wall in Bethlehem. He frowned and said they would never paint a message like that. "We are not a service," he told me. "Besides, it is not true that the Wall saves lives."

Painting the Wall is illegal. The Israelis consider the barrier a "closed military area" and forbid anyone from walking near it. Yusef had had few problems with the IDF, though. Usually he could see them coming in time to toss aside the cans and pretend to be photographing the Wall rather than defacing it. The IDF had only detained Yusef once. They questioned him for six hours but didn't charge him with anything. "I told the soldiers if painting the Wall was really a security concern, I would be happy because it would mean both sides were finally at peace."

Yusef was still taking a few chances. The last message of the day ended up on a slab of Wall adjacent to a steel gate the IDF opened when they wanted to enter Ramallah. Yusef stared at the gate for a moment, shook his can, and sprayed *How about a window.* Tagging the Wall was one thing, but defacing the gate was risky. Faris shook his head. "Yusef is crazy," he said. Yusef looked pleased with himself.

I had been skeptical about the project when I first read about it. I'd spent Friday afternoons amid the weekly tear gas and thrown stones in Jayyous, where young men risked injury and arrest resisting the Wall. I didn't see the point in scrawling *Happy Birthday Jane* on it. Faris told me there were Palestinians who also questioned the purpose of the project. Ramallah's "intelligentsia," those who had grown comfortable under the occupation and no longer resisted it, remained the most cynical. Others complained that the project beautified a structure that is ugly and hateful. Faris scoffed at this. "You do not notice the nail polish on the hand that is beating you."

The detractors are missing the point, I think. Send A Message inspires an ironic form of dialogue: the sender and the receiver are linked by a concrete barrier built to separate. The project exposes the Wall, and the system it represents, to people who might not be otherwise politically motivated. In this way, the banal messages are the most compelling. The senders who submit Nelson Mandela and Gandhi quotes mostly preach to the converted — or at least to the already engaged. But someone who writes a message of love, or a falafel recipe, brings attention to the Wall through a sneaky sort of whimsy. And the silliness subverts the Wall's martial nature. By using this harsh military construction as a medium for a lighthearted exchange, the messages render the barrier no more imposing than a bathroom wall. I didn't see any *For a good time call*…messages, but I'm sure they exist.

The messages also expose the Wall's inability to block the narrative of occupation. For all its military might, the Wall cannot stop the stories from being told. On the contrary, the Wall itself becomes the medium for the story. The Wall is co-opted and hijacked by those who oppose it. Just like the cattle smugglers in India who refashion the barbed fences into pulleys to lift cows over the border, the Send-A-Messagers use the Wall to defeat the Wall. Of course, Yusef's spray paint does not impact the Wall's concrete reality. Nor do the messages tear the Wall down. But they mock the Wall and rob it of its emotional power.

███

There is no better way to mock a Wall, any wall, than by going over it. The concrete slabs stand especially high along the outskirts of Ramallah — but not high enough. In 2007, Mohammad Othman went over.

Mohammad had received an invitation to address the United States Social Forum in Atlanta as a representative from Stop the Wall. He applied for a visa through the American consulate website. After a few weeks, the consulate in Jerusalem called him and told him his visa had been approved and was ready to be picked up. "I told them that I did not have a permit to enter Israel so I could not pick up the visa," Mohammad told me. He asked if the visa could be mailed to his home, but the consular officials insisted he retrieve the documents in person.

Mohammad paid a construction worker he knew in Ramallah a hundred shekels, about thirty dollars, to attach a rope to the top of the Wall using an electric crane. Mohammad found the rope at night and pulled himself, hand over hand, up the twelve metres of concrete. Then he pulled up the rope, tossed it over the other side, and shimmied down to where friends waited to drive him away. He might have been shot if discovered, but such breaches of the Wall were common at the time. Illegal workers from the West Bank entered Jerusalem over the Wall every day, and Palestinians with cranes made extra income setting up the ropes. Eventually the IDF grew weary of seeing ropes dangling contemptuously from the Wall every morning, so they added an electrified fence at the top of the barrier.

When Mohammad arrived at the consulate in the morning, the American officials fingerprinted him and told him to wait. Then they announced his visa application had been denied after all. Mohammad asked why. According to their records, the officials said, Mohammad had murdered a man in the United States thirty-five years earlier. Mohammad had never been to the States, but that did not sway them. Neither did the fact that Mohammad was not even thirty-five years old. "These are FBI records," they said and told Mohammad to leave.

I travelled to Jerusalem through the Wall rather than over it. My bus from downtown Ramallah dropped passengers at the Qalandiya checkpoint. I followed a line of Palestinians with entry permits through the grey gates and turnstiles, showed my passport to a bored IDF soldier frowning behind bulletproof glass, then emerged out the other side of the barrier. My passage through the Wall resembled any other border I've ever traversed. I crossed without rancour or resistance. After all I'd learned in Palestine, my passage across the line was too easy. It felt unearned.

I looked back at the Wall and pictured myself climbing over it. I had entertained these same fantasies of infiltration in the Western Sahara and the Spanish enclaves. To resist barriers is a human instinct. Walls and fences dare us to defeat them, to find a way over, under, or around. Those who defeat the walls — men like Malainin, Jeffrey James, Rocky, and Mohammad — earned my respect for doing something we all itch to do. I would never cross a minefield, crawl over barbed wire, or risk being shot climbing into Jerusalem. But part of me desperately wanted to do these things. I would never truly understand what it meant to live with the walls unless I tried to circumvent them myself.

My driver honked his horn, interrupting my fantasy. I sat down inside my bus, waited for the other passengers, and carried on safely and legally into East Jerusalem.

In 1967, once Israeli troops wrested control of Jerusalem's Old City from the Jordanians, they immediately charged their way to the Western Wall, the ancient retaining wall of Herod's Temple and the holiest site in Judaism. The Israelis flattened the Arab neighbourhoods close to the Western Wall to make room for a huge plaza where devout Jews, tour groups, and wedding and bar mitzvah parties could gather before praying at the Wall. The Arabs displaced by the demolition were transferred to the Shuafat refugee camp on Jerusalem's eastern edge. Now another wall, the Apartheid Wall, has excluded them again. At Shuafat, the Wall makes a rare turn west of the Green Line, taking land from Israel, to exclude the camp and its forty thousand residents from Jerusalem.

The Wall's route through Jerusalem is intricate and evolving, and its effects on the population are wide-ranging. Almost 170 kilometres of the Wall worms through what is known as the Jerusalem Envelope. The barrier includes settlements on its west side and isolates Arab neighbourhoods to the east. Thousands of hectares of farmland have been lost to the barrier. So has a third of the Al-Quds University campus. The Wall divides the Arab neighbourhood of Dahiyat al-Barid in half; now residents living on the Jerusalem side need permits to live in their own homes. In all, more than fifty-five thousand Palestinian residents of Jerusalem, close to a quarter of the city's total Arab population, have been excised from the city.

The Israeli government insists that security needs dictate the route of the Wall, but in Jerusalem it is clear there are demographic concerns at play. Since 1967, the percentage of Jews in Jerusalem has steadily shrunk. The Israeli government seeks to preserve a Jewish majority in the city by exiling Arabs to the other side of the Wall. This hasn't worked. As the Wall began to rise around Jerusalem, Palestinians living in the West Bank worried that the barrier would exile them forever. They feared being kept from their families, the markets, and the holy sites within the Old City. So Palestinians poured into Jerusalem in a dash to buy up homes in the eastern part of the city. Arabs from other parts of the West Bank quickly occupied the houses they had left on the other side of the Wall. As the percentage of Arabs in Greater Jerusalem went up, the ratio of Jews to Arabs decreased.

The Wall causes other problems for Israelis in Jerusalem. Palestinian hospitals in East Jerusalem lost their West Bank patients to the Wall and had to close their doors. Now East Jerusalem's Palestinians crowd the beds in Israeli hospitals. The Wall also severed the ancient connection between Jerusalem and Bethlehem, historically its sister city. Forty percent of the Jerusalem economy once flowed from Bethlehem's Palestinians, who visited Jerusalem to pray at al-Aqsa and shop in the souks. The Wall killed this trade. This is to say nothing of the resentment the Wall inspires in those it edits out of the city. The Wall casts historical hatreds in concrete and embodies the comfortable idea that Palestinians should be feared rather than trusted. The barrier fuels the rage that led to the sort of violence the Wall, according to its builders, was meant to protect against. Instead of easing the Israeli-Palestinian conflict, the Wall has preserved it.

I don't know if most Israelis are aware of Jerusalem's divided neighbourhoods, its overcrowded hospitals, and the downward curve of its Jewish share. I don't know if they've heard about the farmers exiled from their fields or the martyred olive groves. Regardless of what they may or may not know, most Israelis favour the Wall because they believe the barrier protects them. There have been attacks since 2002 — three "bulldozer terrorists" drove their front-end loaders into Israeli cars and buses, and rockets continue to fly out of the Gaza Strip — but the blast of suicide vests has not been heard much in the last few years. The buses and cafés around Israel feel safe. Blood rarely splatters. The Wall is working.

Or perhaps it isn't. Members of both the IDF and Shin Bet, the Israeli secret service, have made the controversial claim that the Wall is not a major factor in preventing attacks. Terrorists can easily bypass the barrier by walking through its many gaps; less than 60 percent of the Wall is finished, and almost a third of the construction has not even begun. In fact, attacks began to taper off in 2002, long before there was enough of the Wall built to make a difference. There are other reasons for the recent ease in violence.

Israel's security structure learned hard lessons from the United States, whose FBI and CIA agents failed to share enough of their secrets to prevent 9/11. Now Israeli intelligence works closely with the IDF. Also, since the death of Yasser Arafat in 2004, Israel co-operates more effectively on security with the Palestinian Authority. The most compelling reason for the drop in violence, however, is a counterintuitive one: the ascendance of Hamas. The Islamic organization, once a wellspring of suicide bombers, was elected to government in Gaza and shifted its focus away from terror and towards politics. In 2009, the head of Shin Bet flatly told a parliamentary committee there is no security reason for continuing to build the Wall. After all I'd seen in Palestine, I suspect there never was.

■■■

After Mohammad took his photos of the flowers on Jayyous's southern hills, we saw an old man sitting on a stool in front of a shack near the fence. He smoked a water pipe and sipped tea prepared in a soot-blackened pot while his wife bent over the weeds in their garden. "The Wall has given me grey hair," the man said, lifting his wool cap and dragging his fingers over his head. The land immediately on the other side of the Wall belonged to him. The fields had been in his family for decades, but now he was without the permits to farm them.

When Israel disengaged from Gaza in 2007, Palestinians destroyed the greenhouses the Jewish settlers left behind. I've heard Israelis say that this is proof of Arab barbarism and hate. Yet here in Jayyous, Israeli bulldozers ripped up thousands of trees, including part of this man's family olive grove, to make space for the Wall. Some of the bulldozed trees were hundreds of years old. Palestinians call them *zeitun rumi*, "Roman olives," in reference to their antiquity. The man had some of his felled trees dragged behind his shack. Now he hacked them apart for firewood to light his pipe and boil water for his tea. Each day he sat and stared out beyond the barbed wire and the sign that warned of mortal danger to what was left of his land. His trees were withering from neglect. Weeds grew tall at the base of trunks that seemed to twist around themselves for self-defence.

The spring after my visit, the Israelis moved the Wall around Jayyous, returning some of the land and two of the freshwater wells to the village.

The shabaab of Jayyous ripped out the abandoned Israeli fence posts and danced on the access road. They waved flags and shouted "Jayyous!" as if in victory. The largest part of what was once Jayyous, however, including the most fertile fields and all the village's greenhouses, remains behind the Wall. The man with the grey hair and wool cap got back some of his confiscated land, but I doubt he celebrated. His bulldozed trees are gone forever. New trees will take almost a decade before they bear fruit, but first he'll have to plough through the asphalt scar the Israelis left behind.

That fall, Mohammad Othman travelled to Norway to speak about the occupation and about the Wall. He returned home through Jordan and tried to cross the Allenby Bridge into Palestine, but the IDF was waiting for him. They arrested him at the border, interrogated him, and held him without charge. Mohammad spent four months in Israeli custody before the IDF returned him to his side of the Wall.

Walling Absurd
Nicosia/Lefkoşa

The walls edge places that cannot be. In the Sahara, a berm tracks through a nation, the Saharawi Arab Democratic Republic, that isn't real. Fences surround Ceuta and Melilla, cities that are in neither Europe nor Africa, neither Spain nor Morocco, but some unlikely and unknowable collision between them. The villagers who live along India's blurred seam with Bangladesh are nowhere people strung out along a zero line. Palestinians surely exist, but Palestine itself is less a place than it is an idea, an emaciated dream defined and denied by someone else's wall. After leaving Palestine, I travelled to the Turkish Republic of Northern Cyprus, another walled nation recognized by no one. Another place that does not exist. I spent a few weeks in the capital city—named Lefkoşa on one side of the Wall and Nicosia on the other.

I drank Turkish coffee in Atölye Cadı Kazanı café in Lefkoşa—the same drink is called Cypriot coffee on the other side of the Wall—and tried to keep Nilgün Güney's cat off my notebook. Nilgün wasn't paying any attention to her cat's affections. She was telling me the story of the island, and she wanted to start at the beginning.

Because she is a Turkish-Cypriot, the story begins on December 21, 1963. Nilgün's beginning even had a time: 2 a.m., the moment Turkish-Cypriot resistance fighters knocked on the door of her father's house. They told him the Greeks were invading and that he should go with them to help protect his people. Nilgün's father lifted his coat and hat from the closet and followed the soldiers into the Mediterranean darkness. Her mother grabbed a small handbag and Nilgün's school uniform, and they fled to her grandmother's house. They could hear gunfire, and the glow from burning houses coerced the sky to a premature dawn. Nilgün, eleven years old at the time, was upset she had to leave her dolls behind.

Cyprus had emerged from eight decades of British rule three years earlier. The path to sovereignty had been hard fought and bloody. Rival Turkish- and Greek-Cypriots were now co-founders of the new republic and partners in its government. The island should have been bathing in the nuptial afterglow of independence; however, the new constitution was a bloated and unworkable package of veto powers, special provisions, and minority guarantees. Among its assembled absurdities was the regulation of national anthems. The Greek national anthem was to be used in the presence of the republic's Greek-Cypriot president, while Turkey's anthem would be sung when the Turkish-Cypriot vice-president was around. I wondered what they would play if the two men were ever together.

But there were bigger problems with the constitution. The document allowed for the British, Greek, and Turkish militaries to station soldiers on the island, thus undermining any real sense of sovereignty. The constitution also called for unattainable ratios in the civil service and the army and bestowed so much power on both the vice-president and his Turkish-Cypriot minority in parliament that either could defeat any bill. And they often did. Outsiders joked that Cyprus was the only democracy in the world where the majority was officially denied the right to rule.

In December 1963, Archbishop Makarios III, the Greek-Cypriot president, presented a list of amendments to the constitution. He insisted that the changes would make cohabitation of the island possible. The Turkish-Cypriots suspected a trick. They feared Makarios's proposals would move Cyprus towards *enosis*: the union of the island with mainland Greece, which, according to Turkish conspiracy theorists, is the evil dream of every Greek. The Turkish-Cypriots rejected Makarios's amendments. The rejection provided enough of a reason for hardline elements on both sides—the Greek paramilitary faction, EOKA, and the Turkish resistance forces, the TMT—to start shooting at each other.

The women in the community did what they could for the fighting men. Nilgün helped her mother and grandmother cook meals for the Turkish fighters. They gathered sheets and blankets and brought them to schools where gymnasiums became hospitals. While they worked, the women shared gossip about who had been injured or killed. There was talk of massacres, of kidnappings, and of murdered children. Nilgün's grandfather, too grey to fight, listened for news at the cafés. Everyone dreaded hearing the name of a son or husband whispered over coffee or between lines of laundry. All of Nilgün's family survived, but the violence claimed Nilgün's favourite teacher. Later, the school was renamed after the teacher with the honorific *Shahid*, "martyr," placed before his name.

The street battles calmed after a few days, and Nilgün's father rejoined the family at her grandmother's house. The British military started to broker a ceasefire. To separate the warring parties, and in an inadvertent homage to Cyril Radcliffe, a British official dragged a green pencil across a map of Nicosia, drawing a line between the Greek- and Turkish-Cypriot quarters. The Green Line cut the city in half. Soldiers began to heave dirt and sandbags along the new boundary. Nilgün's family home stood along the line but on the "wrong" side, and by the time the ceasefire took effect on Christmas Day, every house on the street was off limits. Two years would pass before the UN moved the Green Line one street back and liberated Nilgün's house from south of the line. Her family returned to find the doors broken down. Thieves had stolen the radio, Nilgün's dolls, and the jewellery Nilgün's mother had hoped to bequeath to her daughter one day. The thieves left behind only the furniture they'd found too heavy to carry away.

Turkish-Cypriot politicians resigned from government and set up a parallel regime of nominal self-rule north of the Green Line. They moved quickly. By the end of January, the North had already established a post office and issued its first postage stamp. A UN peacekeeping force and a Greek-Turkish-British "tripartite truce force" assembled to enforce the Christmas ceasefire, but the killing continued for another six months. Most of the six hundred casualties were Turkish-Cypriots targeted by EOKA. The shootings eventually ebbed, and Nilgün remembers life slowly returning to the way it was before. There was, however, a new "separation in the minds," she told me. Any goodwill between Greek- and Turkish-Cypriots had been scorched black by the December violence. Nilgün's parents started buying from Greek-Cypriot merchants again, but they would never forgive the Greeks for looting their home.

Nilgün sat in that same home, a decade later, when the gunfire started again. It was the summer of 1974. Nilgün was twenty-two years old, married, and pregnant. She was studying fine arts in Istanbul but had returned home for her summer vacation. Nilgün's father was listening to the BBC when he heard that right-wing Greek-Cypriots, aided by a junta based in Athens, had overthrown Makarios and massed along the Green Line. Nikos Sampson, a violent, Turk-hating drunk, led the coup. Sampson's presidency would last little more than a week — no foreign government dared recognize the regime — but the mere idea of such a thug in charge of the island terrorized the Turkish-Cypriots. "They said that they would not touch Turks," Nilgün remembered, "but we heard they were going to Turkish-Cypriot villages and killing everyone. Even children."

Nilgün's father suggested that the family spend the night at a friend's house farther away from the Green Line, in case there were clashes. "We woke at sunrise to the sounds of bombs," Nilgün recalled. "There was no electricity. No water. The shops were closed and we had to eat all the food stocks we had in our houses." There was almost nothing left when, a few days later, she heard, "Turkey was coming to save us."

When Greek-Cypriots tell the history of the conflict, they start here, with Turkey's assault on the island in July 1974. Turkish-Cypriots consider Operation Attila to have been a peace mission meant to rescue Turkish-Cypriots from bloodthirsty Greeks. Greek-Cypriots call it an invasion. Regardless of the nomenclature, the action was a debacle at first. The Turkish army sent waves of its most poorly trained and undisciplined soldiers onto the northern beaches, where they were perforated by Greek machine guns. Those who made it over the sand carried little water or ammunition for their guns. Tanks rattled ashore without enough fuel. Nilgün remembers going outside to watch the contrails of missiles overhead and not knowing which were Greek and which were Turkish. The armies themselves were just as confused. Turkish jets sank two of their own landing craft and one of their own destroyers, while the Greek-Cypriots shot down two supply planes bringing reinforcements from Greece.

Mercifully for the Turks, who outnumbered the Greeks but were losing seven men for every one they killed, a ceasefire was called. The guns did not rest for long, though. Turkey sent fresh troops and continued the offensive on August 14. By then the Greek-Cypriot forces, who had performed so admirably during the initial attack, were exhausted. The Turks routed them within two days and pushed south. Greek-Cypriot civilians in the North, between 140,000 and 200,000 depending on which side does the counting, fled the Turkish troops, who murdered and raped civilians as they advanced. The Turks also seized the homes the Greek-Cypriots abandoned. By the time the Turkish army halted at the Green Line, which they rechristened the Attila Line, about a third of the island was under their direct control. It still is today.

The history of the island is a tale of ceasefires built and subsequently broken. Another was called on August 16. Periodic violence continued for months, however, especially around the Green Line. There was still shooting in the streets in October, when Nilgün gave birth to a daughter. Her bedroom was on the second floor and a window faced south. Every time she heard the guns, she carried her baby girl down the stairs to the basement for fear of stray bullets. For months after the battle, the sound of airplanes terrorized her. And for five years, Nilgün was afraid to step in front of a window.

In the years that followed Operation Attila, Greek-Cypriots migrated south of the line — sometimes voluntarily, often not — while Turkish-Cypriots were similarly compelled to move north. Discussions about a bi-communal federation amounted to nothing, and in 1983 the North declared independence. The Green Line was stretched beyond its bounds in the capital until it linked the west coast and the east with a long snake of buffer zone. The Green Line became a border, with the land above it reborn as the Turkish Republic of Northern Cyprus, or TRNC, a "nation" no one but Turkey recognizes. A place that does not exist.

Nilgün graduated from her studies in Istanbul and became a painter and art teacher. She had another child, a boy this time, but the trauma of the 1974 war stayed with her. She suffered panic attacks and agoraphobia. Her marriage strained and broke apart. "The terror and pain that both sides experienced is something that politics cannot explain," she said, though I suspect Dr. Müller-Hegemann could. Nilgün's symptoms resembled those of East Berliners who lived along the Berlin Wall. Nilgün eventually cured her anxiety with eight months of therapy. She bought a building in the Old

City and turned it into a café so she would have something to pass on to her children. Her son tended the bar and spun records there on the weekend.

Now in her fifties, Nilgün wore her dyed red hair in pigtails and a string of cowrie shells around her neck. She told me the barricades on the Green Line meant nothing to her anymore. Her art did not portray the conflict, she said. Still, all the portraits she painted had curious vertical lines instead of noses that divided each face in half.

We'd almost finished our conversation when her parents came in. They were both aged and shared a quiet dignity. Nilgün told them what we were talking about. Her father was nearly deaf and didn't respond, but Nilgün's mother said she still didn't trust Greek people, not after they looted the family's home in 1963.

"They took our jewellery, my dresses, everything. Then in 1974 they shot at our house." She turned to Nilgün. "You should show him the bullet holes." Nilgün drove me to her old house and pointed up at the south-facing wall to the window she was once afraid to stand in front of. Beside the window, bullet holes scarred the plaster like a pox.

▪▪▪

My time in Israel and Palestine had started to weigh on me. I had spent five weeks in the despair that grew in the shadow of the Wall. Palestine's Mauerkrankheit. I had witnessed street battles, heard the stories of newly landless men and of ancient trees torn from the ground. The five weeks of darkness had left me emotionally exhausted. I thought Cyprus would provide some relief. Unlike Palestine, the Cyprus conflict had gone cold. There had been no real violence there in decades. This Wall, on this Green Line, was a relic. Besides, I'd read that the leaders from both sides of the Wall were talking peace. Unification loomed. After Palestine's daily misery, I was looking forward to a few lighthearted weeks along a wall about to fall.

On my first morning on the island, I surrendered to the Wall's strange gravitational pull, skipped breakfast, and headed directly towards the barricades. I breached the Old City walls, their bricks rough like cubes of brown sugar, through the narrow Pafos Gate. I stopped to peer into the Holy Cross Catholic Church and speak with a worker from Pakistan who was mixing cement out front. The church had hired him to repair the front steps. He offered to show me the inside of the church, but I opted to carry on down Granikou Street to the Green Line. The Wall had been standing for nearly forty years; I don't know why I felt the need to hurry.

The Old City is a perfect circle, and the Wall bisects it neatly. There are two sets of barricades — one on the northern side, one in the south. Between them stretches a narrow buffer zone, sometimes only a few metres wide, that is off limits to anyone but military personnel and UN peacekeepers. In the south, the area near the buffer zone forms an ad hoc museum of abandoned buildings and crumbling barricades. The Greeks call it the *nekri zoni*, the "dead zone."

I tried to walk the entire length of the dead zone from the west of the Old City to the east, but it was impossible. The old road that once traversed the city is now in the buffer zone itself and therefore off limits. Instead, I walked up and down streets truncated by the barricades, trying to stay as close to the Wall as possible. Each time I turned a corner and approached the Wall, I felt a strange sort of thrill at my proximity to prohibited space, and from being at the limit of what is off limits. It was a cheap rebellion, as cheap as my infiltration through the Indo-Bangla fence, but I savoured it nonetheless.

The barricades were older than me — some had been here since 1963 — and were not aging well. The sandbags leaked. Old wooden bunkers sagged and crumbled. The rows of gravel-filled metal barrels bled rust and had become unwitting planters for weeds that grew into yellow flowers. Some barrels were painted in alternating blue and white, the colours of the Greek flag, and reminded me of the cheery Formica and vinyl of 1950s diners. Slats of wood formed gun slits that were now peepholes to look across the short divide from Here to There. And everywhere, of course, the barbed wire spun. The wire became so ubiquitous on my travels along the walls that I hardly saw it unless it raised an impromptu flag by snagging a plastic bag out of the wind.

Across from the barricades stood the bullet-blistered buildings. The upper floors were abandoned. Sandbags stuffed the glassless windows to provide cover for riflemen who hadn't been present for decades. Some of the first-floor rooms housed carpentry and mechanic workshops that wheezed with sawdust and noise, but most of the storefronts were shuttered. Trash filled one shop — broken shelving, empty gas canisters, an old moped frame. The dust dyed everything the same greyish brown. Only a plastic Sprite bottle, recently cast on the pile, added any colour. Against the grey, it shone like an emerald. Soon this too would surrender to the pallor. Time and dust would undye the green in the same way the bombs in Gauhati blanched the market of its colour.

Greek-Cypriot soldiers watched over the barricades. They looked absurdly fresh-faced juxtaposed with such dereliction. Young men in helmets standing guard over a war gone cold. They must've been bored. They had wasted part of their youth smoking cigarettes in their uniforms and waving away tourists who came with their cameras. The Wall was camera-shy. Signs warned that photography was forbidden and to KEEP AWAY! in three languages, as if there was real danger there. Meanwhile, the rain and wind and weeds continued their assault on the walls, trampling the barriers into the ground and sucking history deeper into archaeology.

Captain Mike Solonynko called the Starbucks on Ledra Street "Fourbucks" because a cup of coffee there cost about that much. As he leashed his tiny terrier to an outdoor table, he ridiculed me for cheering the Calgary Flames hockey team. Solonynko was a barrel-chested soldier from Edmonton but was out of uniform, and in Bermuda shorts, when we met. He was serving in Operation Snowgoose, Canada's contribution to the United Nations Force in Cyprus or UNFICYP. The Canadian military started placing peacekeeping troops on the island in 1964, which makes Cyprus Canada's most enduring operation, but Snowgoose itself dates from 1974 and the Turkish occupation of the North. At its inception, Operation Snowgoose involved a battalion's worth of Canadian blue helmets, and over the years twenty-five thousand Canadians have served on the island. Canada's role in the mission has reduced considerably in the last few years. In fact, Canada now contributes a single officer to UNFICYP: Captain Mike. The Oilers fan *is* Operation Snowgoose.

Canada lost twenty-seven soldiers in the conflict — only missions in Korea and along the Israel–Egypt border have claimed more Canadian peacekeepers — but Cyprus is hardly a war zone anymore. The mission is safe enough that Solonynko had brought his wife and teenaged son to Nicosia with him. He told me that the UN's role on the island is to enforce the status

quo. The UNFICYP registers each border post and barricade along the Green
Line according to its location, its dimensions, the number of troops allowed
to man it, and other military metrics. UNFICYP ensures these specifications
are maintained. The blue helmets also watch for individuals violating the
buffer zone, but they do not have the authority to engage such intruders. All
they can do is radio the Greek-Cypriot police and report the breach.

We had drunk eight dollars' worth of coffee when Solonynko announced
he wanted to show me something. He drove me past a Greek-Cypriot
barricade with the slogan NOTHING IS GAINED WITHOUT SACRIFICES AND
FREEDOM WITHOUT BLOOD and parked his car next to a spray-painted sign
that said FUCK UN. Solonynko left his dog in the car and walked me to
another bullet-scarred structure along the dead zone. The building was
a UN border post originally manned by Canadian forces, who named it,
patriotically, Maple House. It occupied the second floor above what had once
been a Toyota dealership. The shop had been shuttered since the 1970s, but
Solonynko claimed an inventory of "brand new" thirty-year-old Toyotas still
occupied a basement showroom. Their odometers read only sixty miles, the
distance from the port at Famagusta, where they arrived, to this dealership.
I'd heard about the Toyotas before and thought it a myth, but Solonynko
assured me the cars exist. He had never seen them himself, though. "The
basement is overrun with vermin," he told me. "Rats and flies and feral cats.
It is not safe to go down there anymore."

Solonynko pointed past Maple House into the buffer zone and across
an abandoned schoolyard marked with faded soccer boundaries to where
a derelict yellow sedan stood on blocks. A sign on the car declared, redun-
dantly, "Yellow Car." Solonynko told me the car itself was an official UN
observation post. When the buffer zone was first marked out by the UN in
1974, the peacekeepers described the Turkish-Cypriot territory at this point
as extending from the front of the abandoned car to the corner of a nearby
building. The Turkish military, however, debated the definition of "front." The
UN took "front" to mean the car's headlights and accordingly drew the line
from there. The Turks, however, felt that the "front" of the car in this case was
the part of the car closest to the next border post. The Turks would secure a
marginally larger scrap of territory if the line was drawn by this measurement.

They settled the argument with a bizarre compromise. The Turkish troops acquiesced to the UN's meaning of "front," but as an expression of their authority over the area, a Turkish soldier stands next to the car for five minutes every hour. This absurdity has taken place at the Yellow Car once per hour for more than thirty years.

The United Nations headquarters in Nicosia occupies the Ledra Palace Hotel just outside the Old City walls and right in the middle of the buffer zone. I visited the hotel after leaving Solonynko and his dog. Now peppered with bullet holes, Ledra Palace used to be one of the finest hotels in the Middle East. The walls boasted walnut panelling and painted frescoes. Chandeliers from Venice hung above solid oak floors. The marble-topped bar was tended by a famed barman who, according to lore, invented the brandy sour for Egypt's King Farouk. The king was a Muslim who, in the company of the more devout, wanted a drink that could be mistaken for fruit juice.

When the Turks invaded the island in the summer of 1974, UN troops evacuated the hotel's gilded guests and moved themselves in. In addition to being the main headquarters and barracks of the UN mission, Ledra Palace's neutral location in the buffer zone made it a regular venue for conflict negotiations. When I visited, though, the place seemed less a locale for peace than a British college dormitory. Baby-faced soldiers cursed with English accents beside the laundry counter on the ground level and scuffed the oak floors with their army boots. A map of Nicosia pinned to a corkboard showed the parts of the city out of bounds to the UN troops. They included strip clubs, cabarets, and, oddly, a McDonald's and a KFC. Outside, T-shirts and trousers were hung to dry from the white balconies of the guest rooms.

Ledra Palace stands in the middle of the main crossing point between the Turkish North and the Greek South. Just past the southern checkpoint, where the Greek-Cypriot soldiers rarely bother to check passports, an old sign leans against a wall. The writing has rusted and bled, but the bitterness of the message is clear:

Enjoy yourself in this land of racial purity and true apartheid.
Enjoy the sight of our desecrated churches.
Enjoy what remains of our looted heritage and homes.

from the inhabitants of those areas who are forbidden to enter.

The lettering may be worn but the grievances remain. Greek-Cypriots accuse the Turkish army of running them out of the North, of stealing the homes they left behind, and of defiling or destroying the abandoned churches. There is truth in all of this, but the sign's final claim is no longer true. As of 2003, the North is no longer forbidden to those from the South.

On April 23, 2003 — a day now dubbed Good Wednesday — the president of the TRNC punched holes in the Wall. He announced that Cypriots from both sides of the divide were henceforth permitted to cross in either direction without restrictions. The move was a shock. Cypriots from both sides of the island didn't believe the opening would last, so they rushed the Green Line before the checkpoints closed again. They wanted to visit the homes, churches, and neighbourhoods they'd left behind. At the Ledra Palace crossing, hundreds of Greek-Cypriots lined up to enter the North and tried to ignore the intentionally provocative banners that read "Welcome to the TRNC. You are now entering the sovereign republic." And, perhaps worse, "Turkish Republic of Northern Cyprus FOREVER."

Stephanos Stephanides, a Greek-Cypriot poet, queued among the crowds and chaos at the Ledra Palace crossing in the first days after the borders opened. I met him for cheaper coffee outside the Old City. Like Cypriots on both sides of the island, Stephanos feared the openings would turn out to be a momentary softening of an ossified conflict. He knew better than to trust the politicians. He wanted to cross the divide as soon as he could in case this was his only chance.

Once in the North, an old friend of his father's took Stephanos to the house in Trikomo where he was born, a house he knew only through stories told to him by his mother. All Stephanos could remember about the house was the green of its balcony. His parents did not live there long — their marriage was brief — but as Stephanos walked through rooms he couldn't recall and stood on the balcony he barely remembered, he could feel the ghosts of his parents' fleeting passion. "It was like something I lived in a previous life."

Afterwards, Stephanos sought out his grandmother's house, the home where he spent his youth after his parents split. He remembered the place fondly but was stunned to find it had been completely rebuilt by its new owners. The house of his memory no longer existed. Stephanos knocked on the door and the new owner welcomed him inside. Stephanos's reunion with his childhood home left him with a mix of joy and melancholy. It changed the way he thought of himself, his past, and all his parents had dreamed. Most striking, though, was having a stranger tell him his own family stories.

"Ten children were born in this room," the man remarked as they toured the house.

"Yes," Stephanos said. "One was my mother."

In the weeks that followed the opening, the island was full of such stories of return, remembrance, and reunion. The island's cynics feared the crossings would lead to clashes when the exiled returned to find their old homes occupied by strangers. This rarely happened. Instead, both Turkish- and Greek-Cypriots welcomed each other. I heard about Turkish-Cypriot families delaying their vacations in case southerners arrived and wanted to tour their old homes. Families kept food ready for such surprise visits from former residents, sometimes served with the silverware they had left behind nearly thirty years earlier. Turkish greetings that had not been uttered for decades awoke on the tongues of Greek-speaking men. Routes to favourite cafés and cinemas were suddenly, surprisingly, remembered. Those who crossed over discovered that the old words and old maps, assumed to be long forgotten, had never left them. They had been etched in the stone of their memories all along. It was a joyous time, and optimistic foreign observers predicted that a "spontaneous unification" would take place.

Cypriots themselves were hardly so naive. The island had lived through these moments of hope before. Glasnost. The fall of the Berlin Wall. The end of South African apartheid. Each of these led Cypriots to believe that their own time was at hand, that the wave of other nations' triumphs would wash away the "Cyprus Problem." It never did. Good Wednesday, for all its tears and joy, wouldn't either. Once everyone who wanted to visit the other side had done so, the novelty eroded. Many people still crossed to work or shop, but the two communities rarely mingled. At the end of the day, perhaps it is not walls themselves that keep people apart.

The year after the openings, Cypriots had a chance to vote on reunification. The United Nations hammered together the Annan Plan, a document designed to broker peace on Cyprus. The referendum on the Plan was scheduled for April 24, 2004, a week before the Republic of Cyprus was to ascend into the European Union as a member state. The Plan echoed the 1964 constitution in its confusion and silliness. Among the policy dictates, the Annan Plan called for a new, and wordless, national anthem and a freshly designed flag. It aimed to replace the old flag, a Cyprus-shaped blotch on a white background that a British poet in Nicosia likened to a "soiled nappy," with one composed of three horizontal bars — one blue, one yellow, and one red. The flag reminded me of a stack of Lego bricks.

Europe and the UN were optimistic. It was to be a shining spring. A lingering conflict would be solved, the unified island would raise a new flag, a new anthem would be performed — though, alas, not sung — and Cyprus would be embraced by Brussels into the European fold.

The Turkish-Cypriots voted in favour of the deal. Two-thirds of northern voters were ready to jettison the TRNC to share a country that actually existed, a nation whose economy was an order of magnitude greater than their own. Voters in the South, however, crushed the Annan Plan. More than 75 percent of Greek-Cypriots voted against it. As with the 1964 constitution, Greek-Cypriots took exception to last-minute concessions made to the Turkish-Cypriot minority. Voters in the South feared they would have to pay to improve the North's crumbling infrastructure. They worried that resettlement policies might allow northern Cypriots to reclaim their now-valuable property in the South. They scoffed at conditions that allowed Turkish troops and British bases to remain on the island. The Greek-Cypriots simply had too much to lose and nothing to gain other than peace on paper.

But the South's rejection of the Plan was not based just on economics and policy. For young Greek-Cypriots who grew up with Western European ideas of style and society, the North was the East. Turkish-Cypriots are unfashionable. Their villages are shabby. Nothing compelled Greek-Cypriots to share their country with people they did not care for. The status quo satisfied them. For anyone under forty, it was all they had ever known.

Stephanos was one of the few intellectuals in the South to speak out in favour of the Annan Plan. This position, according to the Greek Orthodox Bishop of Kyrenia, would condemn Stephanos and others who shared his views to eternal damnation. Stephanos risked future hellfire by joining fifteen other Cypriot poets from both sides of the divide to pen a poem in support of the Plan. It was called "Yes, What a Joyful Word!" and included the saccharine lines:

> Yes, a palm open to the other
> To the different, to the unknown
> I passed through the border amongst
> The rumble of thousands of migrating butterflies
> I know this day of May will be the day
> Oh wall
> Your stones
> We will bury
> In the foundations of our common house
> The whole universe
> Fits into a single word![11]

Stephanos was disappointed when he learned that the stones would surely not be buried in a common house. He blamed the Communist government for not doing a better job of supporting the Annan Plan. "The Left allowed those who wanted it dead to stab it to death."

I wondered, though, what was the point of trying to overcome the conflict's decades-old inertia if the majority of Cypriots were satisfied with the way things were. I asked Stephanos why he wanted reunification, and he looked at me as if I'd asked something foolish. Then he said, "The forces that made the status quo happen are violent and evil. There were mass killings on both sides. A situation that has its origins in blood and violence cannot be allowed to stand. It must be put right."

Katerina's grandfather, a Greek-Cypriot baker, used to have a Turkish-Cypriot business partner. He also once helped a Turkish-Cypriot friend hide from army officials who wanted to arrest him. Katerina doesn't know why. This was before 1974 and before Katerina was born. Unlike her grandfather, Katerina has never known a Turkish-Cypriot. And she's never seen the North.

Like all Greek-Cypriot children of her generation, Katerina learned all about the Turkish invasion they never lived through. "We knew that day was 'the bad day,'" she told me in a slick restaurant outside Old Nicosia. Katerina remembers the nightly television spots that flashed images of occupied villages of the North with the message "We Don't Forget." She said that twice each July, sirens blast the summer air on the anniversaries of the 1974 coup d'état and the Turkish invasion of the island.

Katerina learned to revere Greece and distrust the Turks. Her history classes focused on ancient Greek civilization, on the Greek invention of democracy, and on Greece's refusal to aid the Nazis — anything that said "we are the good guys and they are the bad guys." She and her classmates never heard about the 1963 atrocities committed against the Turkish-Cypriots by the Greeks — not in their classrooms anyway. In the pages of southern textbooks, Cypriot history, aside from the British and Turkish invasions of 1828 and 1974, merely comprises episodes in the glorious history of Greek civilization. Religious education too is purely Greek. The only faith Katerina ever learned about was Greek Orthodox Christianity. According to her schooling, there was no other way of believing.

Except, of course, for not believing at all. Katerina's family were leftist atheists and her mother kept her children at home each time the school scheduled a visit to the church. "We thought Holy Communion receiving was a gross and unsanitary ritual," she says with some scorn. Katerina remains an atheist and considers the calls to prayer that echo daily from Greek churches as well as Turkish mosques an "intrusion." She voted against the Annan Plan on policy grounds, not because the Bishop warned that her eternal soul was at stake.

History in the North was taught with the same one-sidedness. Cyprus was described as part of the great narrative of Ottoman glory. The 1974 operation was a Turkish victory over Greek oppression. The books whipped up fear that all Greeks dreamed of *Megali* — a vast and fanciful Greek nation that would devour Cyprus, all the Aegean Islands, and the Turkish regions of Western Thrace. Both sides of the island published history books based on the underlying dogma, embodied by the Wall itself, that Turks and Greeks cannot get along.

In 2006, Turkish-Cypriot educators put aside the old lesson plans rooted in antagonism and rewrote the history books. The new texts do not portray the Greek-Cypriots as a national enemy, and the narratives focus on social history rather than military sagas. Students read more stories of bi-communal football teams and fewer accounts of gun battles won and lost. Cyprus now stands as the mother- and fatherland, not Greece or Turkey. The island is home to unhyphenated Cypriots. Not surprisingly, right-wing parties in the North reacted against the textbooks, and they have become an election issue. If they ever come to power, the rightist parties promise to unwrite the new history and return to the familiar narratives of Us and Them.

Textbooks in the South remain how Katerina remembers them. The Greek Orthodox Church wields too much power to allow a dilution of Greek history in the schools. Katerina, though, is no fool. She knows what is propaganda fed to her by a government she hardly respects and a Church she refuses to kneel before. I was having trouble, though, understanding what Katerina actually believes in. She scoffs at the notion that Turkish- and Greek-Cypriots are hard-wired for hate and feels that the bi-communal activities meant to bring the two groups together are therefore unnecessary. Yet she wanted me to understand that she isn't a "dopey 'Turkish-Cypriots-are-our-brothers-and-sisters' person." She would like to see the Cyprus Problem resolved, but not at any cost and not if it means giving in to the unreasonable demands of the North. She considers the annual clamour of military exercises in the North to be a warning to the South. "They remind us, the other side, that the Turkish military is there. Two seconds away. Ready to strike," she said. Though she has never known war, the sound of fireworks reminds her of gunshots. "Greek-Cypriots are comfortable and living without fear of real, everyday conflict since the sides are pretty separated," she added. At the same time, she recoiled when I suggested she was relieved the Wall stood between them.

I cannot tell if these are contradictions. I wasn't born in a disputed place; and I've never lived alongside a wall. But it seems that, in spite of Katerina's leftist notions of justice, something about this place has hardened her. Her city, her half-city, bestowed upon her an interior distrust of those across the barricades. It doesn't matter that there hasn't been a bullet fired over the Wall in Katerina's lifetime. The fear is not logical. It is the inheritance, and the affliction, of a divided place.

There was something else. Something about the barricades themselves is imprinted on Katerina. She says she doesn't pay them much attention anymore; they've always been part of her Nicosia. She claimed, however, that the severed streets "are the reason for my poor sense of direction." The throwaway remark seemed a half joke, but the idea fascinated me. The barricades along the Green Line define, with the certainty of barbed wire and barrels, the hard divide between North and South. The whole point of the barriers, of walls everywhere, is to erase all ambiguity. Here is where the South ends — there is where the North begins. Yet the Wall disorients Katerina. Perhaps the act of dividing itself confounds. The fact that a road ends in a heap of sandbags is nonsense. Even though she grew up with the walls, there is a part of Katerina that knows the streets have been robbed of their equilibrium. The city is out of order, and she is infected with the vertigo born of its division.

If Katerina doesn't think much about the barricades, she does think about what she calls "the flag on the fucking mountain." Shortly after the North declared its independence in 1983, two enormous flags appeared on the south slope of Mount Pentadaktylos overlooking Nicosia: one the flag of the new TRNC, the other the flag of Turkey. The flags each span about 450 metres, as long as four football fields, and are made of red-and-white-painted stones. A message beneath the Turkish flag reads "How lucky is he who calls himself a Turk." Greek-Cypriots tend to blame the Turkish army for creating the flags, but according to another story, the stones were painted in memory of a 1974 massacre in the mixed village of Tochni. Greek-Cypriot militants rounded up all the Turkish-Cypriot men of military age, bussed them out of the village, and shot them. Afterwards, the militants pushed the eighty-seven bodies into a mass grave. Only nineteen men survived the massacre. They and the widows and orphans of the slain fled north and painted the mountainside to honour their dead.

Regardless of who painted the stones, the flags were meant to provoke. They can be seen from almost any point in the capital, but Greek-Cypriots have the best view. For them, the flags are monstrosities, gloating reminders of the occupation in the North. Since they appeared, the images have poked a pointed stick in Greek-Cypriot eyes. In 2003, the stick was sharpened when the North began to illuminate the TRNC flag at night. The individual elements of the flag light up in sequence. First the crescent moon. Then the star. Then the rectangle that frames them both. The sequence lingers here for a moment, because until the horizontal stripes are added at the end, this is the flag of Turkey.

Katerina calls the newly illuminated flag a "symbol of the hypocrisy of the Turkish-Cypriot side, who supposedly want a solution more than we do. It shows how it's all bullshit and posing." She couldn't believe it when she first saw the flag lit up on Pentadaktylos. She cannot even rely on the night to hide it anymore. Now she avoids looking north at all.

I met Katerina through her boyfriend, Thodoris Tzalavras, whose black-and-white photos of the dead zone I admired online. Thodoris's images of the interiors of broken shops and homes are startling. In an abandoned tavern, bottles still rest on a shelf above dusty bar stools. Second-floor doors open to a sheer drop — the balcony has long since fallen — and a clothesline hangs between cracked walls. The saddest photo is of a teddy bear with plaid-patterned paws splayed out like a vagrant beneath a busted window frame.

Thodoris is not Cypriot by birth. He was born in Greece but came to Cyprus in 2002 to do his mandatory military service. With his long, straight hair and tangled beard, I could not imagine him a soldier. I would not recognize him clean-shaven and with a soldier's trim haircut. Like Katerina, he has never crossed the Green Line.

I wanted Katerina and Thodoris to come with me past the Wall and into the North. I didn't even bother asking Katerina. I knew she would never cross. She admitted a curiosity about the other side. She told me of a friend who had visited the North — "his girlfriend made him go," she said — who returned to say he had never realized how small the island is. "He told me that, on the other side, the sea is so close." But curiosity was not enough to coax Katerina across. Her family never lived in the North and never left anything behind. There is no sacred ground for her on the other side of the Wall; her heart has nothing there to reclaim. More than this, she refuses to grant the occupation validity by handing her passport to an official of a despised regime and having him clatter her data into a computer.

Thodoris felt the same way. Like Katerina, he has no roots in the North and is hardly compelled to step across the Green Line onto occupied land. But I sensed a softness in Thodoris's resolve that I didn't in Katerina. Thodoris had an artist's inquisitiveness about the aesthetics of the other side. He wondered what the northern dead zone looks like. I tried to exploit this when I met with Thodoris alone one afternoon. We shared a bottle of KEO, a Cypriot lager, and I told him, "As an artist interested in the dead zone, you really should see it from both sides."

Thodoris nodded. "There is a part of me that wants to cross. To see what it is like. And maybe one day I will. But for now, I have to say no."

"What if you go with me? We will go for the afternoon. I'll pay for everything so you don't have to feel uncomfortable about giving your money to the occupation. We will just walk around the Old City. We'll have lunch. Or coffee. Then we will come back."

Thodoris paused long enough to let me think he was actually considering my offer, but he wouldn't sell out so cheaply. Not for lunch and Turkish coffee. He shook his head.

"All right, but before I leave Cyprus I am going to ask you one last time."

He laughed. "You can ask again. But I will say no again." He sipped from his beer. "You only want me to go with you so you can write about it."

He was right. My intentions were hardly altruistic. I wanted him to cross because I wanted to understand something I could not understand on my own. I was fascinated by what it would mean to cross through the Wall for the first time. I wanted to see what happened to his face as he passed under the signs of the TRNC. I wanted to follow his eyes and see his body tense. I wanted to count how many times he looked over his shoulder to the place he had come from. I wanted to know if he immediately felt like returning or, perhaps, yearned to go farther, to take a bus north to the sea and discover for himself just how small is his adopted island.

Later, I realized how selfish this was. My crossings through the walls — not just in Nicosia, but everywhere — always felt to me like delicious rebellion. I was the child who sees a door marked "Keep Out" and rushes up to touch the knob. But these are not my struggles. As much as I learn about the walls, and as much as I try to empathize with those who inhabit their shadows, the truth remains that the walls are not meant for me. I don't have the right to coax anyone across. I'd asked Thodoris to betray his own values and defer to an authority he believes is unjust. I'd asked him to give in and to give up.

I wondered if my own crossings were a sort of treachery. When I was in Palestine, Aidan told me he'd never been to Israel and declared it with a tone that implied visiting Israel meant betraying Palestine. Aidan took a side and aligned himself with the Palestinians. To enter the land of their occupier would be scandalous for him. I, on the other hand, professed support for the Palestinian cause yet spent my Jerusalem nights drinking coffee and wine in Israeli cafés. In the Sahara, I shared tea in Saharawi tents, heard stories of war and torture and separation, and locked eyes with refugee women who wanted to know what I would do to help the Saharawis. Then I betrayed them by travelling to Morocco and spending money in the hotels and restaurants of the enemy. I could imagine what Malainin would say if he saw me in the souks of Marrakech, bargaining for cheap souvenirs with my wife on holiday. In Cyprus, I passed through the checkpoints every day without a thought. I weaved back and forth like a drunk across a line that meant so little to me and yet striates the hearts of so many, including those I'd befriended.

The walls impose a simplified identity on those who cannot cross them. You are either from here or from there. You are either one of Us or one of Them. The walls allow for no nuance, no mutually agreed upon story. Along the Indo-Bangladesh border, the walls disregard any bonds between Bengalis on one side of the line and Bengalis on the other. The West Bank Wall does not care what Israelis and Palestinians might have in common. On Cyprus, the barricades reject any sense of a blurred Cypriot identity. Though the island is tiny, the Wall renders irrelevant anything the two sides might share. With unambiguous authority, the Wall declares, "You are either Turkish or Greek." There are no Cyprus flags along the Green Line, only Turkey's crescent and star and the cross and stripes of Greece. The walls divide with medieval clarity.

The walls impose no such identity on me. But they do demand I declare an allegiance. Just as the walls disregard any nuance, they scoff at neutrality. The walls create two sides and insist I take one. When I flashed my passport and flitted back and forth across the fortified lines, I not only displayed a lack of sensitivity to those who cannot do this, but I broke the rules of the game. I'd allied myself to both sides of the Wall, which is the same as allying to none. Instead, I occupied a No Man's Land. My own private Dead Zone.

It rained hard in the morning, but the sky cleared and the aroma of orange blossoms hung like honey from the trees on Ledra Street. They seemed to have bloomed overnight to herald the approaching heat of summer. I tried to stay beneath them as I walked, bathing in their invisible sweetness.

Ledra Street had not always been so kind. In the 1950s, EOKA killed so many British troops and Greek-Cypriot collaborators here that the road was dubbed Murder Mile. Now the street shone as the main shopping district of the Old City. Outlets of European chain stores were selling jewellery, shoes, and, oddly, coloured Palestinian kaffiyehs—yellow and green and pink—which were in fashion. The McDonald's and Starbucks hummed with the conversation of sun-pinked and plump British tourists. "Taverna" restaurants offered apathetic versions of Cypriot cuisine to foreigners who didn't know the difference. The orange blossoms provided the only charm to this road of commercial tourism.

I turned right down a side street to the café where I sat nearly every day for three weeks and spent far too many euros. The weather was warm during my time in Nicosia, and the café workers dragged every table and chair outside onto the street. The seats filled quickly with Cypriot bohemians, big-haired philosophers, and women in hippie head scarves who all drank espresso frappés. I ordered small Cypriot coffees in quick succession, but my regular server eventually cut me off. "You drink too much coffee," she said. "It is not good for you. Can I bring you a lemonade instead?"

After my coffees and lemonade, I returned to Ledra and entered a souvenir shop called Fanos. The store was one of the few original shops on the street and was named for its owner, Fanos Pavlides, who had worked there for more than sixty years. I'd wanted to talk to Fanos since I arrived in Cyprus, but he always put me off. He was always too busy. This time when I walked in, Fanos was trying to sell a bottle of zivania, the Cypriot answer to grappa, to a pair of female Slovakian tourists. "We used to drink whiskey on Cyprus, but we switched to zivania because it doesn't give a headache," Fanos said. "Your husbands will love it." The women were not convinced and settled instead for a few postcards before leaving the store.

Fanos was not happy with the sale, and not happy to see me, but the store was empty and he had no excuse to refuse a conversation. Clad in the sweater vest, shirt, tie, and jacket ensemble—apparently the required dress for aging men of the eastern Mediterranean—Fanos sighed and sank into a chair behind a cluttered desk. I asked him about Ledra Street. "I started working here in 1945, when I was a teenager. We sold bicycles at the time."

"You were a teenager in 1945? How old are you now?" I asked.

"Eighty-four years old."

"Really?! You don't look older than sixty."

"It is because of the zivania," he said, his sales pitch lingering. "If you drink zivania, you don't get wrinkles." He pinched and rubbed his cheeks.

Fanos lifted a packet of old photos from his desk drawer and flipped through them until he found a picture of Ledra Street in the 1940s. He pointed to a boy on a bicycle in the middle of the frame riding away from the camera. "This is me. I am wearing short pants. They were the uniform of the Cypriot volunteer forces." The next photo in the stack showed a Greek Orthodox priest. Then came a portrait of Winston Churchill who, in 1907 and before he was prime minister, said that unifying Cyprus with Greece was "an ideal to be earnestly, devoutly, and feverently cherished."[12]

Fanos jabbed a finger at the photo. "Churchill promised independence to the Cypriots if we fought for Britain in World War II. He broke this promise. Instead, he gives freedom to colonies in Africa!" He threw up his hand in disgust. "Those people did not even know how to eat!" I wondered why he kept the photo.

Fanos had little to say about the Cyprus Problem other than telling me that the Turkish-Cypriots are born thieves. He knew this because he used to buy stolen bicycle parts from them. Fanos crossed the Green Line with the crowds in 2003 but was not impressed with what he saw. "They have nothing," he told me. Fanos asked if I'd spoken to any Turkish-Cypriots on the other side about the conflict. I started to tell him about Nilgün, but he interrupted me. "Not a woman! A woman knows nothing!" The zivania may have kept Fanos looking young, but there was nothing modern about him.

Ledra Street used to end at the Green Line just a few metres past Fanos's shop. The road had been blocked for decades. The British first laid barbed wire across the street in 1956 to separate warring Greek-Cypriot and Turkish-Cypriot militants. They removed the wire after independence in 1960 but laid it back down at the end of 1963 when the two sides started fighting again. The Ledra Street barricade was strengthened into a proper wall in the chaos of 1974. In addition to the cigarette-smoking boys in uniform charged with prohibiting photography, the Wall had a viewing platform where tourists could line up along a rail and stare out over the dead zone at the TRNC. The Wall that severed Ledra Street was one of Nicosia's most popular attractions, a compelling symbol of the Cyprus Problem.

In another surprising gesture towards peace, the Wall on Ledra Street came down in April 2008. Now anyone holding a passport or proper identification could walk across. I stepped past the Greek-Cypriot policemen along a slim strip of asphalt. A row of cheery flower pots ran down the middle, dividing those going from those coming. This was the buffer zone, but unlike the crossing at Ledra Palace, there was nothing here to remind crossers of war. No signs mentioned stolen land and missing persons. Instead, festive fabric curtains on either side of the road blocked my view of the necropolis of abandoned streets and shops. Silhouettes of children holding balloons and women carrying shopping bags were printed onto the fabric to draw my eyes down from the bullet-scarred walls of the dead zone. The pastel corridor ended at a bank of white Turkish-Cypriot inspection huts. I handed my passport to a grim uniformed woman on the other side of the glass. She clacked my information into a computer then stamped a separate piece of paper with my entry visa to the TRNC.

I'd moved to a hotel in Lefkoşa—rooms are cheaper in the north—and so I passed back and forth through the Ledra Street checkpoint at least twice every day. I paused to wave at the quartet of border police who sat bored at a card table near the checkpoint drinking tea out of tulip-shaped glasses. One evening I saw all four men crowded around a nearby "claw game" machine. One officer wiggled the joystick and swung the metal claw over a bin of stuffed toys while his brothers-in-arms shouted advice and encouragement. Sitting on their card table were a few empty tea glasses and three teddy bears.

The international community recognizes the entire island as a single nation, the Republic of Cyprus. The northern half of the Old City, though, feels like a completely different country. There are no Starbucks here. No slick European fashion boutiques. Instead, shops sell cheap clothing and shoes to women in head scarves. Young men browse soccer team jerseys from the Turkish Super League. Restaurants deal in *pide* and *lahmacun*. Conical slabs of doner kebab slowly turn on their vertical spits, wafting an aroma of spiced meat. There are *okey salonus* where old men play dominos and bars that blast Turkish music into the street and pour huge glasses of Efes lager. Turkey's flag waves from the tops of buildings. Portraits of Mustafa Kemal Atatürk, the father of modern Turkey, scowl down over every shop and café.

A blue line painted on the ground guides tourists around Old Lefkoşa, but after a couple of hours buying crafts from the vendors at the Büyük Han and visiting the Selimiye Mosque, a fourteenth-century cathedral converted by the Ottomans into the world's only "Gothic mosque," most visitors have lingered long enough. The kick for these day-trippers is treading over disputed ground, walking below bullet holes, and telling their friends back home that a boy with a rifle waved their cameras away. I can't blame them — I felt the same excitement passing through the fences in Tripura, after all — but the thrill is artificial. When the walls are not meant for us, our crossings through them have no meaning. Our steps have no historical weight and none of the urgency born from memories of war. Instead, we are tourists exchanging holiday dollars for an inauthentic experience. We pass through the walls too lightly.

I drifted off the blue line and towards the Green Line. The barricades were not derelict here in the North. This wall was a true wall, strong and permanent and with red signs declaring FORBIDDEN ZONE. I wondered if the Turkish army made the Wall appear imposing to give the impression that those on the other side posed an actual threat. The Wall's groomed strength suggested that without the barricades, and the Turkish troops standing guard over them, the murderous Greeks would lay siege to the North as they had done nearly a half century ago. The young Greek soldiers on the other side provided the counter-illusion: the brave and smooth-faced youths were all that kept savage Turks from overwhelming the rest of the island. Coming from Palestine, where real violence seethes under a veneer of calm, this seemed foolish. Nothing had happened along this Green Line in decades. As I'd seen, the walls make for great theatre.

I turned a corner and crossed through the stream of young girls that flowed out of a school bearing Atatürk's name. They pulled tiny-wheeled suitcases made of pink vinyl. Their youth and colour struck against the drab dereliction of the old houses. The Wall in the North might stand sturdy, but most of the Old City was crumbling. Bullet holes scarred the buildings along the Green Line. Wooden shutters sagged and dangled on their frames. White plaster had gone grey. The paint flaked and the masonry cracked. The city lived, but apart from a few newly freshened neighbourhoods in the western quarter, Old Lefkoşa felt poor and mistreated. Families lived in these homes, but the windows were broken.

There were no Mediterranean hipsters or Wi-Fi in the café where I paused, but my Turkish coffee cost half as much as it did on the other side of the line. I drank two — no one was concerned about my health here — and watched a tableful of men play cards and smoke. There was a television in the corner and holes in the tablecloths. I sat and debated whether or not to find the Museum of Barbarism. I'd struggled with the decision for days.

The museum gets no mention in guidebooks or in the tourist pamphlets available near the Ledra Street crossing, but somewhere in Lefkoşa stands a house where Greek-Cypriot militants murdered a woman and three children in December 1963. The house, since turned into the museum, belonged to a Turkish-Cypriot army doctor named Nihat Ilhan. He wasn't at home when the EOKA gunmen came calling on Christmas Eve. They found his wife and three sons hiding in an upstairs bathroom and shot them to death in the tub. The room has been left relatively untouched since then. Visitors to the museum see the bullet-cracked tiles and bloodstained walls. Bits of brain crust the ceiling.

I'd seen the gruesome black-and-white photographs: four white faces staring up out of a tub of black blood. The museum wanted me to know what Greeks were capable of, but I decided that seeing the photos was enough. I didn't need to be in that room.

I opted instead for more jovial surroundings and found Avcılar, a Turkish-Cypriot tavern restaurant I'd read about. It was still early for dinner and I was the only diner in the place. My waiter suggested a bottle of raki. I poured a healthy dram into the glass, added water, then used tongs to drop in a few ice cubes. The raki turned snow-white as if by magic and had the licorice tang of aniseed. The waiter did not hand me a menu. Instead, he brought out tiny plates of food. Chunky hummus with smoked paprika. Almonds. Fava beans, both marinated and pureed. Thin slices of salty beef *pastirma*. Yogurt tzatziki. Pickled celery. Fatty dried lamb. Three kinds of cheese. They arrived rapidly. I could barely keep up and eventually lost count. I remember that grilled quail was my main course and fresh watermelon was the dessert. By the time my coffee arrived, I'd eaten close to twenty different things, although the raki dulled my mathematics.

As I ate, a group of men collected at a table with the owner. One man appeared to be hearing impaired and mentally challenged. He held a scented candle covered with glittering pink hearts in his hand. He seemed very proud of this and showed the trinket to each friend who arrived. When the men noticed I was alone, one of them brought over a plate of fresh strawberries to augment my dessert. Another passed over some fresh almonds, still tender and sour inside their fuzzy green jackets. A third man walked over and refilled my raki. Then they decided it would be easier if I just joined them. I surrendered.

The raki kept flowing, but a better brand than I had ordered. We drained the bottle and switched to Johnny Walker Red. We kept one eye on the soccer game on the television — Beşiktaş eventually beat Kayserispor — and the other on our never-draining glasses. A few men spoke English and one pointed to the tavern owner and said, "He is a fascist." The owner shrugged.

Two more men entered, a Turkish-Cypriot journalist and a man from Abkhazia who played professional soccer for one of the local teams. The Republic of Abkhazia — bordering Russia, Georgia, and the Black Sea — is another political anomaly that considers itself an independent state even though almost no one else does. I wanted to talk to the man about going from one place that does not exist to another, but he only spoke Russian and Abkhaz.

A woman joined us. Her arrival excited the man with the pink candle because, as it turned out, it was a gift for her. He waited until she went to the ladies' room and placed the candle on her plate. When she returned, she acted flattered. The man beside me told me that the woman too was a fascist and that her name was Zahra.

"That is a lovely name," I said. My wife was pregnant and we were looking for baby names.

"A lovely name for a lovely woman, don't you think?"

"Yes," I said, not wanting to argue even though I found Zahra a little snaggle-toothed.

"The Canadian says Zahra is beautiful," the man announced to the table.

I blushed and Zahra turned away, troubled by the multiplying admirers at the table.

Another hour or two passed, I couldn't tell how long, and I eventually excused myself to leave. The men refused. "You can't go anywhere. We are going to eat."

"I've been eating for hours," I said.

"You don't understand. We are going to have the chef's specialty. Macaroni."

My family is Italian; this hardly inspired me. The man read my expression and added, "This place is famous for its macaroni. It is not cooked in water."

"What is it cooked in?"

"Grouse stock."

I sat back down.

After half an hour, the waiter set a steaming platter of grouse macaroni on the table. The chef had dusted the pasta with shredded cheese and dried mint, and the men shovelled a heap of noodles onto my plate. The pasta tasted richer than any I'd ever eaten.

I ignored the urge to ask Zahra and the men about the Wall. I realized that I might be missing a fine opportunity, but I didn't want to darken their boozy generosity with talk of war and politics and capitalized "Problems." To talk about the Wall would have meant barricading out the spirit of the evening. After the quail, the strawberries, and all that raki, we'd come to a place beyond walls. The TRNC might not exist, but these men, the tavern, and the macaroni certainly did. The night felt more real than any of the fabricated histories and selected memories I had heard since I arrived in Cyprus.

It was two in the morning by the time the men permitted me to leave. They did not, however, accept my money. The whole table bellowed in protest when I pulled out my wallet. I insisted, but the fascist owner was suitably rigid. He kissed my cheeks and walked me to the door.

■■■

Giulio Savorgnano knew the old walls would not hold. It was 1567. The Venetians ruled Cyprus, but the Ottomans controlled the rest of the eastern Mediterranean and an attack was inevitable. The Lusignan kings who purchased Cyprus from Richard the Lion-Heart at the end of the Crusades had built the walls that surrounded Nicosia, but they were too weak and ruined to repel the sultan's armies. The king charged Savorgnano, the island's chief military engineer, with protecting the city.

Savorgnano levelled all fourteen kilometres of the old ramparts, ordered eighty Greek Orthodox churches and monasteries demolished, and rebuilt the walls with the cannibalized bricks. (The Venetians were Catholics and had no interest in the sacred structures of Greek Orthodoxy.) The new ramparts enclosed the city in a tight circle less than five kilometres around. Savorgnano then breached the new walls at equal intervals with eleven bastions to form a star-shaped *trace italienne*, an Italian military innovation whose "points" repelled cannon fire better than a flat wall. Afterwards, Savorgnano dug a moat around the entire structure and uprooted all the olive and fruit trees around the city to open up a field of fire. Just as in Palestine, trees fell in the name of the walls. Savorgnano wanted Nicosia's defenders to have a clear shot at the invaders he knew would eventually march on the city.

They would come because the sultan wanted his wine. The Ottomans had a peace treaty in place with Venice, and the Grand Vizier counselled against an invasion, but Sultan Selim II, called Selim the Sot behind his back, was a notorious alcoholic. The conquest of the island would provide him with a reliable source of *commandaria*, a sweet Cypriot wine he used to fuel his palace orgies. (It would not be the last time a notorious drunk took over Cyprus. Almost four hundred years later, EOKA coup leader Nikos Sampson, a reincarnation of Selim the Sot, would do the same.)

Selim's army landed on the island in the summer of 1570. The commander, Mustapha Pasha, led 100,000 soldiers and 10,000 horses from Limassol on the island's southern shore to Nicosia's new walls. Savorgnano's ramparts held, but after almost two months of siege the defenders ran out of ammunition. The Ottomans came over the walls at dawn on the forty-fifth day and within six hours massacred more than a third of Nicosia's citizens. They enslaved those they spared. Once again the churches were disassembled for war when the Ottomans melted down church bells to cast new cannons. The sultan got his wine. Four years later, smashed on *commandaria*, Selim slipped on a bathhouse floor, split his skull, and died.

The Venetian Walls stand relatively intact today. Savorgnano's star-shaped city remains a symbol of a unified Nicosia. The two sides of the Old City share the eleven bastions equally: there are five in the south, five in the north, and one standing in the dead zone manned by UN soldiers. On both sides of the Green Line, the Venetian Walls divide the ancient heart of the capital from the modern city that rose up around it. But the Venetian ramparts mark a new divide—an ethnic divide. They draw a convenient line between native Cypriots and the migrant workers. Nicosia's oldest walls hem in the city's newest souls.

Aside from the *konsomatris*, bar hostesses-cum-prostitutes who come primarily from eastern Europe, most migrant workers in Old Lefkoşa are settlers from central Turkey. These Turks have little in common with Turkish-Cypriots, who might identify as Muslims but are hardly devout. Nilgün told me her family only goes to the mosque for funerals, and "they might fast during Ramadan but only to lose weight." By contrast, the Turkish migrants are rural and pious. Their women wear head scarves and the men attend Friday prayers at the mosque. Many Turkish-Cypriots feel that the migrants dilute the "Cypriotness" of the Old City. They pine for the days when the streets smelled of *molohiya* and *kolokas*, traditional Cypriot foods, rather than the foreign stink of Turkish *lahmacun*. They call the migrants *fica*, a word for the seaweed that washes ashore and litters the northern beaches and complain that Turkey sent "the wrong Turks."

In Old Nicosia, the migrants come from everywhere. The Holy Cross Catholic Church holds only one service per week in Greek; the rest are in English for Indian, Filipino, and Sri Lankan worshippers. Signs on lampposts advertise for Nepali hairdressers or ethnospecific apartment rentals—rooms for "Pakistani boys" or "Asian girls" or "Europeans only." At night, Filipina and Nepali prostitutes stand along the ramparts, and blond bar girls from Moldova size up my intentions in dark taverns.

Two Bollywood video stores, a pair of halal butchers, and three Lebanese snack bars serving falafel and shawarma sandwiches stand on the short stretch of Trikoupi Street between the ramparts and the Omeriye Mosque. The mosque, a converted church the Ottomans retrofitted and refloored with the tombstones of Catholic noblemen, serves the city's new Muslims. After Friday prayers, the men jam the street—mostly Pakistanis and Bangladeshis, with a few Arabs and black Africans in the mix. Some don Muslim skullcaps and grow their beards long. Others wear blue jeans and backwards baseball caps. Few, if any, are native Cypriots.

The city most belongs to the migrants on Sunday, the only day off for the hundreds who work as domestic help or attend the universities on student visas. On Sundays, Chinese vendors sell noisy plastic toys such as wind-up robots, flashing guns, and creepy dancing dolls to tourists on Ledra Street. Filipinos play volleyball on outdoor courts built in the Venetian moat. Costanza Bastion, where the Ottomans first breached the walls in 1570, now hosts a Sunday market where migrants shop for cheap clothes and shoes. Stacks of shoeboxes, the detritus of the day's trade, reminded me of the smugglers inside the fences at Melilla.

The south Asians spend their Sundays in the Municipal Gardens just outside Old Nicosia, converting the park into a weekly Little India. They picnic on the grass and eat rice and curry with their fingers from foil packets. Some sell homemade Indian snacks from plastic containers. Men read Hindi newspapers or browse bins of Bollywood bootlegs. Others sit next to the marigold beds and drink green bottles of Carlsberg until their eyes glaze.

One Sunday, I found a spot on a bench next to two Indian men, one Punjabi, the other from the Gujarat. They came to the park on Sundays to ogle the "Lankan girls." Both men studied at the university. "It is easy to get a student visa to Cyprus," the Gujarati told me. Coming as a student was the simplest way into the country and thus an easy way into Europe. They liked Cyprus but would rather have been on the mainland. I told them about Rocky Ghotra and the Indians in Ceuta. They responded with a story about a man in Cyprus who was told by a crooked immigration agent he could catch a train from Nicosia to London. He spent three days looking for the station before someone told him he was on an island.

The Cyprus Problem meant nothing to these migrants. The barricades were not for them any more than they were for me. The only "wall" that mattered to them was the sea dividing them from continental Europe. Unlike Katerina, they'd inherited nothing from this disputed land. I wondered how the conflict would change now that the island's divided capital was swelling with migrants indifferent to its division.

I left the men to their Sunday girl-watching and returned to Old Nicosia. In the Laiki Yitonia district, amid the lace shops and tourist pap, a Nigerian man named Chidi sold west African groceries with his pregnant Slovakian wife. He told me business was better before Cyprus changed to the euro from pounds sterling and before the government deported most of Nicosia's Nigerians. Luckily, enough Africans played on the city's soccer teams and wanted his imported smoked fish, palm oil, and dried silverbeet leaves.

Chidi was grinding ebolo seeds for soup — "the Ghanaians love it too much" — when I asked what he thought of the Cyprus Problem. He shrugged. Chidi was not invested in the conflict nor did he bother to take a side. Still, the lingering hatred between the Cypriots reminded him of the fighting in 1970s Nigeria between the Ibo and the Hausa. "You still have hatreds from that war. From that fight. If they could wipe away memory, everything would be okay, but they cannot wipe it. As long as people continue to celebrate the day of the dead ones, you cannot wipe it away."

A Chinese proverb claims, "Everyone pushes a falling fence." I thought I might find one on Cyprus. The leaders on both sides of the island were leftists and might even be friends. They were talking peace. The papers said conditions had never been better for a deal. I imagined reunification was so imminent that I might be there to watch the Wall tumble. Maybe I would even help push it down.

But what the Cyprus Problem lacks in momentum it makes up in inertia. The conflict has barely inched forward or back in decades. Cypriots hardly need the United Nations to enforce the status quo. Those on both sides of the Wall laze in the comfortable fear and distrust passed from parent to child like jewellery from mother to daughter. Even if the two leaders agreed on a deal, I doubt Cypriots would feel compelled to accept it. The dispute has hardened into flag-painted stones and fossilized bits of brain. You cannot wipe it away. Of all the absurdities that colour the conflict — the young men and fresh paint on aged barricades, the drunken usurpers, a giant flag and a one-man army, a wordless anthem, a yellow car — perhaps the greatest farce is the notion that the Wall is ever going to fall.

Shun Thy Neighbour
The U.S.–Mexico Border

Chicana writer Gloria Anzaldúa described the U.S.–Mexico border as the place "where the Third World grates against the first and bleeds."[13] If this is true, the hemorrhaging is most severe in Arizona. More than half of America's border barriers stand along Arizona's desert boundary with Sonora, Mexico. Nearly five hundred kilometres of walls, fences, and vehicle barriers bristle among the cacti and thorny mesquite. California, New Mexico, and Texas have also erected walls on their borders, but Arizona seemed the most important place for me to go. And no one in Arizona seemed as important to meet as Bill Odle. "A lot of people will tell you they live on the border," Bill told me on the phone, "but I actually do."

I waited for Bill in the parking lot of an abandoned and shuttered steakhouse called the Brite Spot. It was late autumn, a sort of boundary season that draws an arid line between the late summer monsoons and winter's gentle rains. Bill's Dodge pickup truck crunched off Highway 92 and into the gravel lot. National Rifle Association stickers were pasted on the back window, and a red, white, and blue bumper sticker declared "Freedom Isn't Free." The truck looked ready and able to devour my rental Chevrolet Aveo. Bill, in tinted glasses and a black cowboy hat, waved me towards the passenger side door. He said hello when I climbed into the cab; both his beard and voice reminded me of a lion. We rumbled back to the highway while I tried not to stare at the pistol strapped to the seat between us. As a Canadian, I possess a simultaneous repulsion for and fascination with the American right to bear arms.

Bill veered the truck onto a dirt road heading south and we drove until we reached the border, here marked by a fence more than four metres high built with steel posts and panels of tight metal mesh. He parked the truck in the striped shadows the posts threw over the dirt road and turned off the engine. I would soon learn that Bill was hardly partial to long silences, but he sat quietly for a moment as we both stared up at the barrier. He sighed before he spoke. "Historically, defensive things like this—the Great Wall, the Maginot Line, the Berlin Wall—none of them worked. And they were all put up by losers."

The Treaty of Guadalupe Hidalgo gave birth to the U.S.-Mexico border in February 1848. The two countries signed the treaty to end the Mexican-American War and drew a 3,200-kilometre line between them. The border begins at the Pacific, where it slices eastward across the beach between San Diego and Tijuana. The line severs California from Baja California, bifurcates the Sonoran Desert through Arizona, and edges halfway across New Mexico. At El Paso, Texas, the border merges with the middle of the Rio Grande. The river becomes the border for the final 2,000-kilometre stretch across the continent until it empties into the Gulf of Mexico.

For most of the border's lifetime, only strands of barbed wire and the occasional marking stone defined Here as opposed to There. More substantial walls grew along parts of the border during the 1990s, but not in the southern ranchlands of Arizona, and certainly not before Bill and his wife Ellen, fleeing the noise of San Diego, bought a fifty-acre plot on the international line a decade ago. They constructed a home out of straw bales, powered it with wind and sun, and faced the front window south so they could stare at the rolling ranchlands of Sonora, Mexico. Their morning sun rises over the peaks of the Sierra San José and sets behind the Huachuca Mountains to the west. "We moved down here to get away from the city," Bill said. "I liked the idea of living on la frontera."

In 2006, President George W. Bush signed the Secure Fence Act into law. Lawmakers developed the Act in response to the vulnerability Americans felt in the wake of the September 11 attacks. Even though none of the hijackers infiltrated the United States over a land border, the government's preoccupation with border security intensified. The Secure Fence Act was designed to halt illegal migration, drug smuggling, and potential terrorist penetration across America's frontiers. The Act charged the newly formed Department of Homeland Security with maintaining "operational control" of the borders. The DHS planned to accomplish this through increased surveillance of the Mexican and Canadian borders and the construction of over a thousand kilometres of physical barriers along the southern line. Bill and Ellen's small share of the borderland was included in what the Act described as a "priority area."

Bulldozers and dump trucks rumbled onto Bill's property in the fall of 2007 and tore into the ground of the Odles' desert idyll. The builders took five months to erect their barrier. The Wall, alien to the southwestern ideal of the open range, strains Bill and Ellen's Mexican view through tight wire mesh. The Wall enraged Bill, and the ex-Marine and Vietnam veteran turned into a much-quoted voice against the barrier. "Hell, I came out here to get away from people," he said. "Now I end up in books."

In his truck, Bill explained, "This fence thing, it doesn't stop people. Flat out. That's a given." He told me about the countless migrants he'd seen climb up one side of the fence and drop down into America. Some migrants use crude handmade ladders and ropes to get over. Bill collects them as souvenirs like the Spanish border guards in Ceuta and Melilla. The more sophisticated human trafficking rings on the Mexican side have purpose-built trucks with retractable metal ladders. Most migrants, though, don't bother with such equipment. Any able-bodied person can scale the Wall along Bill's property without a ladder. The metal panels are easy to climb. Bill watched women shimmy over, even pregnant women, and children as young as four. He said, too, that a Sierra Club volunteer from Tucson could scramble over the Wall and back again in a minute and forty-eight seconds.

Supporters of the Wall, especially those who live far from the border, don't understand the impotence of the barriers. Raw steel bars make for good theatre and look impressive on television newscasts, but they are easily defeated. "You got some lard-ass in Dubuque, Iowa, or some damn place," Bill said, "and he's got his big fat American ass sitting on an overstuffed couch, looking at a wide-screen TV, eating super-saturated fats, and he sees a picture of this fence and thinks, 'That'll stop 'em.' Well, it'll stop *him*, but not some kid coming up from five hundred miles south who is twenty years old and wants to work."

Bill sympathizes with those kids, the young migrants who cross over the border in search of employment to better the lives of their families in the south. He understands that the vast majority of migrants who come over the Wall are simply looking for work. But a wall that fails to stop migrants also fails to stop those whom Bill terms "the bad guys." The Wall barely slows the armed drug runners who flow across the border lugging burlap bundles of dope. Bill drove the Dodge to a spot along the Wall and showed me a mesh panel one of the *narcos* cut out in the middle of the night. "It was one of those dead quiet nights," Bill said. "And my dogs were goin' jake." The traffickers lowered a truck over the barrier with a vehicle carrier and replaced the panel. The next morning Bill noticed the reattached panel and fresh tire tracks on the ground.

Bill said that members of the Mara Salvatrucha, a transnational gang of drug traffickers, human smugglers, and murderers, have been caught crossing the line. "Those are the real bastards. They use machetes on people and shit like that." And if the *narcos* slipped over the border, so could terrorists. "We got people who tell us that they want to cut our heads off," Bill said. "They are ordained or required to do this. And they've told us that. And we know it. And we have to do something. We have to protect ourselves."

"Are you worried living out here?" I asked.

"Hell no. Ninety-nine percent of the time it is just like this. It's nice. It's not like being in downtown Washington or Los Angeles or some of those hell holes. I mean, shit! At night, if I hear something, I do like any other red-blooded American boy: I wake up my wife and ask her to check it out."

I laughed out loud.

"She is a better shot than I am." Ellen holds a membership in the Shooting Stars of Cochise County, a local all-female gun club. "She is one of those kind of women who fit into this kind of country. Real sweethearts. Tough and strong in every sense."

We drove west to the banks of the Rio San Pedro. Bill's property, and the Wall, ends here. Normandy Barriers—heavy iron rails welded into erect Xs designed to stop vehicles—extend in a line down the riverbank and across the stream bed. The river, high and fast during the late summer monsoons, barely trickled in the autumn afternoon. Cottonwoods lined the riverbank and the leaves on the trees had gone gold. Bill said their Latin name was

Populus fremontii, that nine of the eleven species of American hummingbird nested in its branches, and that mountain lions and bobcats prowled the shade for prey. His knowledge of the local flora and fauna surprised and impressed me. I realized I might be in the company of the only tree-hugging member of the NRA.

The San Pedro watershed supports the habitats of hundreds of animal species. Over a hundred birds breed in the trees that crowd the riverbanks, and another 250 species migrate and winter there every year. The San Pedro ranks as both a national conservation area and a United Nations heritage site. Bill growled that he was "no fan of the UN" but he appreciated the biological value of the San Pedro and the serenity he found there. "The world's fucked up, but you can come here and walk along the river and suddenly it's pretty nice. You can get down here and see no other human structure. The trees and the colours and all that stuff. It is really glorious."

The Wall, though, desecrates this glory by funnelling migrants into the riverbed where they trample through the sensitive watershed. The Wall also fragments natural habitats and disrupts the migrations of local animals. From his front porch, Bill has heard javelinas slam their heads into the Wall trying to break through. He's followed deer running along the border road searching for an opening to continue their migration south. After a mile or so, they give up and return north. "Some people say, 'Fuck the wildlife. Who cares about a deer?' Well, I do, goddammit. It really ticks me off."

A white Border Patrol truck approached us towing a tractor tire on a chain. The dragged tire smoothed the dust along the border so agents could better spot the footprints and tire tracks of border crossers. I'd seen this sort of thing in Palestine: the Israel Defense Forces similarly groomed the sand flanking the West Bank Wall to track any Palestinians who dared to breach the line. The truck's driver stopped in front of us, and when he rolled down the window, Bill joked, "You are going to wear that tire out draggin' it around like that."

The agent laughed.

"You keeping busy?" Bill asked. The question was Bill's way of finding out if the agent had caught anyone lately.

The agent shrugged. "A bit slow today." He reported that the fall harvest created enough jobs in Mexico that migrants didn't need to cross the border to find work. He warned us that the *narcos*, however, were still coming across. "Be careful," he said.

"We are just going down to take a look at the river," Bill told him. "The trees are turning colour."

"I know. It reminds me of home," the agent said.

"Where's that?"

"Michigan."

"Okay. Well, keep your head down. And your eyes open." I couldn't tell if Bill was being sarcastic or not. The agent drove away.

For all his spleen directed at the Wall, Bill harboured no ill will against the Border Patrol agents. In fact, he wanted to see more of them. Bill preferred agents on the line to a failing barrier. The Border Patrol operates highway stops where they pull over northbound drivers and check suspicious vehicles for both migrants and narcotics, but these checkpoints are set up miles from the border itself. I had seen one on the other side of the highway as I drove to meet Bill; it was almost twenty miles from the frontier. "Jesus Christ, they catch an incredible amount of drugs and illegals. My point is, why don't you have that shit at the border? Get all this stuff forward. Not so damn far back." He didn't believe a physical barrier could succeed unless it was simultaneously patrolled by agents on the ground. "If you put up a wall, you better have somebody watching it. And if you have somebody watching it, why the hell do you need a wall?"

Bill figured that if the government conceived of a sensible program that matched temporary workers from south of the border with businesses in the United States, and if American employers who hired undocumented migrants were punished, illegal migration would stop itself. "Another thing I would do," he said, "and you might not expect this from me, is decriminalize pot. Don't legalize it—then it infers the government will give out permits and collect taxes, and those bastards have too much money now." He believed that decriminalizing marijuana would kill the bulk of the narcotics trade across the line. Laws against hard drugs such as heroin and cocaine should remain and be enforced, Bill said, but he didn't care if people smoked weed. "The only time I smoked it I had a bunch of beer in me, so I don't know if it worked or not," he admitted. "I don't know if people still put it in brownies."

The sun began to set over the Huachucas, and we climbed back into the Dodge. Before he started the engine, Bill stared up at the Wall again. For only the second time that afternoon, he was quiet, and for the first time I saw a sort of sadness hang behind his profane eloquence and Wild West rage. The Wall more than angered Bill — it had betrayed him. Bill is a patriot who loves his country. The Wall's folly and failure represented a sort of treason.

"I'll buy you a beer and tell you how this is fucked, but you better have an appreciation for some of the good things this country stands for," he said. "And here we are with our own government not protecting us and doing something that is wrong. And we're the country that has the Statue of Liberty, for Christ's sake!" He shook his head. "You know, I sailed across the Atlantic, and you come into New York harbour and you see the Statue of Liberty. Wow. It's really something. It really means something. Now you look at this. A goddamn fence like that."

Kat Rodriguez, director of an immigration rights organization in Tucson called Derechos Humanos, wore a pink sweater and a button that read "No Papers." She sat behind the messiest desk I've ever seen. Swaying heaps of documents and file folders covered every inch. She told me the U.S. government designed the Wall to kill people.

Barriers stand along nearly 80 percent of the Arizona–Mexico line, but only about 40 percent of these walls, around 200 kilometres' worth, were designed to stop migrants and smugglers travelling on foot. These pedestrian barriers are concentrated mostly around Nogales, Douglas, and Sasabe, larger border towns where migrants could easily disappear once they've crossed the line. With the urban areas effectively walled off, migrants trudge instead through unpopulated areas where there are no pedestrian barriers. The most desperate take their chances crossing the hostile scorch of the Sonoran Desert. The most unlucky of these die there. Between 2004 and 2011, the Border Patrol recovered the remains of nearly 3,000 men, women, and children from the borderlands. About half of the bodies, 1,573, were found along the Arizona–Sonora line. In the fiscal year ending just before I arrived in Arizona, 253 bodies were found — the second-highest number on record. Kat blamed the late rains. "The monsoons came three weeks late this year," she said. *Coyotes*, the guides who lead the migrants across the desert, rely on rain and cool weather. When the rains don't fall, the migrants do. During my month-long stay in the borderlands, another sixteen bodies were pulled out of the desert.

"The feds act shocked by the deaths," Kat said, but she wanted me to understand that these deaths are intentional. Dead migrants are a platform in the government's strategy. Kat extracted a photocopied report from the archaeology of papers on her desk. The document, prepared by the U.S. Border Patrol back in 1994, outlined America's strategic plan for border security. The Border Patrol acknowledged that policies concentrating border walls and enforcement in urban areas would disrupt the traditional routes and funnel migrants into inhospitable landscape. The report stated that "illegal entrants crossing through remote, unihabited expanses of land" could find themselves in "mortal danger." This risk of death, they reasoned, would deter migrants from crossing in the first place. The U.S. Border Patrol aimed to deter migrants by making their migrations deadly. The walls—where they stand and, especially, where they don't—transform "illegal entry" into a capital offence, a crime punishable by death.

The desert kills, but the dead do not dissuade the living. "A fact not talked about," Kat said, "is that most migrants don't die in the desert. Most make it across." The majority of migrants successfully cross the border on their first attempt, and almost everyone who wants to reach America eventually does. I had read about success rates as high as 85 percent. "This is why the desert is not the deterrent the government supposed it would be," she told me. "And because it all operates out of the Department of Homeland Security, none of this is questioned."

In 2003, the U.S. government absorbed the Immigration and Naturalization Service into the newly formed DHS, thus wedding immigration to national security. "This was a disaster," Kat said. Many Americans consider the DHS untouchable. The Department stands between America and more falling towers, and so softening the Department's immigration policy, or even criticizing it, is akin to trampling on the American flag. Some considered Kat's advocacy for undocumented migrants fundamentally un-American and treasonous. "I've been called a *reconquista*," she said, as if her messy office acted as a front for returning Mexican territory lost to the United States back to Mexico. "The border doesn't do what people think it does. Instead, there is pain, death, and horror associated with that wall."

"And it costs billions of dollars," I added.

She nodded.

I felt I was missing something. The other walls I had visited also stood as expensive failures, but in each case there was some segment of the population that valued the barriers and justified their existence. I could understand the impulse for Americans of a certain stripe to want to seal the border against "invaders," but I could not imagine who would defend the current policies. The political left deplored the human abuses inherent in the strategy, and the political right abhorred the costly waste of a system that did not work. "I don't get it," I said. "Why would any American support this? This makes no sense."

Kat grinned. "You have to squint your eyes, tilt your head, and look at it through the lens of corporate greed. Then it's perfectly clear." She explained that the U.S. border strategy is a well-oiled machine designed to stuff huge profits into the pockets of a handful of agencies and corporations. The Wall enriches the Border Patrol, whose agents and staff received $3.6 billion in 2010. The Wall enriches the Boeing Corporation, which signed a $7-billion contract with the DHS to erect a "virtual fence," called SBInet, built of cameras and high-tech sensors. The Wall enriches Elbit Systems, an Israeli defence electronics manufacturer that sold cameras and unmanned drones to the SBInet project. Elbit technology was already monitoring the Wall in the West Bank, so equipment tested on Palestinians now serves to protect America from Mexicans. The virtual fence never worked properly, and the DHS cancelled its contract with Boeing in 2011, but only after a billion tax dollars had already been spent.

"And then there is Streamline," Kat said. On average, Arizona's Border Patrol apprehends around 700 migrants every single day. Officers promptly bus the vast majority of these migrants back to the border and dump them across the line. Each weekday, however, the Border Patrol selects seventy migrants, about 10 percent of their daily catch, for Operation Streamline. These detainees end up in the federal courthouse in downtown Tucson, where they stand before a judge and face criminal charges. There, the migrants have the opportunity to plead guilty to misdemeanour illegal entry. If they do, most receive time served and are deported immediately. Those with multiple entries on their records serve up to six months. The convictions and prison sentences meted out by Operation Streamline are meant to deter other migrants from sneaking across the line.

Operation Streamline's success in discouraging illegal migration is difficult to quantify, but it is suspect at best. The price of the operation is more easily measured, and the numbers are hard to believe. Court costs for Operation Streamline in Arizona alone top out at about $5 million annually. Attorney fees amount to $3.6 million. For the use of its fleet of unmarked buses to ferry nabbed migrants to the courthouse, to prison, and back to the border, a company called G4S Secure Solutions charges Arizonans $76 million a year. Streamline's greatest beneficiary, however, is the Corrections Corporation of America. The private prison Goliath charges Arizona taxpayers $10 million per month to warehouse prisoners serving sentences for immigration-related crimes, most of whom will be deported anyway after doing their time. And all this pays for a program that processes only a tenth of the migrants the Border Patrol manages to detain.

Kat glanced at the clock on her computer. "You should go to the hearings. They start in about a half-hour. Every time I go, I cry."

███

Seventy men and women shuffled through the doors to their seats at the front and side of the courtroom. The migrants wore the same clothes they'd been captured in. Dirty jeans. Torn shirts. Sweaters snagged with burrs. Bits of grass and brush still littered the hair of some men. I'd read that the Streamline courtrooms stink with the odour of unwashed migrants still grimy from their cross-border torments, the reek of nights spent marching in the desert and of their failed evasion of *la migra*. But I could not smell anything from my seat in the back of the gallery. I didn't notice all the migrants were cuffed and shackled until my ears picked up the soft tinkling of their chains. The migrants aimed their reddened and weary eyes at the floor and nervously bounced their knees as they sat. The chains connecting the manacles on their wrists to the fetters on their ankles rattled. Even once the proceedings started, and the amplified voices of magistrate and counsel dominated the room, the jingle of chains endured like a musical score. After a while, the chains were all I could hear.

Most of the migrants had the dark skin and small bodies of Mexico's indigenous people. They seemed even smaller hunched over in their seats in the enormous courtroom. Their ordeal in the desert, their capture, and their final mutation from migrant to defendant had shrunk them somehow. They'd been defeated. Their lawyers, big men, lounged on the benches behind their clients in ill-fitting and wrinkled suits, looking bored and overfed. As they waited for the hearing to begin, one man showed off his new iPad to his colleagues. Another reads a Terry Brooks novel.

When Justice Glenda E. Edmonds entered the courtroom, the lawyers straightened and stood and signalled their clients to jangle to their feet. Judge Edmonds, evidently well practised in Spanish names, quickly read out each defendant from a list. Once she called roll, a court official handed out pairs of headphones to the defendants so each could hear Judge Edmonds's instructions translated into Spanish. Edmonds told the crowd of defendants that, if they pled guilty to the petty offence of illegal entry and agreed to be sentenced, the court would drop the much more serious felony charge of illegal re-entry. She explained that pleading guilty would result in a criminal conviction on their records, and that, if they were found in the United States without documents again, they would face incarceration. Finally, she told them they would all be deported.

The judge called up the first eight defendants on the docket to stand before her. She asked each of them individually if they understood the charges against them, if they knew they had a right to a trial, and if they agreed to waive that right. The defendants murmured "Sí" to every question. Then Edmonds asked each migrant his or her nation of citizenship and when each arrived in Arizona. Most defendants were Mexican, but a few had made longer journeys north from other parts of Latin America. (In the parlance of the border, these migrants are called OTMs — Other Than Mexicans.) Nearly every defendant had arrived sometime within the last few days. Edmonds asked if they had entered through a "port of entry." They answered no. Finally, she asked the defendants to plead either guilty or not guilty to the charge of illegal entry. Every one said *"Culpado."* Guilty.

Each of the eight defendants received a sentence of time served except for the last man, looking forlorn in saggy jeans, who already had a misdemeanour theft conviction on his record from 2005. His lawyer told the judge the man had a two-year-old child. He said the defendant's father had recently died and now the man must act as the breadwinner both for his own young family and for his mother. "He is twenty-five years old," the lawyer said, "a corn and strawberry farmer and a hard worker." As he stood before the judge, listening to his lawyer plead for clemency, the man's quaking shoulders rattled his chains. Then he started to cry. Judge Edmonds ordered someone to bring the defendant a tissue, then gave him two days in prison.

After Judge Edmonds meted out her sentences, the bailiff led the migrants single file out a side door. They passed in front of me as they left. Some grinned like children caught stealing candy. Most, though, just looked at the floor. Except for the corn and strawberry farmer who was headed to jail, each migrant would board a bus to *la frontera*, where border guards would unshackle them and escort them back across the border.

Another group of eight defendants stood to face the judge. Like the first eight, they answered her questions, whispered "*Culpado*," were sentenced to time served, and escorted out. Then another eight. Judge Edmonds was quick and efficient. The last few octets of defendants, though, had records stained with multiple illegal entries, and Edmonds sentenced each to a prison term ranging from thirty to ninety days. Some of these repeat offenders had been caught crossing less than a month previously. One pair of women, Angela Bustamante-Santiago and Olivera Reyna-Lopez, had shown impressive persistence. The Border Patrol busted and deported Angela and Olivera on November 15, then caught them crossing together again three days later. Judge Edmonds sentenced Angela and Olivera to thirty days, and their lawyers requested they be housed together in prison. I couldn't help but admire Angela and Olivera's doggedness and mourn their bad luck.

Many defendants cried as the sentences came down. Bailiffs brought them tissues and Styrofoam cups of water. Edmonds granted a request for a married couple to serve identical sentences so they could be deported together when they finished their jail time. Tiny mercies for diminished souls. Once all the migrants had been sentenced and led out the door, Judge Edmonds rose, everyone stood, and the day's hearings ended.

The entire proceedings – the processing through of seventy migrants – took about ninety minutes. An assembly line of broken men and women that moved with cold efficiency. The U.S. Constitution grants all persons within the United States, even non-citizens, the right to "due process of law." I did the math. That afternoon, Operation Streamline granted each defendant a minute and twenty seconds' worth.

███

I turned off Arizona's Highway 86 and followed Ofelia Rivas's white van onto a road heading south through the Tohono O'odham Indian Reservation. The Baboquivari Mountains, sacred to the O'odham, rose to the east beneath the vast desert sky. Signs along the roadside warned of crossing tortoise, but I only had to brake for a tuft-headed quail that scuttled across the tarmac. White shrines adorned with crosses and flowers marked the places where locals had died on the road. The shrines reminded me of the stone-circle mosques along the highways through the Saharawi refugee camps. In fact, much of the reservation echoed what I'd seen in the Sahara. The O'odham villages, composed of single-storey structures built on hard-packed sand, resembled the Saharawi camps. The saguaro cacti, with their plump, imploring arms, stood in the place of the Sahara's camels as the desert's marriage of the elegant to the absurd. The words *Saharawi* and *Tohono O'odham* both mean "Desert People." Like the Saharawi lands and the other walled places I'd seen, the Tohono O'odham reservation represented the homeland of another nation that does not exist, at least not with any true sovereignty. And both the Saharawi and the O'odham found their traditional land bisected by a wall.

The reservation shares its southern edge with 120 kilometres of the U.S.–Mexico border. Traditional O'odham territory, though, continues far beyond the international line and all the way to the Sea of Cortés, where O'odham men used to make pilgrimages to collect sacred salt. The less solemn rituals of U.S. "spring break" now defile the traditional gathering site. Long before there was a Mexico or a United States, the O'odham wrestled an existence from this desert. They planted tepary beans in the annual flood plains, hunted rabbit and javelina, and picked the rhubarb, spinach, and purslane that grew wild on the land. They tapped mesquite trees for sap and ground its pods into flour, plucked tender buds from cholla cactus, pit-roasted agave, and braved the tiny spines of prickly pears. Unlike the Sahara, the Sonora granted its Desert People a surprising abundance.

The desert is less generous to those who scramble north across the border every night. The new barriers elsewhere along the frontier funnel migrants into the reservation, where the Wall, erected in 2008, remains permeable to migrants on foot. I heard a rumour that water jugs sold to migrants in Mexico are labelled with a silhouette of Baboquivari Peak; migrants are told that as long as they walk towards the peak that matches their jug, they're headed in the right direction. Even with the mountain as a signpost, however, hundreds of migrants die on the reservation. More corpses are recovered from the Tohono O'odham lands than anywhere else along the border. The previous July, 44 of the 59 bodies recovered from the borderlands had been found on the reservation. If the United States designed its border policy to kill migrants, these sands are the killing fields.

I'd read about Ofelia before arriving in Arizona. The respected Tohono O'odham elder acted as a spokesperson for the rights of America's indigenous peoples. In 2003, Ofelia founded O'odham Voice Against the Wall, an organization that sought to address issues around the hardening of the border through O'odham lands. Ofelia did not respond to my first few emails, and I feared she didn't want to speak to me. I worried even more when she finally replied. Her message included a link to a news story about my own government's mistreatment of Canada's First Nations people, as well as the troubling question, "What is your manifesto?" I wrote back and told her I wasn't sure I had one. Apparently, my lack of an answer satisfied her, and Ofelia invited me to her home. We met in the parking lot of the Tohono O'odham High School, where she picked up her grandson, and I followed her to Ali Chuyk, an O'odham settlement adjacent to the border.

As we approached the village, two Department of Homeland Security dump trucks rumbled down a side road towards the highway. By the time they reached the road, they were behind us. Ofelia immediately slowed down and pulled her van into the middle of the highway to block the trucks. I pulled my car onto the shoulder. I had no idea what she was doing. When the trucks stopped at Ofelia's roadblock, she stepped out of the van, walked slowly to the front grille of the first truck, and took a photo of the licence plate with a small pink camera. Then she went to talk to the driver. I couldn't hear what Ofelia asked him, but I heard the driver reply, exasperated, "We have permission to be here, ma'am." Ofelia told me later that she'd demanded to see their identification, and after she photographed their DHS badges, she asked to see permits allowing them to work on the reservation. The men, unused to being challenged by a 55-year-old Native woman, patiently unfolded their permits that proved the DHS had contracted them to build access roads for the Border Patrol. Satisfied, Ofelia returned to her van and pulled it aside to allow the trucks to pass. Both drivers were shaking their heads as they drove away.

Ofelia's home, a single-storey shack, stood at the very end of the road. A fence made of branches and barbed wire — her own wall — surrounded the property. She stepped out of her van and swung open a gate with a sign that read: "U.S. Border Patrol. Do not enter without a lawful search warrant." After I parked the car, I told her I liked the sign. "I have a bunch of them if you want one," she said, inviting me to sit at a table in the shade of a canopy. Two white fridges stood against the cracked stucco walls of the house. A rusty bed frame without a mattress sat in the dust, and a plastic bin of empty Pepsi bottles lay next to a stone hearth and grill where Ofelia made tortillas. Only the black satellite dish on the roof appeared modern and new.

Ofelia sat across from me and folded her hands, knotted with arthritis like tree roots, on the tabletop. She wore a thick flannel shirt against the November breeze and a floral orange skirt. Her hair was straight and black, and when she started to speak, I had to lean forward to hear her. Like all the O'odham I met, Ofelia spoke in soft, reverent tones, as if she was continuously occupying sacred space. And she was. According to O'odham *him'dag* — the canon of beliefs, stories, and rituals that governs O'odham life — all O'odham territory, from the northern reaches of the desert to the Cortés seashore, is holy land. "We are directed by Creation to maintain the area by doing our ceremonies," Ofelia whispered. "By doing our prayer offerings. Doing our songs to specific mountains. Gathering medicine." Because their land spanned beyond the international line, the Wall not only divided the territory, it desecrated it.

Some of the traditional ceremonies occur on the other side of the border. The annual rebirthing ritual called the *vikita* — named for the white fluff on the base of an eagle feather — takes place in the ceremonial grounds at

Qitowak, about thirty kilometres south of the line. The *vikita* ritual "has been going on since the beginning of the world," Ofelia told me. "We wait for the saguaro fruit to turn red, because that is when we have the ceremony." The ripening fruit is the O'odham call to prayer. The elders cross the border with medicine bundles holding the sacred implements of the ritual. I asked Ofelia what the bundles contain, but she would not tell me. "There are certain secret things that are held by the singers in a sacred way," she said with careful ambiguity. "And some items related to rain and water, and the clouds that represent the directions, the colours, the animals and the plants."

Before the increased security along the border, the O'odham passed freely back and forth across the line, following their traditional routes. Ofelia's parents' villages were on opposite sides of the frontier, and Ofelia used to cross all the time. When she was a child, only a barbed wire cattle fence marked the borderline. "We didn't realize it was a border, really, until 9/11," Ofelia joked. Now the keepers of the O'odham faith need to face those who hold the line. The DHS has ordered two of the ceremonial routes closed and forces O'odham to make long detours to checkpoints enforced by the Border Patrol. The agents now insist on searching medicine bundles for drugs and contraband. According to O'odham belief, only the celebrants of the O'odham rituals are permitted to handle the sacred items. The border searches pollute the sanctity of the bundles and, according to Ofelia, violate treaty rights of the Tohono O'odham. After some of the O'odham explained to the guards that they were ceremonial dancers, "the agents said, 'If you men are dancers, then do a dance.' They made them dance! Isn't that so inhumane?" Ofelia told me about a checkpoint near the Yaqui Indian reservation farther east where a guard broke open the antlers on an elder's ritual headdress to make sure there were no drugs hidden inside.

The abuse occurs all over the reservation, not just along the border. "If their job is to enforce and monitor the border, then why aren't they on the border?" Ofelia asked. Border Patrol vehicles follow O'odham as they leave their homes and arbitrarily pull them over for searches and questioning. O'odham have been harassed, held at gunpoint, and beaten up. One morning, a Border Patrol agent pulled over a tribal elder and asked where he was going. When the elder said he was going to the grocery store, the agent demanded to see a grocery list. "So now all the poor elders have to make a little list every time they go out in case they are asked," Ofelia said. "It's humiliating. They've beaten up so many people. Intimidated enough people. Every other night there are helicopters going back and forth. People feel like they better be good little Indians."

All Tohono O'odham are considered American citizens under federal law, regardless of which side of the international line they live on. They should be allowed to pass freely over the border. New protocols, though, require border agents to check the identification of everyone who crosses the line. Federal agents only allow "southern" O'odham to cross the line to use the medical facilities on the reservation. They are not permitted to leave the reservation at all, and the Border Patrol operates checkpoints on the highway just outside the reservation boundary to ensure everyone who passes has a visa or is a documented American.

Even O'odham born north of the border sometimes have trouble proving their citizenship. Ofelia was born in her mother's dirt-floor home that stands next to Ofelia's house. No one recorded the official details of Ofelia's birth, and like most O'odham of her generation, she had no birth certificate or proof of citizenship. Only a collection of forms from the Indian health services proved she existed at all. Now all O'odham have to scrape together a paper reality in order to walk the lands their Creator bequeathed to them.

For most of her life, Ofelia lacked sufficient documents to obtain a U.S. passport. Recently, though, a friend of hers who works with legal aid dug through Ofelia's medical records and amassed enough paperwork to satisfy the passport requirements. Ofelia sat in the passport office with the application form in front of her. She hesitated before signing, and the moment after she wrote her name at the bottom of the form, she wanted to take it back. "I said, 'I don't want this,' but it was too late. They took the paper from me." Ofelia remembered the moment with sadness. "I absolutely believe that by signing that document I renounced my sovereignty as an O'odham. It just destroys my system. My whole system." Ofelia would rather be a citizen of a place that does not exist than bow before a government that has desecrated and humiliated her culture.

I thought of Bill Odle. Bill and Ofelia shared nothing other than their proximity to the international border. He was the cowboy. She was the Indian. I suspected she would have as little time for his patriotism as he would have for her disdain of America. Yet both saw the barriers as an affront to the spirit of the land they loved. For Bill, the Wall betrayed his sacrosanct notion of America. For Ofelia, who had no such love for America, the Wall lacerated the blessed desert and defiled the *him'dag*. For both Ofelia and Bill, the true tragedy of the Wall came not from its corporeal crimes but from how it cut through their souls.

Like Bill, Ofelia sympathized with the migrants who crossed the border to find work in America and do the jobs Americans wouldn't do. "No one here is going to pick onions and cut lettuce," she said. "It is beneath them as American people to be picking the fruit and vegetables they eat all the time." She had a special empathy for the indigenous farmers who trekked across the border, such as the tiny men and women at the Streamline hearings. They, like the Tohono O'odham, were the original inhabitants of the land where they lived. When she encountered migrants passing through the reservation, she gave them water and packets of crackers and cheese, and she kept water in her van to offer migrants she saw along the highway. Aiding the migrants was a crime, but "everybody does it," Ofelia said. "My sister used to put out a bucket of sandwiches and water every day. People came through all the time."

The Tohono O'odham do not oppose a secure border. They even campaigned for one. In the 1990s, Mexican *narcos* used the reservation as a highway to run drugs. The cartels recruited young O'odham girls into their gangs, broke them with drugs, and sold them for sex. Then they used the girls to carry drugs into America. "These O'odham girls were the first drug mules," Ofelia said. The Tohono O'odham Nation pleaded with the federal government to secure the border against the smugglers, but the government showed little interest in stopping the drug trade. A delegation from Washington came down to visit the border. Afterwards, they told the O'odham that the reservation was sovereign land and therefore the responsibility of the tribal council, not the federal government. After 9/11, though, the border became their business. The government declared the reservation U.S. property and the frontier a vulnerable infiltration point for terrorists. Abused Indian girls could not inspire the feds as effectively as Osama bin Laden had.

Ofelia was hardly ambivalent about 9/11. Her own daughter was living in Manhattan that September. Taren had moved to New York City to study cuisine at the Culinary Institute of America. On the morning of September 11, her instructors had scheduled Taren's class to serve breakfast at the World Trade Center. Their subway train was delayed and the students never made it downtown. Otherwise, Taren might have been in one of the Towers, dressed in chef's whites and flipping omelettes, when the planes hit. "I had a little radio and was listening to the one station coming out of Phoenix. The radio was describing what was happening minute by minute, but I didn't have a phone," Ofelia told me. Desperate to reach her daughter, Ofelia drove to Tucson to borrow a friend's telephone.

Taren survived 9/11, but she didn't survive post-disaster New York. In the months following the attacks, the city grew harsh towards the brown skinned, regardless of their ethnicity. "People on the subway called her 'towel head' and told her to go home," Ofelia said. Eventually, defeated by the ignorance and fear born of the attacks, Taren abandoned her studies and drove her car all the way from New York home to the reservation.

I found the connection between Ofelia and September 11 remarkable. On that terrible day, Ofelia sat in a chair, pressed her ear to a radio, and feared for her daughter. Now the Wall, conceived on that same day by that same fear, stood four hundred metres away on a line the O'odham used to ignore. Ofelia did not fear for her daughter anymore, but for her people.

I told Ofelia how the Wall in northeast India divided the border communities and imposed a sense of difference between them. Bengalis in India felt estranged from Bengalis on the other side of a line that, until the fencing rose, no one noticed. Ofelia told me the O'odham experienced a parallel phenomenon. Since the Wall had gone up, many O'odham had started referring to their members south of the border as *Mexicano* O'odham and those in the north as *Americano* O'odham. Dividing Here from There created an Us and a Them. Ofelia rejected the distinction—"I am not *Americano* O'odham. I am just O'odham"—but many O'odham north of the line distrusted the O'odham who came up from Mexico to use the reservation's health clinics. They suspected they were not O'odham at all, but Mexicans pretending to be O'odham. Ofelia said, too, that O'odham in Mexico perceived O'odham in the United States as being advantaged. Every wall implies difference, and O'odham in the south presumed the difference was economic. "They say that you guys have more privileges because you are living in the United States," Ofelia said. "I say to them, 'You want to come to my house and see how much privilege I have? I have no running water. And some people live poorer than me. Your water is cheaper. Your electricity is cheaper.'"

For the first time that afternoon, Ofelia raised her voice. "The only way I am privileged is that I went to boarding school in Nevada. After four years, I got a document that says 'Completion,' but it is not a diploma. How can I be privileged when I was taken from my home? I missed the ceremonies. I missed my elders that passed away and who I never met again. I missed the growing season. I missed the cactus when it ripens. I missed everything. How can I be privileged? Because I speak English? When I went to school, they would hit me if I didn't say the words. So I had to say the words."

She sat silent for a moment and looked down at her hands. When she raised her eyes, she asked if I would like to see the Wall. We got into my car and she guided me along the paths to the border. It was late afternoon, and shadows extended from the fence across the dirt road on the American side. Aside from the occasional gust of the November wind that shook the cholla cactus and swept dust into our eyes, the borderline was quiet. Ofelia was quiet too, and her presence lent the scene a kind of sacred stillness. She told me we were lucky—the silence was too often punctured by helicopters and Border Patrol ATVs.

A row of steel posts, linked with three strands of wire cable, stood along the borderline. The posts were sunk five feet into the ground and filled with concrete slurry to stop trucks from barrelling through. The posts were spaced far enough apart, however, that anyone on foot could step through the Wall. The DHS originally wanted to build a solid wall here, something akin to the post-and-mesh barrier along Bill Odle's property. Environmentalists and members of the O'odham Nation objected, but Ofelia figured the DHS was deterred by the cost, not anything else. Besides, the DHS kept their options open. She pointed to metal clips on the tops of the posts where the government could hang steel panels and seal off the border to foot traffic. "They did it in Yuma," she said. "The National Guard came in with plates of metal and put it together like Lego. It could change at any time. I feel like they are preparing for war."

The Wall travelled straight along the border except where it abruptly veered off the line and curved around a tall saguaro to place the cactus on the south side of the barrier. The diversion around the cactus baffled Ofelia. "How did the Border Patrol decide this cactus was a Mexican cactus?" she laughed. Then she stepped across the border to pose for a photo in front of the saguaro. She invited me over the line and I squeezed past the posts to join her on the other side. I stood there for a moment before stepping back into the United States. Stories of remote drones and omniscient Border Patrol spooked me. I live across America's other border and know how easily one can find his name on a border-crossing black list. I didn't want to risk being forever banned from the United States for the thin prank of pushing past some fence posts into Mexico.

"People have to realize that the barrier is permanently there," Ofelia said. "And because it is permanent, it changes forever who we are."

Before I said goodbye to Ofelia, she told me about the elders who died the year the Wall went up. "That year we lost eleven elders. One after another, they passed away. It just seemed like they couldn't comprehend what was happening." Seeing their sacred land bifurcated and dishonoured poisoned them somehow. The Wall Disease can be terminal. "Almost every month we were having death ceremonies. I had longer hair back then, and I kept cutting it to honour the elders who died. By the end of the year, my hair was gone."

∎∎∎

America's southern borderland is holy land. I met a Presbyterian minister in Douglas, Arizona, who said living on the frontier altered his perception of the Christmas story. Now he saw the birth of Christ as God's migration across the border between the earthly and the divine. O'odham converts to Catholicism make a yearly pilgrimage across the border to Magdalena, where they kneel before a statue of Saint Francis Xavier. Mexican migrants seek help from Saint Toribio Romo, a murdered priest canonized in 2002, who devotees believe appears to border crossers en route and guides them safely through the desert. At Saint Toribio's shrine in central Mexico, vendors sell the "migrant's prayer book" filled with verses for migrants to recite during their journeys north. Alongside love potions and devotional candles, Tijuana's apothecaries sell clay statues of the unofficial saint Juan Soldado, another patron of the migrants. They believe Soldado was wrongfully accused of, and executed for, the gruesome rape and murder of an eight-year-old girl, and they visit his tomb near the border to pray for safe passage over *la línea*. The migrants' journey from south to north, over the line and through the desert, is itself a kind of Passion in the biblical sense of the word. Each migrant navigates his or her own Via Dolorosa. They despair and agonize and endure. Some will fall and bleed, their flesh pricked by thorns or cactus spines, their knees rasped on rock. Many will die, but each prays for redemption at journey's end.

I wanted to walk the paths of the hopeful migrants once they have subverted the Wall. I contacted No More Deaths, an Arizona-based activist coalition committed to making the borderlands less deadly for the migrants who cross over. Representatives from various faith communities and humanitarian groups founded No More Deaths in 2004. The coalition works to raise awareness of the migrant plight and to influence U.S. border policy, but their main course of action is to keep migrants alive. No More Deaths maintains permanent water stations in the desert, marked with blue flags on tall masts, where migrants can drink. Their volunteers also hike the migrant trails themselves and leave jugs of clean water and food caches where they know migrants will pass.

No More Deaths invited me to join two of their volunteers as they led a group of high school students from Los Angeles along one of the trails to a migrant shrine. I met Steve Johnston and John Heid in Tucson, and we drove south to the edge of Arivaca Lake where the students had gathered. After John handed out plastic jugs of water to the students, Steve led us through a lakeshore copse of cottonwoods to where a migrant trail emerged from a mountain pass. The detritus of migration lay all along the path. Dusty carcasses of backpacks. A shredded L.A. Dodgers jacket. A pair of discarded blue jeans. Old toothbrushes and spent deodorant sticks. An empty bottle of cologne. As the migrants reach the end of their journey, they switch into clean clothes and leave their torn and filthy gear behind. They wash themselves as best they can—a final ablution of toothpaste and mouthwash—before they meet up with a vehicle that will spirit them away.

We found black plastic water jugs bearing labels from Altar, a Mexican town just south of the border that acts as the main staging ground for journeys north. Migrants connect with coyotes in Altar and buy supplies for the crossing. John told me all the migrants used to carry white water jugs, but an enterprising bottler in Altar realized black jugs are harder to spot by *la migra* patrolling the desert. We also found discarded Red Bull cans. When the migrants begin to tire, their coyotes give them Red Bull, but the intake of sugar and caffeine can cripple bodies already weakened by days walking in the desert.

Those who support the hardening of the border consider the litter left behind by the migrants as yet another reason to wall up the frontier. Even volunteers with No More Deaths have been charged with littering by U.S. Fish and Wildlife for leaving behind jugs of clean water. No one denies that the migrant debris pollutes the desert's sanctity, and volunteers clear away whatever garbage they can each time they hike the trails, but these objects have a resonance beyond mere trash. They are the jetsam of migration: the relics of otherwise invisible men and women the passerby can know no other way than by plastic combs and tuna cans. Coiled carcasses of toothpaste tubes. A living archaeology. On this day in the desert, the ordinary implements of daily life stood as the biographies of men and women I could not see.

Our caravan continued to crunch along the path. The students became quiet. Their voices, loud with teenage laughter at the start of the hike, lowered into something more reverential. The sight of the trash seemed to strike them into silence. Until then, the migrants were just ideas. Phantoms. Seeing what they left behind revealed them as living, moving beings with hair to comb and teeth to clean. They had bodies that needed to be nourished. Just as the walls lend a physicality to notions of difference, the artifacts granted the migrants a flesh-and-blood reality. The hike grew to seem like a pilgrimage.

Farther along the trail, beneath a mesquite bush, John pointed to a white water jug half filled with filthy grey water. "Water from a cattle tank," he said. "The migrants would drink that. It can make people very sick. Out here it is lethal, because if you get diarrhea so bad you can't go on, you are left behind. That is a major cause of death out here in the desert." Following John's instructions, the students dumped the cow water onto the ground and placed a few jugs of clean water in its place.

We followed Steve single file into a mountain pass. He paused in front of a small crevice in the rock wall that smelled of burned wax. Soot blackened the tiny cave, and a few charred and broken candle holders lay on the ground.

"This was the shrine of Jesús Malverde," he said. "The patron saint of the drug runners." Malverde used to steal horses in the early 1900s and was eventually captured and hanged by Mexican authorities. The *narcos* later adopted Malverde as their saint. They appreciated his criminal success and, as dope dealers, related to his name: the word *malverde* means "bad green." The shrine used to feature a painting of Malverde, but Border Patrol agents tore it down. They didn't like the idea of a site where *narcos* could find spiritual comfort.

We reached an eight-foot rock wall. Steve and John helped the students climb over. The trail continued to an enclave bounded on all sides by high cliffs. The grey stone granted the space a solemn cathedral coolness. A natural niche in one wall had been transformed into another shrine. Migrants had placed icons of the Virgin of Guadalupe into the niche, as well as tiny prayer books featuring the image of Saint Toribio Romo on the covers. Metal dog tags bearing the words *El Otro Lodo*, "The Other Side," hung with rosaries and scapulars on notches of stone. Soot from candles blackened the roof of the shrine. The migrants had paused here and pressed calloused hands together as prayers to Santo Toribio fell from their lips. They carried the implements of devotion — beads, crosses, prayer books — in their backpacks alongside the other necessities of their journey.

"A lot of people carry votive candles," John said. "We've come across shrines where the candle is still lit. Can you imagine if you were coming for the rest of your life up here? What would you carry? Would you want to carry candles to light along the way?"

Before we turned around to hike back, John gathered the students around him and read a poem called *"La Ruta de las Mujeres,"* "The Women's Route," written by Arizonan United Church minister Reverend Delle McCormick:

> I walk the path that you took
> hours or days ago.
> Stones and slope and thorns
> threaten each step with
> danger.
>
> I see where you slept
> under the mesquite tree

home to spiders, snakes, ants —
familiar to coyotes, Gila monsters,
God knows what.

A piece of plastic,
grass woven into the branches
for shade against the merciless sun,
a tuna can, toothbrush,
tortilla cloth, used bus ticket —
all part of your story,
your life lost in this desert.

Nearby a tiny silver spoon
engraved, a love letter,
your bible, a pair of panties,
birth control pills,
breast cancer medicine,
a baby bottle, diapers,
one *chancla*, perfume bottle,
a pair of pants with
a name and number written in the inseam.

O, what you leave behind
haunts me
I know you
Sister, mother, friend,
Lover, aunt.

Some day
we will all be held
accountable for
your suffering, your loss.

Some day, we will
celebrate your courage,

your story, your making
your way to the Promised Land.
Some day we will name this Exodus
and thank God that
some of you make it
across.[14]

Few of the students spoke on the way back. One boy, though, paused to lift a discarded bottle from the path and put it in his backpack as a souvenir.

As a sacred space, the borderlands create their own holy icons. Even the congregation calling for higher fences and sealed borders has canonized a saint. On the morning of March 27, 2010, Robert Krentz and his brother Phil were checking fences and waterlines on their 35,000-acre ranch. The two brothers communicated via hand-held radios, but high winds mangled their transmissions. The last thing Phil heard Robert say was something about an "illegal alien." After Robert failed to show up for a noon meeting with Phil, the family began to worry. A search was launched. A helicopter team spotted Robert's body before midnight. Krentz, along with his dog, had been shot. At sunrise the next day, investigators found a trail of shoe prints heading south from the crime scene. A crew of trackers led by a mountain lion hunter named Warner Glenn tracked the prints to the borderline. The local sheriff, Larry Dever, admitted to the media that he couldn't be certain of the nationality of the shooter, but he believed the killer must have been a migrant. "What we do have is Rob saying 'illegal alien' and if anybody would know, it would be him," Dever said. "Given the location, I guarantee it was not somebody on their way to Wal-Mart."

Investigators in the United States and Mexico have never found the man who killed Krentz or the gun used to shoot him. They have never determined a motive or named an official suspect. Many question Dever's interpretation of events and wonder if Krentz himself was involved in the cross-border drug trade. Nevertheless, voices calling for a hardened international boundary used Krentz as a martyr for their cause and claimed his murder proved the dangers of a porous border. Hyperbole flowed, the language seemingly lifted from the scripts of spaghetti westerns. Days after the killing, Ed Ashurst, one of Krentz's ranching neighbours, told the *Arizona Daily Star* that "Mexican outlaws" were in control of the borderlands and he would kill any illegal alien who dared enter his home. The following June, Arizona Congresswoman Gabrielle Giffords held up a photo of Krentz at a press conference as she announced that more National Guard troops would be sent to the border. "Robert Krentz really is the face behind the violence at the U.S.–Mexico border," she said. The wall builders had their saint.

The activists, on the other hand, had Josseline. When we returned to the car after the hike, John gave me a small laminated photograph of a fourteen-year-old Salvadoran girl standing in a church. Her hair was black and pulled back tightly, her face was solemn, and her hand rested on her hip in a pose that seemed both defiant and awkward, as if she didn't know quite how to stand. The girl's name, Josseline Jamileth Hernández Quinteros, was typed on the back of the photo. Dates written in Spanish bracketed her life — 15 Septiembre 1993 and 20 Febrero 2008 — but the brief message beneath was in English. "This young girl from El Salvador died crossing the Arizona desert."

In January 2008, Josseline and her little brother left their home in El Salvador to join their mother, who was working in Los Angeles. They crossed through Guatemala into Mexico, where a coyote led them and a group of other migrants across *la línea*. Sometime during the journey, Josseline fell ill. When the group reached Cedar Canyon, about eleven kilometres north of the border, Josseline started to vomit and became too weak to walk. Her coyote, though, was on a schedule. He had planned for a truck to pick the group up along the highway and would not risk missing the ride for the sake of one sick girl. He decided to leave Josseline behind. Josseline's little brother wanted to stay with her, but she told him to go. "You have to keep going and get to Mom." The other migrants carried the crying boy away.

Dan Millis, a No More Deaths volunteer, found Josseline's body three weeks later. After she was removed from the desert by sheriff's deputies, volunteers erected a white cross on the spot and decorated it with pink flowers. A Catholic priest celebrated a Mass there in her memory. Many volunteers attended the service, along with members of Josseline's extended family. Her mother, father, and little brother did not. As undocumented migrants, they feared deportation if they ventured too near the line and the agents who patrolled it.

Josseline became a new saint for the borderlands. A young Salvadoran girl who just wanted to be with her mother was martyred by a policy of walls that transformed the borderlands into Golgotha. Many volunteers from No More Deaths carried photos of Josseline in their wallets, and new volunteers made pilgrimages to Josseline's shrine. "It is a way to emotionally engage them," Steve told me. Steve appreciated the symbolic power of Josseline's story but admitted there was a danger in the activists' over-embrace of her tragedy. "Josseline died for a reason," he said. "And that reason has not anything to do with us."

Night fell before we reached Tucson. The Arizona desert sky had a clarity I'd never seen anywhere, not even in the Sahara. The diamond-cut stars did not sparkle in the Sonora, they gleamed steady, piercing the obsidian dark. Looking out the car window, I thought of the migrants who, just then, were walking on the sand, placing one foot in front of the other through the sharpened Sonoran night.

▮▮▮

Patricia would not tell me her last name because in 1997 she went under the Wall. She reached the United States through a drainage tunnel that passed beneath the border wall at Nogales. "The tunnel was really dark and the day was raining a lot, and the hole was very small," she said. For forty-five minutes, Patricia crouch-walked her way under the border, her legs bent and her knees bobbing just below her chin. She was alone with her coyote and followed the splash of his footsteps through the stinking black. Seven other migrants were supposed to form a caravan through the tunnel that day; all but Patricia changed their mind. They were afraid of the rain and of drowning in the sewer. And they feared the *bajadores*, roving gangsters who prowl the tunnels and smuggler routes for migrants to rob, abduct, or assault. The *bajadores* are the pirates of the borderlands.

Somewhere above ground, Patricia's three children crossed through the Nogales port of entry with her sister, an American citizen. The children had no papers, but Patricia gambled that border agents would not bother checking them if the children were travelling with a documented American. Patricia's husband was already in Tucson. The entire family—Patricia, her husband, and the three children—had entered the United States on temporary visas two years earlier, but when Patricia brought her children to visit their grandmother in Mexico, the border officials took away her visa. Hence the underground duck-walk beneath *la línea*.

In the late 1990s, Patricia used to travel across the border often. Her family lived in Nogales, Sonora, just on the other side of the Wall. "I used to see my mother once every three months," she told me. "We could go and come back again and again." The new wall and the heightened security along the border ended these regular visits home. If she were to cross into Mexico now, she would be forced to return through the desert, and she was not willing to make that gamble. And if *la migra* caught her crossing over, she risked an Operation Streamline prison sentence in addition to deportation. So Patricia stayed in Tucson. She called America "the Golden Cage."

The Wall is more successful at trapping undocumented migrants in America than it is in keeping them out. Before the hardening of the border, migration of Mexicans across the line used to be a seasonal phenomenon. The family breadwinner, often a farmer and almost always a man, would tend to his own crops in Mexico then leave his wife and family to travel north and work the American harvest. He would return to Mexico for the holidays. Most Mexicans are devout Catholics. Between Christmas and Tres Reyes, the January feast marking the Magi's manger-side visit to the infant Christ, there were hardly any migrants north of the border. Some migrants used to come and go across the border every six to eight weeks. Their journeys resembled commutes more than migrations.

The Wall ended these fluid comings and goings. Now the crossings were dangerous and expensive. Northbound workers who used to sneak past the barbed wire on their own now had to hire coyotes to lead them along treacherous desert trails. Once in America, these men didn't dare return to Mexico to visit their families, because they knew they might be caught, or killed, on their way back north. Instead, the entire family came up across the line. Women and children now crossed the border to be with their husbands and fathers. Once they made it in, they didn't leave either. The Wall transformed the seasonal migration of individual males into permanent residencies of entire families. Patricia's family was one of these.

Eight months before we met, when Patricia's father was visiting from Nogales, he fell ill and died in Patricia's home. Patricia brought her father's body to the border, where customs officials shuttled the casket to her brother on the other side. Patricia did not attend the funeral. "I couldn't go," she said, "because if I went, I could not come back." As she told the story, Patricia's shoulders started to quake like the Streamline defendants I'd seen. She began to cry. "Now I worry because my mother is alone. And it is cold there and dangerous. I really worry about her because if something happens, I don't know what I am going to do. We have to live with this every day."

"Can your mother visit you here?" I asked.

"She is older. She doesn't like to see the Border Patrol and their scary faces. And she doesn't like the politics here. She says it is too sad to live in America because it is supposed to be the free country, but you are not free here."

For undocumented migrants like Patricia and her family, the politics in Arizona continue to darken. In April 2010, less than a month after the Krentz murder, the Arizona state legislature passed the Support Our Law Enforcement and Safe Neighborhoods Act, known better by its less Orwellian name SB1070. The bill compelled law enforcement officers to demand proof of citizenship from anyone they had reasonable suspicion of being an "illegal alien." SB1070 stirred noisy protest throughout the United States and Mexico, and various businesses and city councils hollered for boycotts against Arizona. Patricia and her husband opted for a more sombre and dignified response to SB1070. They summoned their three children into the living room, sat them on the sofa, and talked about what they should do if police took their parents away.

If she is caught, Patricia would rather serve a prison sentence than sign a voluntary deportation order that would automatically eject her across the border. "I have to tell my children, 'If something happens to me, don't cry. Keep going to school. Keep doing good choices. I'm going to be in jail for three or four weeks. Maybe six weeks. I don't know.'" At her release, Patricia would plead her case to a judge, who in all likelihood would deport her anyway. I asked her what she would do then. "I would find another tunnel," she replied.

Patricia began to cry again. "It is hard to tell them that you are going to jail and will be separated from the family. It is hard to talk about this."

"Do your children understand?"

"Maybe my oldest son does, but my daughter tells me, 'Don't say that. What am I going to do without you for too many days?' It is hard for her to hear what I was saying." Patricia told me her daughter panicked one afternoon when she phoned home and her mother didn't answer. "She called my husband, my friends, my neighbour, my other son. 'Where is my mom? Why is she not answering the phone? What happened to her?'" Patricia shook her head, and allowed herself a brief smile. "We always say in the morning that you have to have a hug and a kiss for Mom and Dad because we don't know what is going to happen today."

Patricia's children were now teenagers. Her fourteen-year-old daughter wanted to be an oncologist. Her middle child, a son, was fifteen and a fine basketball player. He wanted to study law. Patricia's eldest son was seventeen and would soon graduate from high school. He planned to study civil engineering or pharmaceutical science. But these were all fantasies. Since none of Patricia's children have American citizenship, they cannot attend college in the United States unless they pay expensive foreign student tuition, which the family could never afford. "My oldest boy is frustrated," Patricia told me. "He says that if nothing better happens here, he is going to go back to Mexico and go to university there. He has really good grades, and he says, 'Why do I have to study if I am not able to go to university here? They will always treat me as a criminal. It wasn't my fault to come here.'" Patricia sounded weary. "I am not sure if coming to America was the right decision. With everything happening here, maybe it would be better in Mexico."

I thought of Rocky Ghotra in Ceuta, who regretted leaving India to chase European dreams. Patricia never intended to stay in America. Her family came for the sake of her children's education and because her sister-in-law convinced her that jobs were plentiful. "She said, 'Come. It is good. There is no cold. You can have a car. Furniture. There is lots of work and the kids can go to school.'" In the 1990s, the federal government debated granting amnesty to undocumented migrants. Patricia's family had reason to be optimistic, but not anymore.

"Since the Towers, this changed. It all changed."

■■■

Elsewhere in the world, the walls have created accidental Edens. The demilitarized zone between the two Koreas—four kilometres wide, 250 kilometres long, and edged by barbed wire fences and watchtowers—has been devoid of human presence for more than a half century. In that time, the DMZ has transformed itself into an unintended wildlife preserve, now home to Amur leopards, Siberian musk deer, red-crowned cranes, and other nearly extinct species. With no humans to interfere with them, the animals moved in. They might have disappeared were it not for the Wall. The once off-limits borderland that divided Germany likewise surrendered to the wild. The 1,400-kilometre scar from Germany's Baltic Sea coast to the Czech border forms the protected Grünes Band, the "Green Belt," a narrow biosphere teeming with nearly six hundred endangered animal and plant species. A true Green Line. The dead zone in Cyprus isn't dead at all. Plants and animals have been infiltrating the vacant buildings of the Green Line for nearly fifty years. One of Thodoris Tzalavras's most dramatic photos of the dead zone show a tree bursting through the floor and out the window of an abandoned house. Nature, uninterested in the lines men trace over maps and the barriers they build, flourishes in the narrow spaces between the walls.

The U.S.–Mexico wall, however, has generated no such ad hoc paradise. Quite the opposite. In November 2009, fifty marchers joined Tucson's annual All Souls Procession to honour the life, and mark the death, of Macho B. Until the Arizona Game and Fish Department killed him the previous spring, Macho B had been the last remaining jaguar living wild on American territory. The marchers, many dressed as jaguars themselves, carried an enormous papier mâché puppet of Macho B through Tucson's downtown to rouse support for wildlife conservation and to show that, while the Wall fails to deter migrants and drug runners, the barriers succeed at disrupting wildlife.

"There are lots of species on the borderlands that are impacted by the Wall," Randy Serraglio said when we met for coffee at Tucson's Hotel Congress. Serraglio worked for the Center for Biological Diversity, a Tucson-based organization that advocates for the protection of endangered animals. "The jaguar is one of the obvious ones." Jaguars used to roam throughout much of the southern United States until trapping practically wiped them out. In the twentieth century, the wild cats appeared sporadically from across the border in Mexico. "These creatures have huge home ranges," Serraglio said. "They need to control territory and have space to ensure their genetic diversity. They need to spread out." The walls effectively bifurcated their habitat and accelerated an extinction that now seems inevitable.

When the DHS started to fortify the border, wildlife biologists predicted the Wall would cause an ecological disaster. Environmentalists, conservationists, and concerned landowners such as Bill Odle worked to stop the construction. They armed themselves with lawyers who cited federal statutes in their battle against the Wall and took the DHS to court. Protective legislation including the Endangered Species Act, the Arizona Desert Wilderness Act, and the National Environmental Policy Act, among many others, stood in the way of the construction. The Wall was illegal under these laws. The environmentalists had some early success when a judge granted the defenders of Odle's stretch of the San Pedro a temporary restraining order to halt the Wall's construction.

The wall builders at the Department of Homeland Security just shrugged and lifted their trump card, the Real ID Act, from their briefcases. Among its 93-page laundry list of homeland defence appropriations, weapons procurements, and funding for the wars in Afghanistan and Iraq, the Real ID Act authorized the DHS to "waive in their entirety" any local, state, and federal statutes that blocked the construction of the Wall along the southern border. The Act granted the Secretary of the DHS, then Michael Chertoff, the "sole discretion" over such waivers. This sort of power bestowed upon an unelected appointee had no precedent in U.S. law. The Secretary could simply disregard decades' worth of legislation passed by Congress and signed by presidents. And so he did. Chertoff swept aside nineteen laws that protected the San Pedro preserve, and the Wall went up. In total, the DHS waived thirty-six laws to build barriers all along the border. "Yes, I don't want to disturb the habitat of a lizard," Chertoff smirked at reporters, "but am I prepared to pay human lives to do that?"

Environmentalists like Serraglio were unsure what lizard Chertoff had in mind, or whose lives he thought he was saving, but the ecological trauma caused by the Wall, in Arizona and elsewhere, is clear. In addition to its bisection of jaguar territory, the Wall interferes with the migrations of Mexican grey wolves, black bears, and Sonoran pronghorns. The Wall prevents south Texas ocelots from finding Mexican mates. To make room for the barriers, the DHS felled over a hundred rare Tecate cypress, which hosted the already imperilled Thorne's hairstreak butterfly. The Wall even endangers birds. The imposing steel barriers spook the shy and low-flying cactus ferruginous pygmy owls, the world's smallest owl, which nest in saguaros. They can fly over the Wall, but they don't. "The birds see the Wall as a barrier, thus it is a barrier," Serraglio said. "No one would think the Wall would affect a bird. I can hear the right-wingers now. They're gonna go nuts: 'Oh God! Gimme a break. It's an owl. It's a bird. Just fly over. It's absurd.' No, it's not. It's science."

Truly absurd was the solution the government devised for the jaguar migration problem. DHS engineers cut small openings at the base of the border wall at distant intervals along its length. These "cat doors" were meant to allow animals to pass through and continue their migrations. "This is the feds' way of saying, 'Don't worry. We're concerned about the wildlife too. So we want to do something to help,'" Serraglio said. "What are they going to do? Take pamphlets down to Mexico and hand them out to the jaguars to tell them where the door is? Is the pamphlet going to be printed in Spanish or English?"

I told Serraglio that some supporters of the border fence also played the environmental card. They claimed migrants polluted the borderlands with their trash, and a secure wall would ensure the landscape remained pristine. He acknowledged that migrant trash accumulating in low-lying areas can damage the tiny ecosystems those areas cradle. "But trash is ephemeral. It can be picked up," he said. "Trash pales in comparison to the landscape-scale destruction caused by the border wall and the massive destruction by the operational elements." The access roads, floodlights, helicopters, and heavy construction equipment all ripped deep wounds into the borderland. So do the ATVs the Border Patrol uses to chase down fleeing migrants. All these damage the habitat more than the scattering of migrant toiletries.

███

The I-19 links Tucson with the border at Nogales. All along the highway, road signs are posted in kilometres for the comfort of drivers from metric Mexico. Any fragrance of Arizonan goodwill, however, dissipates at the sight of the Wall. In the 1990s, the U.S. Border Patrol erected a barrier wall out of recycled helicopter landing mats to sever Nogales, Arizona, from Nogales, Sonora. The steel panels stood upright and army green, like the scales of some fantastic dragon sprawling over the rolling borderland. The great jazzman

Charles Mingus was born on the American side of Nogales and wrestled his bass in jazz clubs on both sides of the line. The writer Alberto Rios was born here, too. In his memoir *Capirotada,* Rios wrote that the border at Nogales "is both where two countries meet as well as how two countries meet, and the handshake is rough." He recalls when only a chain-link fence marked the borderline. The frontier "used to be an idea first," he wrote, "and then a fence and then a wall. I guess it is still an idea."[15]

For musician Glenn Weyant, the Wall is a musical instrument. I stood behind Glenn on the American side of the Wall and watched him attach a contact microphone to a steel panel with black electrical tape. He ran a wire from the microphone to a compression amplifier and flicked the power switch, turned the volume knob, and stepped forward to play the Wall. Glenn danced his fingers over the steel panels as if trying to tap the Wall's cold reptilian veins. His hand drumming reverberated and echoed out of the amplifier as tiny booms and tinny buzzes. The sounds crossed the dusty border road and floated up the hill where National Guard troops and Border Patrol agents stared, bewildered, at a plaid-shirted man fondling the border they were charged to protect.

Glenn paused. He heard something in the noise that I didn't, a resonance he wanted to explore further. He moved back, tweaked a dial, and fetched a pair of trimmed palm fronds from a burlap rice sack. He drummed the Wall's rust-scabbed support posts with the fronds for a while, then dragged a cello bow along the clips that linked the panels. He bowed gently—steel will eat the bow hair, he'd told me earlier—and the Wall released a metallic moan that sounded the way blood tastes. I tried to ask Glenn a question, but he'd lost himself in the bizarre symphony he coaxed from the Wall.

Glenn began playing the Wall after a 2005 drive into the grasslands of the Buenos Aires National Wildlife Refuge, a nature preserve in the Sonoran Desert near the international border. The refuge is considered public space and welcomes visitors twenty-four hours a day, but there too the handshake can be rough. When he stopped his car on the side of the road to watch a red-tailed hawk, a military helicopter rose from behind a copse of trees, the noise of the rotor blades hacking through the desert silence. The helicopter hovered close enough to blow Glenn's hair back, but through the buzz he could see a trooper in a flight helmet tapping at a computer. Later, he realized the soldier was running the plates on his car. "They were documenting and photographing me," Glenn said. "It was like every conspiracy theorist's dream." After he drove away, a pair of Border Patrol vans appeared on the highway behind him. They didn't pull Glenn over but tailed him until he left the refuge.

Back in Tucson, Glenn vowed to engage with what the border had become: a place where Black Hawks had displaced red hawks as the resident bird. He decided to harness the militarization of the border into an unlikely musical project. He wanted to play the Wall. He drove to Nogales with a box of recording equipment and a collection of drumsticks. He didn't know if playing the Wall was illegal and wondered if the Border Patrol would arrest him, but Glenn wanted to learn what the Wall *sounded* like. He fastened a microphone to the metal surface and connected the wire to an amplifier and digital recorder. Then he plugged in a pair of headphones. Glenn hadn't realized how much his contraption looked like an improvised explosive device until a highway patrol vehicle charged up the border road and a nervous trooper stepped out. Glenn plucked the headphones from his ears and explained to the officer that he meant to play the Wall, not obliterate it. The officer recorded Glenn's driver's licence data in his computer and left him alone.

Glenn expanded the endeavour into what he calls the Anta Project; anta means "end of known territory" in Sanskrit. He began his "soundings" at the Nogales border wall, but when the town's military edges started to feel too paranoid and unfriendly, Glenn trekked into the desert. "Bach played in cathedrals," Glenn told me. "The Sonoran Desert is my cathedral." He played the vertical pipes of the bollard walls that rang like church bells when not properly filled with cement, and stroked the wire fences with his cello bow. "This might seem avant garde," he said, "but I read about a rancher who used to bow barbed wire fences to calm his cattle." Glenn also recorded the natural ambient sounds of the newly militarized frontier. Revved engines of Border Patrol trucks rumbled like bass lines in his recordings. Dogs yapped and peacocks yelped. Desert winds strummed wire fences like some unintentional aoelian harp. If the desert was Glenn's cathedral, then these voices were his choir. In one session, he played a "duet" with a Border Patrol helicopter, drumming the Wall while the chopper blades thumped a beat overhead.

"Some say it is a fence. Some say it is a wall. I say it is an instrument," Glenn said. "If they are going to put this thing up, I am going to transform it. As far as I am concerned, this is not a barrier. It is not stopping people from crossing. Instead, it is a 2,000-mile-long instrument. The government spent millions of dollars to build the world's largest instrument." By playing the Wall, Glenn subverted it. He understood that what he was doing might seem like nonsense, but the Wall itself was ridiculous. "The whole thing is absurdity. It is mind-boggling. And to come out with a cello bow and to bow the fucking thing? That is so far out."

Glenn's wall performances reminded me of Faris and Yusef's Send A Message scheme in Ramallah. Both projects sought to defeat the walls by robbing them of their military machismo. "In a way, I am taking the Wall down," Glenn said. "Do you want to be afraid of it? Or do you want to take people aside and show the absurdity of it? It's like when a kid grows up. The dad is a big angry dude, but when you grow up, you say, 'Oh my God, my dad is a scared little guy.' When you are young, you are afraid. When you grow up, you wonder what there is to be afraid of anymore. Let me embrace this. Let me stop this. The Wall is what the big angry dad put up. So screw it."

Glenn mixed his recordings of border ephemera into sonic collages and sold the symphonies on his website. He donated the proceeds to No More Deaths. The recordings are not music in the traditional sense. They lack any discernible melody or rhythm, and some of Glenn's listeners told him his music was the worst thing they had ever heard. But others found a kind of beauty in his border songs. Some meditated to the sounds. I couldn't hear the music in the recordings that Glenn hears, but the tracks possess an undeniable and compelling ghostliness: a metallic melancholy that screeches and buzzes and rattles like a beast on a chain. Through Anta, I found the soundtrack to my journeys along the barricades. These were the echoes of division. The wailings of the walls.

When Glenn finished his sounding and stepped out of the barricades' cool shadow, he revealed something else: the Wall sang without being played. The steely moans kept floating out of the amplifier. He explained that the panels and posts, like all matter everywhere, vibrate constantly. He had heard the steel expand and creak and pop as the desert day warmed. He had heard the desert breezes conduct the Wall's shiver and rattle. My ear could not sense these sounds, but Glenn's microphone could, and his amplifier broadcast the whispers aloud. Glenn's equipment uncovered the irony that a structure built to halt movement is itself in constant motion. And there is democracy to this resonance. The steel reverberates with sounds from both sides of the border equally. It does not distinguish Mexico from America and does not know Here from There. Sonically, then, the Wall subverts its own mission. It unifies rather than divides.

For a few minutes, Glenn and I stood and listened to the barrier's solo dirge, the Wall's weird metallic jazz. Then he turned to me. "Would you like to play a duet?"

I selected a rubber mallet and a wire whisk from Glenn's bag and moved up to the Wall. I hesitated at first. This sort of whimsy felt misplaced in the shadow of all the sadness I'd witnessed, here and elsewhere, along the walls. The barriers were serious. I began to tap the steel with the mallet, apologetically, until I heard my hammering echo through the amplifier behind me. Then I drummed a little faster. I found a clip of metal wire hanging from one panel and I teased it with the whisk until the clip fell into the dirt. While Glenn rapped the Wall with palm fronds, I dragged my mallet over the corrugations and pounded a vertical post with the side of my fist to listen to the boom. I stopped feeling foolish as the Wall transformed beneath my hands. Perhaps not into a musical instrument — not by my rhythmless rapping — but into something else. Something less than what it was meant to be. We rendered the steel into sound. Rattling an egg whisk along the Nogales barrier felt more subversive that my brief step across the line with Ofelia. Glenn and I were taking down the Wall.

Months after I left Arizona, the Department of Homeland Security uprooted the steel panels dividing Nogales and erected a new wall built of metal tubes filled with slurry and spaced four inches apart. The updated barrier allowed the Border Patrol to see through to the other side and, some argue, struck a more aesthetic pose than the rusting sheets of steel. The drug runners, though, adapted quickly. Soon after the renovation, drug enforcement agents in the United States started to find oddly shaped bundles of narcotics during drug busts. The packets were small and just under four inches wide. The agents realized the *narcos* had specifically designed the bundles to be passed through the new barrier at Nogales.

After my duet with Glenn, however, I was less interested in how the new wall failed than in how it sounded. Glenn wrote to tell me:

> My first take was dull and dead compared to the old wall which, as you know, was sheets of metal rather than slurry-filled pipes. It's an industrially produced medieval monster. However, I'm getting to know it and I've begun discovering "how" to play, amplify and transform it. I've also been learning where to place the custom mics I've built and where they pick up sound the best. Yesterday the wind there was real crazy and the wall was literally humming from the vibrations. That was a nice surprise. So it's like any new instrument. There is a bit of a learning curve, and it will require lots of practice and some seasoning over time, but I'd say it is already showing great promise as a multi-million-dollar instrument rather than a symbol of fear and loathing.

Early on a Saturday morning, I returned to Nogales on one of the shuttles that plied the highway from Tucson to the border and crossed *la línea* into Mexico. Nobody at the border post checked my documents. I followed the Wall west along Internacional. Murals were painted on the backs of the panels Glenn and I had drummed upon a few days earlier. One depicted the Virgin Mary surrounded by candles and the word *viajeros*, "travellers," written above. Another showed a map of Mexico with footprints walking north to the American line. One depicted a skeleton wearing jeans, a red T-shirt, and a single shoe lying among cacti in the desert. *Muerte*, "death," was written underneath.

I arrived at the Comedor de los Migrantes, the Migrants' Canteen, just before they served breakfast and walked past a growing line of Mexicans clutching deportation documents. A white-bearded Jesuit priest named Father Peter Neely opened the gate for me and introduced me to the assemblage of volunteers. The Comedor offered breakfast and lunch, and some comfort, to the recently expelled.

The Comedor occupied an open-air cement terrace shaded by a corrugated tin roof. Long tables covered in blue-and-white plastic tablecloths filled most of the space, and a sheet of blue tarpaulin formed a front wall. Volunteers had duct-taped maps of the borderlands to the tarp. Arced lines on the maps showed the distances migrants on foot could reasonably travel per day. The map-makers knew that coyotes notoriously understated distances to their clients and convinced them they could reach cities like Tucson or Los Angeles after a short hike. Steve Johnston of No More Deaths told me that migrants found hitchhiking near the Arizona border often asked for rides to cities as far away as New York, believing America to be much smaller than it is. Red spots on the same maps marked where dead bodies of unsuccessful migrants had been found. They dotted the maps like a pox.

When the Comedor opened, I watched as volunteers checked each guest's documents. Father Neely said the canteen served only those migrants whose deportation orders proved they had been ejected from the United States sometime within the last fifteen days. In the past, coyotes used to mix with the crowd and recruit clients over lunch. After they checked their papers, the volunteers greeted the migrants with a sincere welcome. Each received a handshake and a "Buenos días" as they stepped up the concrete steps. The volunteers addressed each man as "Señor," every woman as "Señora" or "Señorita." Mike, a volunteer, told me, "This is something they don't get elsewhere." The comfort of a kind word and a warm human touch was rare along the borderlands. The Comedor's guests had spent the last few days treated first as cargo, then as criminals. The last stranger to touch them wore a uniform. Their hands had been shackled, not shaken.

I counted about a hundred diners. A relatively slow morning, according to Father Neely. Usually the Comedor served 130 guests for breakfast and another 100 for lunch. Most of the migrants were men, though more women than usual had appeared at the Comedor in recent weeks; none of the volunteers knew why. For the most part, the migrants didn't know each other, but they shared a common disappointment. For all their efforts, none of them had reached America. Some looked more hopeful than others. Mike pointed to one young man wearing a backpack, three pairs of socks, and tennis shoes. "As soon as he finishes breakfast," Mike said, "he will try crossing again." Most migrants keep trying to cross the line, but Father Neely said Operation Streamline hearings and threats of jail time deterred many. This was the first time I had heard that an American immigration policy actually worked.

Once the migrants had crammed themselves into their seats, a young nun with a bright voice welcomed them all to the Comedor. She asked how many had been deported the previous night. Half raised their hands. The nun told them they could get food and clothes at the Comedor, and make phone calls, and that once each week an American nurse would come to treat the ill and injured. "We know that you have suffered," she said. "We know that in the desert you can be separated from your group. You can be assaulted and kidnapped. We would love to have you feel that God has not abandoned you." The sister encouraged the migrants to take the time to be silent, to meditate, and to pray.

The volunteers served breakfast: *pozole* soup with hot tortillas and coffee poured into tall plastic cups identical to those Rocky's friends filled with chai in Ceuta. I watched some of the women pass their hot tortillas from hand to hand to warm their chilled fingers. Everybody seemed cold. They shivered in hoodies and sweatshirts too thin for the November morning. Their knees shook in worn jeans. When the migrants finished their soup, local seminary students spooned out beans and *carnitas* for them into pink plastic bowls.

After the meal, most of the diners left the Comedor, but one migrant family agreed to speak with me. The father and mother and I sat in the corner of the Comedor while their two young daughters played with a stray orange cat. *La migra* had apprehended the family the previous night as they crossed the desert through the Organ Pipe Cactus National Monument, just west of the Tohono O'odham lands. This was not their first time crossing the border. The family had crossed together twice before and lived in Compton for a while before being deported. The father had tried crossing the border alone nine times and was successful twice, once passing over the line near Mexicali and once over the Wall at Tijuana. He explained how he climbed onto his coyote's shoulders, grabbed the top of the Wall, then shimmied down the other side "like a fireman." The *migra* were kinder in California, he said. One of the Border Patrol officers who caught him told him, "Better luck next time."

I asked him why he didn't try crossing through Mexicali or Tijuana again. "It is too expensive. Now, to cross at Tijuana costs $4,000 each person." The new wall between California and Tijuana, barriers erected since his fireman's shimmy, made crossings far more difficult and thus more expensive. By the end of 2011, the price would balloon to nearly $10,000. As in Ceuta and Melilla, hardening the border increased the price for passage, and the smugglers got rich. In Sonora, their coyote charged the man $1,500 for him and his wife and $1,700 for each daughter. Crossing with children bore greater risks, and coyotes knew they were more precious cargo.

The family spent two days in the desert with their coyote. "You are walking and suffering a lot of cold," the father said. "And you are checking for drug traffickers. If they see you, they can shoot you if they feel threatened. They are always armed." He said he saw a group of about thirty or forty *narcos* in the desert, and his family waited until they passed before continuing.

The family hid during the day and walked only at night. Their coyote was jumpy. Every couple of hours he thought he heard a sound and gestured for the family to get on the ground. Eventually, a Border Patrol officer on horseback crashed through the brush where they hid. The coyote escaped, but the family was detained. "Getting caught was very sad," the father told me. "Because you've been walking a long time. You've made sacrifices to get there. It is sadness." He was angry that the Border Patrol deported his family but the *narcos* made it through. "When we were caught, we were treated like criminals. It is not fair. We were going to work. Not to harm the country. The people they should catch they don't catch, and I don't know why."

"Were your girls scared?" I asked.

The mother smiled at her daughters, who were chasing the cat beneath the table. "No. They were very brave," she said. "In the desert, my youngest was telling me, 'Don't worry, Mommy. We are going to get there. Courage, Mommy. We are going to make it there and live better there.'" The mother began to cry. Her husband turned his face to the Comedor wall.

After making it over the Wall near Tijuana the previous year, the father travelled to Seattle, where he poured concrete for a construction company willing to hire him under the table. After he felt secure in the job, he travelled back across the line into Mexico to fetch his wife and daughters. He wanted them all to live together in Seattle. Instead, they ended up in Nogales, among the other deportees, wondering what to do next.

As I listened to the man speak, I realized he was telling my own family's story. After World War II, my grandfather left his wife and daughters in Italy and travelled to Canada to seek a better life for his family. He found work pouring concrete and doing construction. He worked and saved until he felt financially secure, then he sent for the rest of his family. Sitting across the table from this man was like sitting across from my own grandfather a half century ago. The only difference between the two men was that my grandfather had three daughters instead of two, and there had been no walls for him to climb.

My grandfather is in his eighties. The daughters he brought to Canada granted him seven grandchildren and seven great-grandchildren. I named my son after him: Amedeo. My grandfather can look out over the Calgary skyline and point out all the buildings he helped to construct when he first immigrated here. I couldn't see how his contribution to the city, and to the country, would be any less had he lacked an envelope of papers claiming that he legally belonged. When people on the border talk about solving the immigration problem, sometimes I wonder what the problem really is.

Before returning to Canada, I travelled to the southwestern edge of California to see where the Wall ended. Despite its steely strength elsewhere along the border, the Wall whimpered at the Pacific. On the white sand between San Diego and Tijuana, the Wall fragmented into a row of tall posts that leaned like drunks in the surf at Imperial Beach. The ocean didn't care about political boundaries. It dumped kelp on both sides and crusted the fence posts with salty rust.

The border was born on this beach. Just up the hill from the shoreline stood a white stone pillar that marked the first gathering place of the U.S.-Mexico boundary commission, where, in 1849, after the end of the Mexican-American War, leaders of both countries began to trace a line between them. In 1971, First Lady Pat Nixon inaugurated a state park on Imperial Beach and declared the area around the boundary monument to be Friendship Park, a focal point and meeting place for citizens of both nations. At the time, only three strands of barbed wire separated north from south. "I hate to see a fence anywhere," the First Lady said. Members of her security detail cut through a section of the wire so she could step across the line and embrace the Mexican children whose parents came to meet her. "I hope there won't be a fence here too long," she told them.

The new walls were born here too. In the 1990s, crowds of illegal migrants from Mexico fled the collapsing peso and scrambled over the border to find work in the United States. Most crossed over the line along the 23-kilometre stretch from the Pacific coast to the San Ysidro Mountains south of San Diego. In 1994, Border Patrol agents apprehended half a million illegal migrants in this section alone, far more than anywhere else along the frontier. Bill Clinton's government launched Operation Gatekeeper in an attempt to stop these crossings. Gatekeeper allocated funds to increase the number of Border Patrol officers and called for a physical barrier on the line. The United States replaced Mrs. Nixon's barbed wire fence with a barrier of helicopter landing mats freshly surplused from the first Gulf War. The border boasted a spine of corrugated steel, and the term Friendship Park started to sound like a punchline.

The new barrier did not extend all the way to the ocean, however, and the row of steel fence posts that remained on the beach became a rendezvous point for people from both sides of the border. For those without the documents to cross *la línea*, this was the closest they could get to their families inside America. Mexicans on either side of the border unfolded lawn chairs on the sand and talked to each other through the fence posts. They exchanged gossip, *caramelos*, and warm tamales wrapped in foil. Fingers stretched past the posts to pinch children's cheeks. Mothers held the hands of their deported sons. Husbands reached through to caress their wives' faces. Lovers kissed through the Wall, too. They pressed their faces between the fence posts; their lips crossed the line like smugglers and met like diplomats. When they finally pulled away, the cold steel had chilled and reddened their ears.

"It was beautiful and extraordinary," Reverend John Fanestil told me as we walked on the thick white sand to the Wall. Fanestil used to celebrate Mass on the beach each Sunday and served Communion through the fence posts. "I saw people introduce new grandchildren to grandparents," he said.

"And families who'd travelled four days by bus to stand here and look at their relatives on the other side." He told me about one young man who had served time in an American prison and whose five-year probation prevented him from leaving the United States. "He told me he'd done some terrible things in his life, but he never elaborated," Fanestil told me. The man had two children with a woman on the other side of the border. She brought them to the Wall to see their father each Sunday. He mussed their hair through the fence posts and tried to convince their mother to marry him. She eyed him from the other side and tried to surmise if she could trust him, if she could love this man forever. "This was literally the only place in the world they could see each other," Fanestil said. "And the only place where they could touch."

The touching ended in 2008 with the Secure Fence Act, which, at the beach, manifested as a new wall. A fifteen-foot-tall steel barrier rose several metres north of the borderline, creating a no man's land between the new wall and Clinton's steel panels. "They fenced off the fence," Fanestil said. Now shiny white Border Patrol SUVs drove up and down the fresh asphalt roads that flanked the new barriers. Compared with the rusted recycled panels that made up the first border wall, the "Bush Walls" looked clean, futuristic, and serious. Signs declared the area, inaugurated more than thirty years earlier as an international meeting place, to be "U.S. Government Property" and reminded visitors it was "under 24 hour surveillance."

The old fence posts remained on the beach, but once they erected the new wall, the Border Patrol declared the posts off limits. Officials warned Fanestil that passing Communion wafers across the border violated customs regulations. Fanestil ignored the ban until one Sunday in 2009 when a line of Border Patrol agents formed a human wall in front of Fanestil and his congregation. The agents, armoured with helmets and flak jackets, seemed rather overequipped for a confrontation with a reverend armed only with a chalice full of holy wafers. Like the Wall itself, the scene made for great theatre. After choirs on both sides of the border sang hymns together, Fanestil declared that he was in the service of a greater power than the Department of Homeland Security and walked past the agents towards the Wall. The agents handcuffed Fanestil and led him away. They eventually released him without charge.

The Border Patrol planned to eliminate access to Friendship Park altogether, but pressure by activists like Fanestil led to a pathetic compromise.
For four hours every weekend, and for only thirty minutes at a time, Border
Patrol agents permitted visitors to pass through the Wall into a half-circle
plaza abutting the tall barrier of tight wire mesh that stood along the border.
However, a second fence surrounded the plaza to ensure visitors couldn't
physically reach across the line. Families who came to meet here had to speak
through the mesh. They could not pass anything to each other. And they
could no longer touch. The Wall robbed the border of what little remained of
its humanity. The California Parks Department called the plaza Friendship
Circle. Visitors called it *la jaula*: the cage.

When we arrived at the gate, Father Fanestil tapped the window of a
Border Patrol vehicle to ask the slumped agent inside to let us into the cage.
We walked to the edge of the circle, the white boundary stone just beyond my
reach. A family stood on the other side of the fence and Fanestil called out,
"Hola!" They introduced themselves as the Zamora family and the father,
Peter, told me they used to live in San Diego together until U.S. immigration
deported him back to Mexico. Now the rest of the family went to Tijuana on
the weekends to visit Peter and they came to the Wall together to peer back
into America. From through the mesh, I asked Peter what he thought of the
American half of Friendship Park.

"Man, it is ugly," he said. "Usually it is the other way around. We always
saw green grass on that side." Peter gestured to our humourless border guard,
who had returned to his truck. "Tell that guy to grab a shovel. Make your
side look nice. He's not doing anything."

Peter told me he had been impressed by the Wall at first, but now he
found the barrier dehumanizing. "You know the dog pound? That's what it
feels like now. I'm gonna start barking." Then he joked that the worst thing
about the Wall was that he couldn't discipline his teenaged daughter from
across the line. "If she acts up, how am I supposed to pull her ear?" The girl,
standing beside him in red-rimmed sunglasses, crossed her arms and blushed.

I returned to Friendship Park about a year later. Builders contracted by the
DHS had removed the remaining helicopter landing mats and the fence posts
leaning in the surf. When I arrived, workmen in hard hats and orange vests
were installing a new wall built of rustproof steel pipes spaced ten centimetres

apart and filled with cement. The updated barrier would stretch almost a hundred metres out into the ocean. As a blue construction crane lifted the new fence posts into place, Mexican teenagers in swimsuits milled around the borderline and dared each other to step across the briefly unbarricaded *frontera*. Border Patrol agents on the U.S. side watched them closely to ensure they didn't move too far into America.

I walked up from the beach to the place where I'd met the Zamoras. It was gone. As part of the renovation, the wall builders had dismantled *la jaula*, blocked all access to the 1849 border pillar from the north, and bulldozed America's half of Friendship Circle.

The new wall at Imperial Beach cost $4.3 million and rendered Friendship Park the most ironically named public place in America.

The Mutilated City
Belfast

Psychiatrists believe there are many factors that compel people to cut themselves. Some slice their arms and legs to express rage or emotional pain. Some "cutters" draw blood to relieve a persistent sense of unreality; pain feels real even when nothing else does. Others cut for control, carving lines into their bodies when their flesh seems their only jurisdiction. For some, the cutting brings pleasure rather than pain. Shallow wounds summon endorphins that bloom into bloody pharmacological joys. The sensation, though, can cause addiction. Cutters learn to crave what their blades can bring. They open more and more wounds until their bodies become relief maps. Geographies of intimate scars.

Walls, steel fences, and barriers scar the map of Belfast. Some slice several kilometres along major roadways. Others block narrow lanes a few metres long, or lacerate schoolyards and parks. The walls cut neighbourhoods into tiny enclaves of Catholics and Protestants. Bright paint attempts to beautify some of the Walls, but profane graffiti mars most. The scrawled-upon walls demand "KAH" and "KAT"— Kill All Huns and Kill All Taigs, derogatory terms for Protestants and Catholics. Barbed wire spins cruel calligraphy atop steel fences. The entire city feels bristled and spiked. I arrived in Belfast in June 2011 and spent a month walking alongside the barriers. Nowhere in my travels did the walls create such intimate incisions. No city I had seen engaged in such compulsive self-harm. And nowhere did the walls seem less likely to fall.

On my first Belfast morning, I walked from my hostel in downtown Belfast to the eastern reach of Falls Road. From here, a near-continuous series of barriers cuts a line west between a Catholic area known as the Falls and the predominantly Protestant Shankill. I walked past "Solidarity Wall," where murals honoured nineteenth-century abolitionist Frederick Douglass, expressed support for Basque separatists, and called for a free Palestine. I turned the corner onto Northumberland Street beneath a painting of Barack Obama, who, in a 2008 speech to a multitude of rapt Berliners, said: "Not only have walls come down in Berlin, but they have come down in Belfast, where Protestant and Catholic found a way to live together."[16] I found it hard not to smirk at Obama's claim as I crossed through the 2-metre-high steel gate separating the Shankill from the Falls, Protestant from Catholic, and walked to Cupar Way.

British army chief Sir Ian Freeland erected Belfast's first "peaceline" on Cupar Way in August 1969. His soldiers unspooled a line of barbed wire to separate Protestant and Catholic rioters just as his colleagues had done across Ledra Street in Nicosia six years earlier. When the line went down, Freeland said, "This will be a very, very temporary affair. We will not have a Berlin Wall or anything like that in this city."[17] Freeland could not have imagined that the barricade would outlast the Berlin Wall or that the barrier would mature from a line of wire into a three-metre wall of concrete. The Cupar Way Wall grew further when sheets of corrugated metal were added, then again as tall spans of wire mesh were fixed to the top. Now the triple-level wall stands six metres high and stretches for more than half a kilometre.

The Wall multiplied as well as it grew. Since 1969, the Northern Ireland Office, or NIO, has put up forty more "official" peacelines. The Housing Executive, responsible for providing social housing, has also erected barriers. And so have various other developers and agencies. If one tallies all forms of "defensive architecture" purpose-built to separate Catholics from Protestants—gates, strategically planted hedges, vacant lots that form no man's land between communities—the number of barriers carving up the map of Belfast approaches one hundred. Their proliferation, though, remains poorly documented. No one knows the location of all the barriers, who built them, and when. They have grown constantly and organically over the last four decades, and few records are kept. What is certain, though, is that Obama got it wrong. No interface barrier erected in Belfast has ever come down. They have propagated, extended, and grown — but they have never fallen.

Freeland coined the term "peaceline," but few in Belfast use the term much anymore. The word was as much a misnomer as "the Troubles," which sounded more like a stomach upset than a thirty-year conflict that claimed the lives of more than 3,500 people. Protestants and Catholics have wrestled over Ireland since the 1600s. The Troubles, though, refers to a distinct period of struggle, beginning with riots in 1969 that pitted Protestant Unionists who supported sustained British rule in Northern Ireland against Catholic Nationalists who wanted the North to sever all ties with London and form a unified Ireland with the Irish Republic. Civilians made up the majority of the casualties, but the conflict itself was fought by various elements of the British armed forces, the police, and Loyalist and Republican paramilitary organizations. Their acronymed names gave rise to an alphabet of Irish violence: UVF, UDA, UFF, UDR, RHC, INLA, and various manifestations of the IRA. I struggled to keep the initials straight.

A series of ceasefires in the 1990s coaxed the guns out of paramilitary hands, and in 1998 both sides signed the Good Friday Agreement, effectively ending the Troubles. No signed document or press-conference handshakes, however, could abruptly bring together two communities who'd fought each other for four hundred years. And the agreement could not stop the Walls from going up. More barriers stand today than before the Good Friday Agreement. The last wall built by the Northern Ireland Office, a 4.5-metre weldmesh fence, was erected in 2007 through the playground of Hazelwood Elementary School following attacks on Catholic homes in the area. The most recent wall, though, was erected by the local Housing Executive in 2010 on Hillview Road alongside a new property development as it was being built. The Wall went up even before there was anyone for it to protect.

Coloured graffiti and bright posters on the Cupar Way Wall attempted to mask the grey severity of the concrete and had turned the barrier into a tourist attraction. As I walked past, a quartet of young Americans scrawled on the Wall with black markers. Sightseeing buses and taxis regularly ply Cupar Way and invite their charges to add their names and personal messages of peace to the thousands already scribbled over the concrete. "When the guns stop you can hear the birds of freedom," wrote Maeve from Australia. Adam from Houston implored, "May God help us all." Perhaps all my time along the world's conflicted edges had made me cynical, but I harboured no patience for condescending clichés about peace and brotherhood. They were gestures of foreign vanity penned by the momentarily engaged. (I laughed out loud at one contribution, however: "Do what John Lennon said.") Besides, all the wall art and feel-good nonsense did not keep one's eyes from glancing upwards at the wire mesh and imagining a brick sailing over it.

▪▪▪

"I abhor the day I went around with a petition to put that wall up," Teena Patrick told me.

I reached Teena through the Interface Residents Group, one of many organizations in Belfast that promoted peaceful coexistence between those who lived on the "interfaces" — the term used for the borderlands between Catholic and Protestant areas of Belfast. Teena picked me up in her yellow Nissan and drove along the interface barrier standing on Springfield Road. The Wall divided the Nationalist communities on the west side from Unionists in the east. The barrier consisted of a brick wall slicked with greasy "anti-climb" paint and topped with a vertical expanse of tight wire mesh that reminded me of the graph paper I used in high school chemistry labs. The Wall spanned about four hundred metres, from the gate at Lanark Way to the barrier blocking Workman Avenue. There, a corrugated metal door allowed pedestrians to pass through, but only during daylight hours: the door was locked shut at night. The Wall severed four residential streets that once connected the neighbourhood to the shops and pubs on Springfield Road.

In the late 1980s, before the Wall, men regularly hurled bricks and petrol bombs at Protestant homes along Springfield Road. When fearful residents of the houses closest to the road fled the attacks, Republican arsonists set their homes on fire. A whole row of Protestant houses were torched and destroyed. The government erected a small fence, but the barrier did not stop houses from getting "bricked" almost daily. Teena and other Protestants in the area realized that they would continue to lose homes without a proper barricade. Teena went door to door to collect signatures on a petition demanding the government erect a barrier along Springfield. Initially, the residents called for a fence made of corrugated iron, but then they decided what they really needed was a wall.

Some residents refused to sign the petition. They didn't want to see a wall rise in their neighbourhood. Teena understood their concerns. She had no love for the barricades standing elsewhere in Belfast and the divisions they enforced. But her community needed preserving. "When times are bad, we want a quick fix," she told me. Enough residents signed, and Teena brought the petition to the Northern Ireland Office. "It didn't take long for the Wall to go up," she said. A wall was cost-effective. Erecting a barrier was far easier, and cheaper, than actually policing an interface. In 2005, the NIO augmented the Springfield Wall by erecting a steel fence on top to protect a row of newly built houses from thrown stones and bottles.

Looking back, Teena wondered if they might have challenged the violence in a different way. Perhaps the community could have held the police and politicians to account for the damage done to their neighbourhood. But she wasn't sure. "The Wall protected us from loss," she said. "But we imprisoned ourselves." The police locked the gates on Workman Avenue and Lanark Way during times of tension in the city, often with little warning. This forced residents with their own cars to make long detours around the Wall to reach Springfield Road. Residents on foot, especially the elderly and the infirm, were effectively trapped either inside or outside the Wall. Teena regularly received phone calls from neighbours who'd stepped off a city bus from downtown only to find themselves locked out of their own neighbourhood.

As with the other barriers I'd seen, the residents of Belfast built their walls for their own peace of mind — to feel protected and secure from outside dangers. But the walls had turned against them. An abruptly locked gate could exile them to the other side. For those living along the interfaces, the walls were Frankenstein's monsters: far easier to build than to control.

Still, there were few calls to take the Springfield Wall down. Residents on both sides saw a need for the protection the Wall provided. At best, Teena hoped the Wall could be granted a facelift to make it look more aesthetically pleasing and less crudely militaristic. I didn't tell Teena that I found this idea profoundly depressing. I didn't believe that brightening the barriers with a lick of paint or ornamental brickwork would soften their tragedy. This was not the same as Glenn Weyant in Arizona, or Faris and Yusuf in Ramallah, who used art to subvert their walls. Prettifying the Belfast barriers was a cheap attempt to forget what the walls had set out to achieve. I remembered what Faris in Ramallah had said about painting the West Bank Wall: "You do not notice the nail polish on the hand that is beating you."

Teena drove her Nissan through the gate on Lanark Way. She parked on the edge of an empty lot where a group of teenage Protestant boys kicked a soccer ball around. Boys like these were the most affected by the Walls. "Because of gates and barriers," Teena said, "young people are afraid to cross gates and barriers." The structures themselves breed fear. Just like the fences standing along the Indo-Bangladesh border, Belfast's walls declare that danger lurks on the other side, and that those who live across the line wish us harm. The reality of the threat becomes irrelevant; the perception is all. "If you are told, 'Don't go out. Be on your guard. Watch out,' you don't want to cross," Teena said. "Not to visit your relatives. Not even to go to work."

Belfast's youth have never known a city without the walls. "Those kids have never lived in a shared space," Teena said. They lack the psychological strength to cross through the shadows of their fortified lines. Before young people cross through the gates, they always look first to see if anyone from the other side is watching.

"Where do they learn to be afraid?" I asked her.

Teena laughed at my question. "They learn on the interface. You don't live on the interface without being challenged about being on one side or the other." Young people from either community know each other only through conflict, and they base their conflict purely on relative geography. More than religion, in Belfast your neighbourhood defines you. A few days earlier, a group of twenty Catholic teenagers came across the interface at Lanark Way and began hurling stones at houses. The Protestant kids rallied and began to stone the Catholics in turn. I asked Teena the reason for the "invasion." She told me there was none. Sometimes kids cross the interfaces just to spark a reaction. "I don't understand where half of their anger comes from. Or half of their hate. I know some come from lovely families."

Teena aimed to coax these angry teens away from the violence they saw on the streets. "I try to talk young people into doing something different." In her work with Belfast youth, she employed the mediation skills she'd learned during her service with the Ulster Defence Regiment (UDR), an infantry division of the British army formed to defend Northern Ireland against bombers and gunmen. Teena enlisted in the UDR as a young woman. "I always thought it was right to serve my country," she said. She had wanted to sign up for the regular British army, but a pair of tattoos disqualified her. She had her husband's name encircled with a heart inked on one wrist and her own name on the other. The UDR was less strict about the tattoos. Had her inscribed wrists not kept her out of the regular British forces, Teena might have been sent to Cyprus to stand between Turks and Greeks. Instead, she stood in Belfast trying to keep Catholics and Protestants from killing each other.

Teena spent fifteen years as a Greenfinch, the name given to the UDR's female soldiers, eventually being promoted to corporal. Her English father served in the Royal Marines and was already a member of the UDR by the time Teena signed up. Her brother and sister also served in the UDR. The family supported Teena's military service at first but opposed her decision to stay with the regiment after she had children. "Some nights my son was crying and keeping my other children awake until I came in at four in the morning," she said. "I had no idea." Republican militants often targeted UDR soldiers and their families, and Teena's children knew never to answer the door and to keep the blinds closed. "You didn't tell anyone where your mommy worked."

Teena had her tattoos removed when her son was born, but the inscriptions on her psyche endured. Like the walls themselves, her inner defences were still standing. Even now, whenever Teena entered a room, she tried to sit where she could see a door. And she always dropped her purse on purpose before getting into her car so she could surreptitiously check for a bomb underneath as she bent to pick up her bag. "It's something that doesn't leave you," she said.

Belfast was filled with men like Breandán Clarke—men with close-cropped hair, iron handshakes, and bodies built like welterweight boxers. Their muscles were tightly packed into small frames that seemed hardly able to contain them. They walked the streets like unsprung snares. As a small man myself, I admired how dangerous these men looked. I envied their fighter's stride.

I met Breandán at the offices of the North Belfast Interface Network, which represented some of the poorest and most conflict-ravaged communities in Belfast: Ardoyne, Cliftonville, and New Lodge. These neighbourhoods suffered a disproportionate amount of sectarian violence. During the Troubles, more than four hundred civilians were killed in the one-square-mile area these communities covered, and fourteen interface barriers divided the neighbourhoods into tiny fragments. The NBIN strove to improve community relations and responded when tensions seethed into violence.

Before the ceasefires in the latter half of the 1990s, the conflict was waged mainly by, and between, the acronymed paramilitary groups. The British army and the Royal Ulster Constabulary also added their guns to the thirty-year tussle. Once the paramilitaries laid down their guns, a natural entropy took over the conflict. For the first time, a young man did not need to enlist to participate. These men, born too late to have fought in the "official" Troubles, inherited a more amorphous conflict that combined the medieval with the modern. Instead of semi-automatic rifles and intricately designed time bombs, today's combatants fight with fists and bottles. But they communicate, coordinate, and strategize through sophisticated cellphones and social media. Barbed wire and brick walls are irrelevant in an age when teenagers plan their fights on Facebook.

Breandán told me that boys from opposite sides of the divide often brought their video-game combat onto the streets. Two boys playing online games would arrange to meet on the interface to transform their virtual battle into a real fist fight. Other boys rushed to join in and the girls egged them on. "Two boys playing *Call of Duty* turns into a 150-person riot," Breandán said. The new violence may have a contemporary spark, but the street dynamic has hardly changed since he too was a fist-fighting teen. "The toughest guy in Ardoyne still wants to fight the toughest guy in Glenbryn," he said. I suspected Breandán, in his youth, was himself the toughest guy in Ardoyne. Breandán and the NBIN, along with other community groups, tried to prevent these conflicts before needing to intercede. "Once you get to the stage of intervention, you are already tits up."

Breandán and I left the NBIN offices and walked to Alliance Avenue, where a twelve-metre-high wall divided the Catholics in Ardoyne from their Loyalist neighbours in the Glenbryn Estate. During the course of the Troubles, almost twenty people were killed along the half-kilometre stretch of Alliance Avenue that forms the interface. The British army laid a temporary barrier along Alliance in 1971. The barricade matured into a permanent wall built of brick, mesh screens, and corrugated steel panels akin to the Gulf War landing mats I "played" in Nogales. Here, though, the Wall stood directly behind the houses, denying sunlight to the back windows of over a hundred homes.

I asked Breandán what he thought of the word *peaceline*. "The Wall doesn't bring peace," he said. "The Wall becomes, largely, a congregation point. It becomes a target. A site for graffiti." Besides, the Wall along Alliance Avenue never stopped gunmen from attacking Catholic homes. Snipers erected scaffolding next to the Wall and shot into windows, or tossed bombs onto rooftops, using the Wall for cover. Breandán recalled touring Sinn Fein officials through the neighbourhood during the Troubles. They were drawn to the barriers and invariably stopped to peer down the alleyways at the walls, not realizing they were putting themselves within rifle range of Loyalist gunmen. Breandán, a faithful Republican, always made sure to stand between the officials and the Wall. "I would be 'sandbagging,'" he told me. "If someone is going to get it, it won't be one of the bosses."

The walls no longer provide cover for snipers. Instead, they impose a sense of territorial constraint on Belfast's youth that renders them unwilling to stray beyond their fortified familiar. Young people in Belfast favour segregated communities more than their parents do. Boys experience this geographical conservatism more than girls. Their tiny neighbourhoods become entire worlds they feel both duty bound to defend and afraid to leave. The walls may provide some protection from hurled objects, but they prevent people from either community from ever seeing each other beyond ossified binaries of Catholic and Protestant. Us and Them. The "solution" entrenches the problem. Breandán told me there were kids in Ardoyne who lived almost their entire lives within the single square mile of the community. He called these walled-in youth INLA, co-opting the initials of the Irish National Liberation Army to mean "I Never Leave Ardoyne."

Breandán and I walked to where the Wall ended at the junction with

Ardoyne Road. Breandán pointed north up the street to where Union Jacks and Ulster flags hung from lampposts. "That's Glenbryn," he said. "That pointy thing is a church. And up there is Holy Cross Primary School."

I recognized the name. "The site of the Holy Cross dispute," I said.

Breandán frowned. "Blockade," he said. His voice was low. "It was not a 'dispute.' It was a blockade."

Holy Cross, a Catholic girls' school, stands on Ardoyne Road directly across from Protestant Glenbryn. In June 2001, Glenbryn residents decided they did not want Holy Cross girls walking past their houses on their way to school. The reason for their abrupt objection was never clear. Some in Glenbryn accused Nationalists of using the daily commutes of the schoolgirls as cover for stone throwing. Others feared the Provisional IRA was somehow collecting intelligence on the neighbourhood during these morning walks to class. Whatever the reason, Glenbryn demanded the girls take an alternate route to Holy Cross. The Catholic families refused. Loyalists in Glenbryn staged protests along the road and, in the final week of June, blocked the school gates. The police decided not to intervene, and the girls of Holy Cross, barred from entering their own school, broke for summer vacation a week early.

The two-month holiday did not ease the tension between the communities. Protests resumed when school reopened in September and they lasted for fourteen horrifying weeks. The intensity of the protests varied from day to day, but at its worst the Holy Cross conflict blackened into some of the sickest and most shameful scenes Belfast had endured in years. Each morning, parents and police officers in full riot gear escorted the Catholic schoolgirls, clad in their uniform red jumpers and black skirts, up Ardoyne Road. Loyalist protesters lined the street to blare foghorns, throw stones, and set off firecrackers. They shouted profanity and insults at the girls, called them "Fenian whores," and held up pornographic images for them to see. One morning, someone threw a bottle of piss. "They exposed those girls to the fuckin' most heinous and horrific ordeal," Breandán said.

Like the migrant trails in Arizona, Ardoyne Road from Alliance Avenue to the school gates became for these girls a Via Dolorosa, their morning walk a Passion. Images from the blockades show girls crying in red-faced trauma, gripping their parents' hands while their bodies twist with fear. At the same time that the 9/11 attacks were commandeering the rest of the world's attention, the girls of Holy Cross endured a far more intimate terrorism.

The daily blockades bred nightly violence. Riots shattered the streets of northern Belfast for seventy straight nights. Strike marks from bullets fired during the Holy Cross riots still perforate the Wall along Alliance Avenue. A visit by Archbishop Desmond Tutu provided no calm. Only once First Minister David Trimble came to Holy Cross at the end of November did the conflict finally settle. More than a decade later, though, the memory of the blockades still hangs over the city. In Belfast, the phrase "Holy Cross" refers more to the clashes along Ardoyne Road than to the name of the school itself.

In the narrative of post-Troubles Belfast, this corner of Ardoyne and Alliance has become sacred ground. The two hundred metres of asphalt stretching north from the intersection to the Holy Cross School is now a sort of historic battlefield, one soaked with the tears of uniformed schoolgirls rather than the blood of uniformed men. Yet the corner itself, with its quaint brick homes and front gardens, seems too small and innocent to be gilded with such dark significance. Perhaps another tragedy of the walled places comes from their ability to debase quiet neighbourhood corners and short residential lanes into the front lines of miniature wars.

In the wake of the blockades, Glenbryn residents demanded another barrier be built across Ardoyne Road at this junction to prevent the Nationalists from Ardoyne crossing Glenbryn. The Wall would have forced the Holy Cross students to access their school through a rear entrance. Nationalists rejected the idea of the barrier. "This is not Birmingham, Alabama," Breandán said. "We're not taking a back door to anyone. That's our school."

Breandán wanted to show me how he aimed to defeat the walls. We walked south from Ardoyne to Flax Street, a road completely closed off by a steel wall topped with a garland of triangular metal spikes. A large-scale high-resolution photograph had been pasted over the Wall that depicted the actual view down Flax Street if the barrier were not there. According to Breandán, a photo covering the other side of the Wall showed the view from the other direction. In effect, the photos allowed passersby on both sides of the barrier to see through the Wall.

An artist with Draw Down the Walls, a project co-founded by Breandán, created the photographs on the Flax Street barrier. Draw Down the Walls uses the arts to examine Belfast's interface barriers. Among other things, the project strives to inspire youth, especially those living in the neighbourhoods bifurcated by the walls, to imagine a city without barriers. One of DDTW's aims, according to Breandán, is to "disappear the walls." To take them down artistically if not physically.

Breandán told me about his friend Tom, who'd found himself stuck in a traffic jam on the other side of the barricade one afternoon. A bomb scare had shut down Crumlin Road during the evening rush hour and Tom sat on his bus waiting for police to usher the traffic through. Tom could see his own flat in the photo on the Flax Street wall. Were it not for the Wall, he could have walked home in a couple of minutes. The image showed Tom the absurdity of the barriers and how they destroy the logical movement of the city. Over pints at the local pub, Breandán told Tom that his Draw Down the Walls group had put up the photo. "Tom says to me, 'I tell you what, that's brilliant. That's nailed on. It's absolutely nailed on.' And I says, 'Actually, it's pasted on, but let's not get semantic about it.'"

Farther down the road, Breandán showed me another wall he wanted to "disappear." This brick wall stood almost two and a half metres high. Steel and concrete reinforced the metre-thick walls. Breandán told me the government had built this wall to withstand a tank attack. "It'll last a thousand years," he said. Now, however, the barrier was obsolete. The neighbourhood dynamic had changed since the Wall went up and it no longer separated Catholics from Protestants. Everyone agreed this wall could come down, but removing such a fortification was expensive. Breandán had a better idea. He wanted to plant a row of Japanese knotweed trees along the barrier. The knotweed grows highly-invasive roots that would lay siege to the Wall, split the brick and, over time, tear the Wall down. Breandán saw the project as a sort of long-term art installation.

Breandán left me at the top of Crumlin Road. I asked him the best way to return downtown. He said I could follow Crumlin directly south. "That's a straight walk down that road," he said. "But if you are walking down that road from here, in that direction, some of the young bucks might take an opportunistic dig at ya."

"You're joking," I said.

"You could walk down there a hundred times and only one time you'd get a thumping. So it is up to yourself if you want to walk that way. Or I'll show you a more circuitous but safe route."

The warning surprised me. I didn't understand how I could be a target of Belfast's sectarian violence. "You really believe they'd go after someone like me? I'm almost forty years old. And it's obvious as soon as I speak that I'm from somewhere else."

"There was this one guy," Breandán said. "An Indian bloke. They saw him and said, 'Where ya from?' And he said India or such-and-such. They said, 'You a Catholic or a Protestant?' He says, 'I'm Hindu.' And they say, 'Aye. But are ya a Catholic Hindu or a Protestant Hindu?'"

I grinned. I'd heard the story before but never believed it was true.

■■■

Ian McLaughlin, a community worker in the Lower Shankill, a Unionist neighbourhood, worked alongside Breandán with Draw Down the Walls. Ian and Breandán came from opposite sides of the conflict. Breandán, a Republican, wanted a united Ireland. Ian was a Loyalist who wanted the North to remain firmly a part of Britain. I would learn, though, that the two men had almost everything else in common.

I met Ian at his office on Shankill Road. He too was short but built like a boxer, with heavy arms and a thick neck. Ian told me that the walls in Belfast started out the same as the Green Line in Nicosia: as coiled lines of barbed wire flanked with British soldiers. He was only seven or eight years old when he watched the British army come into the street to separate Loyalists from Nationalists. His "overarching memory" was of the soldiers unrolling a half mile of barbed wire in the middle of Crumlin Road. "Then they stood behind the wire and pointed their guns into the Loyalist areas. That always stayed with me: 'Why the fuck are they pointing guns at me?'"

The army built the barricades with the rationale that if the combatants couldn't reach each other, they couldn't kill each other. As a young man, Ian felt the walls would stop the violence. "But people on both sides, being very ingenious and fuelled by religious hatred, very quickly saw ways around it," he said. The structures evolved alongside the building animosity. What were conceived as temporary barriers were made permanent. Steel fences replaced coiled wire. Fences hardened into walls just as fear hardened into hate. But the walls did not protect against the militants who hurled pipe bombs, nail bombs, and "coffee can" bombs over the top. Often the attackers didn't know what damage their explosives caused until the media reported it. "I didn't need to see you to launch a perhaps murderous attack on your community," Ian said of the blindly thrown bombs. "But if you were blinded by sectarianism at the time, you probably didn't give a fuck what happened when you threw it."

To counter the projectiles, the government extended many of the walls upwards with panels of wire mesh. Over the years, the walls grew like living things. "And I've grown alongside the structures," Ian said. I thought of Mohammad in Jayyous marking his own growth with that of the olive tree in his care.

Since 1998's Good Friday Agreement, the ruling Democratic Unionist Party and Republican politicians with Sinn Fein have shared power in the Northern Ireland Assembly. Their apparent co-operation failed to impress Ian. "Outsiders might believe that everything is rosy on the hill," he said, speaking of the government buildings at Stormont, "but sectarianism is as raw today in some quarters as it was in 1969."

In many middle-class neighbourhoods, youth in both communities with no "physical recollection of the bad years" feel they've missed out. These boys were brought up hearing stories of the "great riots" and the bravery of the men who fought for either side. They made heroes out of men like Michael Stone, whose shocking 1988 attack on an IRA funeral in Milltown Cemetery was filmed and broadcast internationally. Today's youth watch the assault on YouTube. Hardline Loyalists so revere the ruthless gunman Billy Wright that they tattoo his face on their arms. These boys want to be part of the good fight. "Let's fight for the glorious 32-county Ireland," they say. Or "Let's fight for God and Ulster. Let's fight for the Crown.'

"With the greatest of respect, I've done all that," Ian said. "Fuck that."

I sensed that Ian was admitting something to me. "What did you do? Were you a paramilitary?"

"Allegedly," he said. "Allegedly. Do I have a criminal record? No, I don't. So work it out."

I laughed out loud at the elegant blend of secrecy and candour.

"Everybody has a history, Marcello. Yes, I have one. Am I proud of it? Shit happens."

"Does your violent past — your 'alleged' violent past — give you more or less credibility as a peacemaker?"

"More," he said. "My activities are closely scrutinized by civil society." He reminded me that senior members of the Democratic Unionist Party had served prison time for the crimes they committed during the Troubles, but he had never been to jail. "You cannot hold my past against me if I have a cleaner record than those in power." Ian sat down with ex-militants from both sides of the conflict, including former members of the UVF, the INLA, and the Provisional IRA, as long as they committed themselves to peace. Men who at one time would not sit next to each other in the same room now worked together alongside Ian. "The baggage which I would've been perceived to carry is gone." *Perceived. Allegedly.* The mincing of Ian's words mirrored the cutting of the city.

"Poverty and deprivation knows no wall," he said. The communities living in the shadow of the interface walls endured similar levels of poverty and unemployment. Only those who couldn't afford to live anywhere else — the poor, the elderly, the infirm — lived on the interfaces. Rents were cheaper along the fortified lines because no one wanted to be there. In the past, residents of these neighbourhoods easily spoke in terms of Us and Them. Now, a common sense of hopelessness serves to bind the communities on either side of the barriers. Almost everyone agrees the walls should come down. "Them and us share the same shit on both sides of the Wall," Ian said. "It's not a case of 100% of people here and there hate each other and want to kill each other." But the walls will fall only when the conditions are right, when Protestants and Catholics can occupy the same room, the way Ian and Breandán do, and look each other in the eye.

I told Ian about my walk along Cupar Way. The thought of the walls acting as a tourist attraction frustrated him. He said that if kids in his community drew on the barricades, they would be charged with vandalism "or anti-social behaviour or some shit," but whenever a taxi or tour bus brought tourists to see the Wall, the driver handed out felt-tipped pens for them to write with. "It's something I find hard to deal with. These kids live here every day of the week and you will condemn them for writing on that wall. But some guy who gets off a cruise ship for five hours can come up and draw all over the fucking thing."

███

During the Troubles, Violet and her husband Billy attended a dinner and dance at the Orange Hall on Clifton Street. "My husband's not a dancer," Violet said, her voice small and quiet. "But I remember, coming near the last dance of the night, he said, 'Come on. I'll try to take you round for a dance.' And we were just on the floor and we heard a pop. We thought it was balloons. It was actually a machine gun that riddled the windows near where I was sitting. There was a bullet hole in the back of my chair. If I'd been sitting there, I'd be dead."

Violet and Billy, an elderly Protestant couple, live in the Loyalist Lower Shankill neighbourhood. The Springfield Road Wall rises directly behind their tiny brick house. I sat with them in their living room and we talked about the walls. Unlike the profane and muscled men I'd shared time with in Belfast, Billy was thin and quiet. He perched on the edge of his chair with avian fragility and folded his hands in his lap. Violet was more talkative, but the insulin she was taking made her mouth dry and she regularly left the room for a glass of water.

Billy and Violet both remembered a time before the barricades, when Catholics and Protestants got along together. Billy "chummed with Catholics" as a teenager, and their own sons played with Catholic children when they were small. "We didn't raise our kids to be bigots or sectarians," Billy said. Catholics used to come out and watch the parades with their family. "I still remember those friends, but I lost touch with them during the Troubles."

"Since the Wall came up, we are divided," Violet said. "I can't see them coming down. Not in our lifetime."

"Would you like to see them come down?" I asked.

Violet shook her head. "If it did come down, we're wide open to the Springfield." She could not imagine living in their home without the Wall to protect them. A Nationalist pub stood on the other side of the Wall from their house. Violet and Billy often found broken beer bottles in their garden in the morning, or heard them shatter on their roof at night. Three years earlier, a two-pence coin had hit Billy in the ear while he sat in his backyard. "What if they hit him in the eye?" Violet asked. If nothing stood between their home and Springfield Road, Violet and Billy believed the attacks on their house would escalate from the occasional thrown bottle into a full assault. "If that wall wasn't there, we'd be afraid."

"People were glad to see the Wall go up," Billy said. "But were they really happy about it? No."

"I can't see peace," Violet said. "Not proper peace coming to this country. I just can't."

I glanced out their window to the Wall looming six metres tall over their home, both ominous and protective, sheltering them from violence while shutting out their light. It was no wonder Violet couldn't see peace. From her windows, she could hardly see anything at all. For people like Violet and Billy who lived on the interfaces, the only view was a backward glance into a fright-darkened past.

Violet talked about the young men who fought for the Loyalist cause during the Troubles. They felt they were fighting for their country, but were abandoned by the very system they battled to defend and ended up serving life sentences for their efforts. Protestant politicians who encouraged Loyalist action did not attend the funerals of Loyalist paramilitaries. She harboured special loathing for Ian Paisley, a long-time voice for loyalism and a Unionist politician. "I hate him," she said with a firmness I hadn't yet seen from her. "I listened to him at first, but then he turned his back on the boys and called them murderers. He was the one who opened his big mouth and kept mouthing until things started. I think if I ever came across him..." She stopped herself from finishing the sentence.

Even the Protestant clergy abandoned the boys. Church ministers refused to visit convicted paramilitaries because they considered them terrorists. "I tried to get a minister to see this one lad," Violet began, but again she stopped herself. "If I went into detail, it would be too private." Later, though, after she told me about her compassion for mothers on either side of the conflict who wept over their sons' graves, Violet relinquished the story. The "lad" she spoke of, the young prisoner the Protestant minister refused to see, was her son Thomas.

When he was fifteen, Thomas graduated out of the British army's boys' service. Four years later, the police arrested him for his role in a shooting. The court convicted him and sentenced him to life in prison. Thomas served seventeen years of his sentence, all but the last two in the Maze, a notorious prison purpose-built for convicted gunmen. "They never told me what he did," Violet said. "And I never wanted to know."

The anxiety of losing Thomas to the Maze, and the feeling that her own Protestant community had abandoned him, nearly destroyed Violet. When she visited Thomas in prison, the guards would not let her touch him. At home, Violet continued setting a plate for him at the dinner table. Her thoughts of Thomas completely overwhelmed her, and Violet's other children felt emotionally forgotten. Eventually, her psychological problems grew so severe that she was hospitalized. While Thomas sat in his prison cell, Violet lay in her hospital bed. "I served time with him," she said.

When Thomas was released from prison, he returned to a country he didn't recognize. He wondered what he had been fighting for. His enemies, men with alleged or confirmed ties to the IRA, now occupied the halls of power. "We are not happy about terrorists and ex-terrorists being in government," Violet said. Members of the UDP and Sinn Fein now shook hands for the television cameras and shared power. "They're pretty much up each other's backsides now."

"But isn't this progress?" I asked. Former rivals shaking hands and sharing power seemed a positive step forward to me.

"It's progress, but it is hard to take in, knowing what they've done through the years."

Before I left the house, Violet repeated her opinion that the walls were not coming down, at least not in her lifetime. "My father served in the British army and the B-Specials," she said. "He told me there was never peace in Ireland. And there never will be."

████

Martin Adams — a gay medical worker and former Catholic seminary student who lived with his Protestant boyfriend — wanted me to meet "regular people." By regular, he meant those who lived away from the walls. Martin knew of my interest in the barricades and that I planned on spending most of my time in Belfast meeting interface residents and community activists. He wanted me to understand that a sort of normal life existed for families like his own who were not involved with the conflict in any intimate way.

What passed for normal for a boy growing up in Belfast during the Troubles hardly resembles what I'd call a regular life. "We became hardened to bomb scares," Martin said after he picked me up from my hostel. He told me about hearing tense voices broadcast over a Marks & Spencer's PA, asking shoppers to put down their baskets and leave the store immediately. At the height of the conflict, entering Belfast's downtown meant passing through the "Ring of Steel," a military security perimeter where soldiers padded people down before allowing them to clank through the steel turnstiles. Security personnel lifted babies from their prams to check for concealed bombs and boarded buses to search for explosives.

"I remember thinking, if I were to bring a bomb on a bus, I would keep it in my lap because the soldiers only ever checked under the seats," Martin said. He became so conditioned to the searches that, while on vacation in Dublin, Martin instinctively raised his arms at the entrance to a shop in preparation for a security guard with a metal detector. His father placed his hands on Martin's wrists and gently pushed his arms down. "This is not Belfast," his father told him. "You don't have to do that here."

Martin and I drove over the bridge spanning the Lagan River into east Belfast and passed the house where he grew up. Martin's family was Catholic, but they lived in a predominately Protestant neighbourhood. He attended a Protestant school, where his father worked as the headmaster. All of Martin's boyhood mates were "Prods." He remembered how cool it was to talk to British soldiers in the Protestant neighbourhoods but not among Catholics, who considered the military their enemy.

The conflict did not collide with middle-class families like Martin's in the same way it affected the poor. They did not live on an interface. The Troubles, though, troubled everyone. "I have a recollection of some drama in the house one night in the early 1970s," Martin told me, "and Dad closing the curtains even though it was bright outside. I remember not being allowed to see something." Martin learned later that a family they knew, the Browns, were being "burnt out." The paramilitaries forced the Browns out of their home because they were Catholics living in a Protestant area, then torched the house afterwards as "extra punishment." Martin's parents wanted to shield him as best they could from such violence.

Explosions provided the bass line for Martin's childhood, even far from the interfaces. Martin remembered Loyalist paramilitaries bombing a church they used to attend and Republicans detonating a bomb at the top of the street in an attack on a civil servant's house. "I had nightmares the IRA would come and take my dad," he said. "I remember at night, as a kid and right into my adulthood, lying in bed and hearing a massive rumbling bang of a bomb. And the house shaking. And you normally switched on the news at midnight to hear where it was that got bombed."

Martin's closest encounter with sectarian violence came years later, when there was a bomb scare in the neighbourhood where he worked. The police were late evacuating his building and the bomb exploded just as he and his co-workers were being led out. "Pop. Off it went," Martin said. The blast knocked him to the ground and perforated one woman's eardrum. Paramedics took her to the hospital. "The rest of us thought it was a good excuse to go to the pub." Martin paused, as if startled by his own recollections. "It is funny talking about it now, because it's just so unreal."

When he graduated from high school, Martin studied for three years to become a Catholic priest, but he left the seminary before he was ordained. One night the racket from a British military helicopter hovering overhead interrupted students reciting the night prayer in the seminary chapel. The presiding priest saw how the noise frustrated his students, so he stopped the prayer. "Remember, God loves them too," the priest said, then joked, "Now let's say a Hail Mary for Her Majesty's forces of oppression." While Martin suspected some Catholic priests "might've got a wee bit too involved" in Republican activities, most clergymen engaged themselves in peacebuilding. The Catholic Church opposed the bombing campaigns of the IRA. Martin and his family saw Pope John Paul II when the pontiff visited Ireland. "I remember his speech because I saw it," Martin told me. "The Pope said, 'People of Ireland, on my knees I plead with you to stop the violence.' Of course, the Pope was ignored."

In spite of the Pope's censure and the violence meted out by the IRA and other Republican paramilitaries, the Nationalist side of the struggle always enjoyed better international press than their Loyalist rivals. I wondered if this dichotomy prevailed because Britain, with its dark colonial past, represented an easier and more traditional villain than "underdog" Republicans fighting the good fight. Martin agreed, though he thought cultural stereotypes also played a part. "The world, especially America, wants cutesy-pie Irish roots untainted by British oppression. They see Ireland as a country where people knit you a jumper and there's a donkey tied up outside."

"Where everyone drinks Guinness," I said. I'd spent enough time in Canada's faux Irish pubs to know the stereotype. "And where all the girls have red hair."

"And they're all named Colleen," he added. "I've never even met a Colleen."

Martin drove me past a series of Loyalist murals along Newtownards Road known as Freedom Corner. The paintings honoured Loyalist paramilitary groups with historical vignettes and slogans such as "The Ulster conflict is about nationality. This we shall maintain." A hooded gunman pointed a rifle out from the walls alongside images of the Union Jack, the Red Hand of Ulster, the English rose, and the Irish thistle. My lack of interest in the murals surprised and relieved Martin. He told me that most visitors to Belfast insisted on photographing Freedom Corner, and he felt the propagandist celebration of armed men poorly represented his city. My lack of interest surprised me too. I suppose that after the years I'd spent among wall artists—watching Yusef and Faris in Ramallah transform their wall into a message board, playing a duet in Nogales with Glenn Weyant—these uninspired portrayals did little to impress me.

In recent years, community groups have painted over many of the Troubles-era murals depicting paramilitary groups and sectarian slogans and replaced them with images that might appeal to both communities. New murals told the story of Belfast author C.S. Lewis, for example, or famed local footballer George Best. But more threatening and sectarian murals started to appear in east Belfast in the weeks before I arrived. Martin drove the car past two of them, both painted on gable walls in ominous black, white, and grey. In one, a pair of gunmen wearing black balaclavas and clutching machine guns stared out alongside a message that read "We seek nothing but the elementary right implanted in every man, the right if you are attacked to defend yourself." The artists had painted over a benign mural celebrating a bi-communal football club. Across the road, the other mural depicted three more Loyalist paramilitaries with guns drawn and posing in front of a brick wall. A proclamation read: "We are the pilgrims, master; we shall go always a little further."

"The paint's barely dry," Martin said, looking up at the freshly rendered gunmen. "It worries me, now that I think about it." The move from neutral murals to these menacing images felt like a step backwards to Martin and made him wonder if they foretold a return to sustained violence. "You see stuff like this and you think, 'Oh shit.' Why else would they take the time to put them up?"

Martin believed that in spite of the new murals and the occasional riot, most people in Northern Ireland were satisfied with the status quo. "I was Catholic by faith, but due to my upbringing I accepted that I was a British national. If anyone asks me where I came from, I say I'm from an island called Ireland." He was content with being part of the United Kingdom, especially considering the current economic strength of the U.K. in comparison with the floundering Republic of Ireland. No one with any sense would rush to exchange their pounds sterling for the Republic's quick-sinking euros. "They wouldn't be in any hurry to have a united Ireland," he said.

"What would you like to see happen politically in the North?" I asked.

"I just want it to continue getting better," he replied. "It is working for me. Every year has gotten better. Year on year, Belfast is more like a normal city. I am a gay man, who's out, who has a career in a government thing, and there is no problem with that." He added, "There are no more searches at the city centre. No more being thrown out of places because there is a bomb scare. When I recall these things for you, it seems like fiction. Like they never happened." Martin was not naive. He understood his experience differed from that of people who lived alongside the walls or those who had suffered the deaths of people close to them. Martin lost no one. "I had a blessed and safe experience of the Troubles."

I thought of Teena's life as a mother and soldier. I thought of the girls of Holy Cross and Breandán's work on the interfaces. I thought of the bottles crashing on Billy and Violet's roof and their son's incarceration. Memories are long along the Walls. They form the mortar between the bricks. Nothing about the interfaces seemed fictional or blessed and safe. Even now. I was grateful for Martin's kindness and hospitality—and for the fine chicken korma he prepared for me before I returned to Canada. I consider him a friend. But I suspect his wall-less experience of the Troubles was an aberration. Later, I told Breandán about Martin, about how his family was not affected by the conflict. "How lucky for him," Breandán replied, with something resembling a sneer.

■■■

Shankill Road was gearing up for the twelfth of July. British flags and red, white, and blue bunting hung from the lampposts over the street. Food trucks peddled hot dogs and burgers. Face-painted children tossed around parade batons, tagged the sidewalks with silly string, or drove their parents mad by hammering on tiny tin drums. Souvenir shops did brisk business. Alongside the Ulster flags and Union Jack key chains were T-shirts for infants that read "I'm so cute I must be a Prod." Tough-looking men drank beer on street corners while their equally menacing girlfriends downed neon vodka coolers. All to honour King Billy.

In the summer of 1690, the armies of Protestant King William of Orange defeated the Catholic James II on the banks of the River Boyne. James was William's father-in-law, and while the skirmish no doubt caused some uncomfortable family gatherings, the Battle of the Boyne grew to represent the ascension of Protestantism in the north of Ireland, especially over the Catholic Church. Historically, King William and his triumph on the Boyne make unlikely emblems for Protestant supremacy. William was born Dutch, not English; the Pope and most European Catholic leaders supported his campaign against James; and the Battle of the Boyne hardly stands as the decisive victory over Jacobite rule – William did not finally pacify Ireland for England until the following year. Over a century later, though, after killing a dozen mostly unarmed Catholic Defenders in a village inn, Protestant "Peep O'Day Boys" formed the Orange Institution and anointed "King Billy" their iconic and ancestral hero.

The Orange Institution evolved into the most politically influential religious fraternity in Ireland and throughout the British Empire. Orange Lodges arose, and remain, throughout the Commonwealth, in the United States, and as far afield as Togo. In Canada, four members of the Orange Order became prime minister, and an Orangeman wrote the patriotic though uncomfortably anti-French anthem "The Maple Leaf Forever." Between 1921 and 1969, every prime minister of Northern Ireland and nearly every government minister was an Orangeman, and by 1965 nearly two-thirds of all Protestant men in Northern Ireland belonged. The importance of the Orange Order has waned over the past decade and membership no longer grants such prestige. (I recommend the Loyal Orange Lodge reconsider their ancient acronym LOL if they want to be taken seriously in the digital age.) Still, every July 12 — the Glorious Twelfth — the Orangemen exercise their enduring relevance, or at least their guile, when they march in honour of King William's victory at the Battle of the Boyne.

The festivities leading up to the Twelfth included bonfires on the night of July 11. I turned off Shankill to check on the progress of the woodpile on Lanark Way. In 1690, King William's supporters lit fires on hilltops to guide his nighttime advance through the mud flats of the Belfast lough. In memory of those fires, Unionist neighbourhoods gathered around bonfires the night before the Twelfth. Some of the bonfires were immense and the pyres took weeks to construct. The bonfire on Lanark Way, just inside the Springfield Road Wall, was always Belfast's largest. When I first saw the pyre two weeks earlier, about sixty rings of stacked wooden pallets already formed a cylindrical pyre higher than the surrounding houses. Near the base, the layers of pallets alternated with layers of rubber tires. The two teenaged boys assembling the pyre paused in their labour to wave at my camera from the top of the pile. Then they turned around, dropped their pants, and mooned me.

Now, still a few days before the eleventh, the bonfire stood more than twice as high. Almost fifteen metres tall. It resembled the hive of some enormous, nightmarish bees. A larger crew of boys were working on the pyre and gathered around me as I approached. I asked them if I could take a picture of the structure. I think my interest in their efforts, and my foreign accent, amused them. One of the older boys, an unofficial "foreman" of some kind, told me they fill the centre of the vast cylinder with whatever kindling they can find: scrap wood, broken pallets, even old furniture. "The whole thing is solid," he said. The tires on the bottom weigh the entire tower down and prevent it from toppling over. I was impressed by the architectural logic.

He told me that on the eleventh they would douse the whole thing with diesel fuel and set it alight at midnight. The party, though, kicked off around eight. They invited me to come by. "Ask for Big Neil," one boy said. The rest of them smirked.

▪▪▪

On Sunday, I woke early to visit the interfaces in Duncairn Gardens in north Belfast. Beer bottles littered the morning sidewalks and pint glasses gilded with an inch of last night's lager haunted the ledges of shuttered pubs. Halfway up Antrim Road, a gaggle of men appeared in front of me swilling beer from tall cans. They were young and loud and flushed red with morning drink.

Antrim Road ran through a neighbourhood not known for trouble and far from any interfaces. I knew this intellectually, but my body's reaction to the approaching boys betrayed all reason. I felt my chest tighten and I started to sweat. I'd heard too much about the teenage toughs who itched to lay a thumping on anyone walking on the wrong side of the street. I glanced around to try to determine whether I was in a Protestant or a Catholic neighbourhood—not that it would matter. I tried to think of what I would say if the boys stopped me, and considered which way I could run and whether or not the boys were too drunk to catch me. I hadn't felt this panicked since my first protest in Jayyous when the IDF's sound grenades exploded over my head. The walls had infected me too, and I found myself in solidarity with the perpetually afraid.

I didn't make eye contact with any of the boys when I passed them. Instead, I held my breath. My biceps turned to stone and didn't soften until half a block up. I felt foolish. The boys didn't even notice me. Then I felt a rage as illogical as my fear. I was angry at the city for making me cower before a group of harmless teenagers. Instead of envying the boys for their vigour and tough-guy aesthetic, Belfast compelled me to fear them. The walls divided the city into cells of safety and danger, and as an outsider I didn't have the map. I didn't know where I was walking. I felt as if I were stepping across a minefield.

Safe from imagined threats, I turned off Antrim Road onto Duncairn Gardens, where a collection of walls and gates separated the Loyalist enclave of Tiger's Bay from the Nationalist areas of Parkside and Newington that surrounded it. Here the walls defined microgeographies so absurdly small they could hardly even be described as neighbourhoods. Parkside and Newington each consisted of fewer than half a dozen individual streets, and Tiger's Bay was barely five hundred metres wide. Yet these tiny interfaces had mutated into battlefields for nearly continuous violence between 2000 and 2002.

A brick wall topped with black steel spikes blocked vehicle access into Tiger's Bay from Duncairn Gardens, but a steel door allowed pedestrians to pass through. A CCTV camera, caged in protective wire mesh, watched over the interface from the top of a tall post. Someone had spray-painted "KAH" – Kill All Huns – on a wall across from the door, and a small plaque next to the opening bore a more cryptic message: "After that experience my feet would not take me out of my front door."

My non-encounter with the drunk boys had left me with a lingering anxiety, and I hesitated for a moment before walking through the door. The sky above Tiger's Bay flashed with the red, white, and blue of Union Jacks flapping from lampposts. A black wall rose between the row of houses on the edge of Tiger's Bay and the Nationalist homes on Newington Avenue, one street over. This wall went up in July 2002 to protect the residents of Newington from bottles and bricks thrown over from Tiger's Bay. Before the Wall, families in Newington so feared the projectiles sailing over into their backyards that they chipped in to buy hard hats for the neighbourhood's children so they could continue playing outside.

Two women sat in lawn chairs in front of their house, their freshly painted toenails drying, and while I suspected they were too busy enjoying the sunshine to notice me, I didn't want to linger in their neighbourhood. I passed back through the door and walked up Duncairn Gardens until I found a house marked with a small sign reading *Gurdwara Guru Nanak Devi Ji*. I rang the bell and a Sikh man named Santos answered, invited me in, asked me to remove my shoes, and helped me tie an orange cloth over my head. He led me up the stairs to a small prayer hall, where he showed me how to press my palms together and bow towards an intricate shrine before touching my forehead to the floor. The day's prayer had just ended and I followed Santos back downstairs, where about a half-dozen of his fellow Sikhs gathered for lunch. Santos gestured to a mat on the floor and invited me to join them. Two women emerged from the kitchen bearing metal thali trays heaped with curried potato and eggplant, yellow dal, some soft suji, and a bit of salad.

I had arranged to meet with the Sikhs because I wanted to know what it meant to live in the shadow of someone else's wall. The Indian students I'd met in Nicosia had no interest in the Cyprus Problem or the Greek–Turk binary. I wondered about this same dynamic in Belfast. I wondered how the barriers, and the conflict they enshrined, affected residents who were neither Catholic nor Protestant, nor even ethnically Irish, and had no natural allegiances to one side or the other. The fact that their temple stood right on the interface and in an area known for sectarian violence also interested me. What did it mean to be a neutral party on a battlefield?

The man who sat next to me, Mohan, had lived in Belfast for fifteen years. "It is not very peaceful," he said by way of understatement. "We avoid certain areas. The strongholds of either community."

"What do you think of the walls?" I asked.

"It doesn't look nice. It is an eyesore. But safety is more important than the eyesore. If they can have the Wall, it keeps both sides apart. In God we are all the same, but people here are very territorial." Mohan was a man of faith — more so than the others in the room, it seemed — and he spoke to me in ambiguous religious slogans. He believed the solution to the conflict in Northern Ireland could be found within the lessons of Holy Scripture. "You have to rely on God," Mohan said.

From the other side of the room, Santos scoffed at Mohan's confidence in religion. He believed instead that a revolving cycle of violence and vengeance would prolong the conflict in Northern Ireland, as well as elsewhere. "If your brother dies by your enemy, you will not forget it. You will try to take revenge tomorrow. That is very, very bad. This is why there can be no peace in Ireland. Or in Kashmir. Or in the Middle East. Or anywhere else there is war."

I appreciated Santos's cynicism and asked him what he thought of the barriers when he first arrived in Belfast.

"I thought the other side must be a jail," he said.

"It is a jail for the people who live there," Mohan added.

Santos told me about walking along the Cupar Way Wall and trying to find a passage to the other side. "I asked the people, 'Can I go there? Is it a jail?' They said, 'It is not a jail.' I said, 'Then what is it? Why is it so high?' They said, 'It is a border.' I said, 'A border for what?' They said, 'That is a Protestant area

and you are in a Catholic area.' I said, 'Okay, thank you,' and walked away."
Santos laughed at the memory. He came from India, a nation preoccupied with
marking and guarding international boundaries, and the idea of a city fortifying residential "borders" bewildered and amused him. "This is also a border
area," Santos grinned, referring to the temple's location near the interfaces.

Aside from the occasional road closure, clashes between the residents
of Tiger's Bay, Newington, and Parkside never affected the gurdwara. But
while their temple enjoyed an immunity against sectarian violence, Sikhs
and other visible minorities could not avoid old-fashioned bigotry. A young
man who was listening to our conversation spoke up from the other side of
the room. "Racism here is an altogether different thing. In Belfast there is
hatred. People here intend to harm you. They can throw anything on you.
That is not just racism. That is hatred." He suggested the barricades served
to feed this racism by making it impossible to engage with anyone but your
own community. Outsiders to the fortified monocultures were feared or
despised. For most of Belfast's history, the bigotry manifested solely between
Catholics and Protestants. But the city was no longer binary. Immigration
was providing new Others to subsequently wall out in the same way. The
haters had now added the words *paki* and *nigger* to *taig* and *hun*. "Because
of the fences," the man said, "people are not getting comfortable with the
multicultural city."

Like sectarianism, racism rained from the Belfast sky. Two years earlier,
someone had shattered the gurdwara's windows with stones. Vandals also
stoned a Hari Krishna temple and the homes of Filipina nurses. "These boys
are crazy boys," Santos said of the Irish youths. They targeted his own home
with a petrol bomb. "My house was burned," he said. Santos called the police,
but they never investigated. "They told me it was a minor case." He laughed.
"They said it is happening every hour."

Police did respond to the attack on the gurdwara, however. They came
to the temple and made a report, and the municipality paid for the smashed
window to be replaced. Then the Housing Executive built the Sikhs a wall. A
steel fence now stood over the temple's back garden. The barrier protected
against hurled stones but cut yet another scar into the city's flesh. Belfast responded to every problem, sectarian or otherwise, with barbed wire and steel.
Walls were the de facto policy. When he took me around Ardoyne, Breandán

had shown me an alleyway where young people used to gather to smoke pot. Instead of the police apprehending the teens, the community erected a locking gate to close off the alley altogether. "There's the solution. Build another fucking wall," Breandán had told me. "Rather than do something about the problem, put a fucking gate on." Now walls went up around new housing developments in anticipation of trouble rather than in response to it. Forty years of compulsive wall building had turned into an addiction.

I said to the men in the room, "In Canada, if someone throws rocks, the police don't put up a wall. They find the person who threw the rocks."

"But here there are too many rocks," Santos said.

▓▓▓

In preparation for the bonfires of the Eleventh Night, Peter Craig, Chief Fire Officer of the Northern Ireland Fire and Rescue Service, issued the following community information bulletin titled *NIFRS attendance at bonfires*:

> Each year in Northern Ireland hundreds of bonfires are lit and enjoyed in safety by many people; however, sometimes the bonfire gets out of control and requires the attendance of Northern Ireland Fire & Rescue Service.
>
> FIREFIGHTERS ARE ONLY THERE TO ENSURE YOUR SAFETY! FIREFIGHTERS ARE NOT THERE TO SPOIL ANYONE'S FUN!
>
> At this time we call on all members of the community to remember the difficult job that Firefighters do on their behalf.
>
> FIREFIGHTERS ARE PART OF YOUR COMMUNITY! AN ATTACK ON YOUR FIREFIGHTERS IS AN ATTACK ON YOUR COMMUNITY!
>
> We also ask community leaders and those with influence within the community for assistance to ensure that Firefighters are able to carry out their job without fear of attack or harassment.

PLEASE REMEMBER!
FIREFIGHTERS HAVE NO POWER TO
REMOVE BONFIRES!
FIREFIGHTERS DO NOT RISK ASSESS BONFIRE SITES!

The plea from the fire department added to my gathering dread about the bonfires. I didn't want to miss them; to be in Belfast on the Eleventh Night and not see the fires seemed ridiculous. Ian invited me to attend the bonfire at Lanark Way with him and his family. No doubt I'd be safe in Ian's company. Still, nearly everyone warned me that sectarian and alcohol-fuelled aggression added a darkness to the flame-lit parties and outsiders might not be welcome.

My walk through east Belfast on the afternoon of the eleventh did little for my unease. I paused to watch a group of men finish building a small bonfire pyre at the entrance to Cluan Place, a tiny street of Loyalist homes divided from their Nationalist neighbours in the Short Strand by one of Belfast's tallest walls. Each year, the residents of Cluan Place built a bonfire in the middle of the only road leading into Cluan Place, effectively barricading themselves inside. The flames melted the asphalt and scarred the roadway every July. This year's pyre consisted of a stack of wooden pallets, old chairs, and tabletops. Someone had written FUCK ALL TAIGS and FUCK THE SHORT STRAND on a sheet of wood facing the main road. An Irish tricolour had already been nailed to the pyre and two men were adding the yellow and white flag of the Vatican. Another man stood by waiting to attach a Palestinian flag.

Irish sectarianism breeds strange solidarities. Since the 1960s, Nationalists have aligned themselves to other liberation struggles around the world. They found a natural ally in the Palestinians. Both groups consider their homeland to be occupied by a superior military power that denies them their sovereign rights. Palestinian solidarity movements are active in Belfast, Palestinian flags fly over Nationalist areas, and images of the Palestine struggle appear in murals and in Nationalist pubs. In response, Loyalists in Belfast sympathize with the Israeli side of the conflict. The simple binaries of sectarianism explain much of this: "If my enemy supports Palestine, I therefore support Israel." But the relationship between Israel and loyalism has more nuanced origins. Loyalists, like Israelis, consider themselves the victims of terror, the bombers of Hezbollah akin to the IRA. Many Loyalists admire Israel's heavy response to terrorist attacks, and some feel the British army could learn important lessons from the IDF. Thus, the occasional Star of David flies in Loyalist Belfast — one hung outside a home in Cluan Place — and the occasional Palestinian flag gets nailed to a bonfire. I wondered what Mohammad Othman, the Stop the Wall activist in Palestine, would think of Loyalists' oddly placed hatred of his people and the burning of their flag.

In the evening, I walked up Shankill Road en route to meet Ian and watch the Lanark Way fire. I passed a few more pyres replete with Irish tricolours, Republican election posters, and Gaelic football jerseys before reaching the main street party. Three young women sang pop songs on a portable stage while blissed out, and children bounced on inflatable playground equipment. People danced and drank in the street. The air smelled of deep-fried things. Belfast's city government tries to market the Twelfth as a friendly event for tourists and families of both communities. But the juxtaposition of sectarian venom and family fun disturbed me. Burning flags and bouncy castles. Tiny drums and profanity. Balloons and scrawled calls to Kill All Taigs. I wondered, too, why the city government permitted such displays. Pubs in downtown Belfast refused entry to anyone wearing sports jerseys because team allegiance is regarded as bald-faced sectarianism. Yet on public streets, Protestants were allowed to burn the emblems of their Catholic neighbours. The connection between these wholesome delights and sectarian hate tightened my stomach. What hope was there for the walls to come down if children found joy in the hatred that erected them? For the first time in my life, I felt saddened by the happiness of others.

I turned down Lanark Way, crossing the street to avoid groups of drinkers, and reached the Lanark Way bonfire. The pyre had grown even more since I last saw it. "Big Neil" and his crew had added two enormous wooden spools to the top and fastened a giant Irish flag. Gaelic football jerseys and Sinn Fein election posters were scattered over the sides like ornaments on a Christmas tree. Two boys wearing latex gloves climbed along the top of the tower pouring diesel out of a soda bottle onto the upper pallets.

Midnight was still a couple of hours away, but a crowd of young people had already gathered to drink and dance in the shadow of the monolith.

Ulster techno music blared from speakers in a white van. I walked past the party up the road to Ian's house. He invited me into his kitchen and introduced me to his wife, Margaret. One of his young daughters came in to show me her most recent loose tooth; her two front teeth were already missing. "Some boy kissed out her front teeth," Ian teased. The girl turned away from me and begged Ian to take her to the bonfire. He told her the fire would not be lit until midnight, but she didn't believe him. She cried until he put on some cartoons for her to watch. Then he opened a couple of Budweisers and told me about the sunny day in September 1981 when Mark Stockman was shot.

Ian and Mark both worked at the Mackies factory by day and served as Ulster Defence Regiment soldiers at night. They had to check in their guns at the end of their nightly service; the UDR command deemed the men too young to carry pistols while off duty. Ian and Mark worked in different areas of the factory and planned to meet during their lunch break that day to play darts in the canteen. As they crossed the factory yard from different directions, Ian watched a car pull up and stop behind Mark. A man stepped out, rolled a black balaclava over his face, and pointed a pistol at Mark's head. Mark was facing Ian when the bullet struck. "The look on Mark's face, when he was shot, won't leave me," Ian said.

Mark was dead before he hit the ground, Ian is certain, but the gunman stood over him and kept pumping bullets into Mark's body. Then he raised his gun, pointed it at Ian, and pulled the trigger. The gun clicked. All the bullets were in Mark. "McLaughlin, you should be dead," the man said. He returned to the car, shouted, "Up the Ra!" — the IRA cheer — and drove away. Were it not for the savagery of a gunman so ignited by hate that he'd emptied his pistol into a dead man, Ian would also have lain dead in that yard. As he stood over Mark's body, Ian's first thoughts turned not to vengeance against the IRA for murdering his friend, but to contempt for a British army that failed to protect the men in their service. As a result, a twenty-year-old life lay wasted and bloody in a factory yard.

Ian left the UDR. He handed in his "sausage bag" — his army-issue duffle — to UDR command. Then he went in search of a paramilitary to join. As a former UDR soldier with weapons and tactical training, Ian was a coveted recruit. He "allegedly" joined the Ulster Defence Association because their armed wing, the Ulster Freedom Fighters, were, according to Ian, "the most militant." After watching Mark's eyes as the bullet tore through him, Ian was looking for ruthlessness.

I was grateful for Ian's candour to this point, but he wouldn't speak of his actions within the UFF. According to the Sutton Index, a grisly accounting of deaths during the Troubles, the UFF killed almost 150 people, nearly all of them civilians. I cannot know, and perhaps don't want to know, exactly what Ian was involved in and whether or not he spilled blood. All he said was, "At the time, I didn't give a fuck." Republican forces pursued Ian constantly. He stashed clothing in houses all through Belfast, and for one eighteen-month stretch he didn't sleep in the same place two nights in a row. "It was no kind of life," he said.

"What finally stopped you?" I asked.

"Having a family," Ian said. Becoming a father "mellowed him." By then, he had decided that violence no longer served Loyalist ideals. Still, "no one ever leaves a paramilitary organization." They are either forced out or eliminated. Ian retained responsibilities within the UDA but did not disclose what they were.

"What if your peacebuilding efforts are at cross purposes with your obligations to the UDA?" I asked. "Which master do you serve?"

"This doesn't happen," he replied. "There are no cross purposes. The UDA also sees peace as the way forward."

We stepped out into Ian's back garden while he smoked a cigarette. "If having a family and mellowing with age brought you out away from violence, what would bring you back? Is there anything that could draw you back to that life?"

He dragged on his cigarette and looked past me through the living room window to where his daughter had fallen asleep in front of the television. "If my family was in danger," he said.

We drained two more beers before Ian cut himself off. Violence of some kind always marred the Eleventh Night and Ian needed to keep his head clear. He stayed in contact with other community activists around the city who tried to intervene when trouble inevitably arose. As midnight approached, we walked to the bonfire with another of Ian's daughters. (His youngest was still sleeping on the couch and would be devastated when she learned she missed the fire.) When we reached the pyre, the top of the tower had just been set ablaze. Onlookers cheered and raised their beer bottles when the Irish flag lit up, burned, and disappeared. The pyre grew into a raging column of fire, twisting into itself like some hellish tornado. The heat pushed everyone back. My cheeks began to redden and sweat. Sparks and embers formed new constellations in the sky over the crowd, the larger pieces still glowing by the time they drifted to the ground. Ian's daughter, looking up like the rest of us, caught a cinder in her eye. She cried until Ian plucked it out. When the flames reached the base layers of tires, thick pythons of smoke coiled upwards, black and acrid, until I could taste burning rubber at the back of my throat. I told Ian that no other place on earth would allow this. He agreed.

Ian's cellphone began to ring as the roar of the flames waned. Someone reported that youths were rioting on a traffic roundabout at the edge of downtown. The rest of the night would be busy for Ian as he marshalled community leaders to the scene to try to calm the clashes. I left him to his work. Before I walked away, he told me to call his mobile if I got into any trouble. "I could be there in ten minutes," he said. "Or I'll call someone else to get you." I thanked him for his concern and walked back down Shankill. No one bothered me, but the streets rang with the angry joy of drunken men. Broken bottles crunched beneath my shoes and the filthy tang of burning tires hung in the air overhead.

I hadn't taken a side. I didn't know whether I agreed that Northern Ireland should be part of the Republic or if links to Britain should be maintained. I wasn't certain which community had been most hard done by. I could not see the conflict here with the same clarity with which I viewed the Israeli occupation of Palestine or America's policies along the Mexican border. Along those barricades, the economic and military disparity between the wall builders and the wall dwellers was vast, and the walls' victims were easy to discern. In Belfast, though, the wounds all seemed self-inflicted. I couldn't tell whom to blame.

I was certain, though, that the Twelfth exposed the ugly face of loyalism. The Twelfth celebrated bigotry and appeased hate. I didn't believe for a moment that the bonfires of this evening and the parades scheduled for the following day had as much to do with a 400-year-old battle as they did with a contemporary loathing of Catholics. No one could speak of "shared futures" or of walls coming down while standing in the glow of bonfires and burning flags.

■■■

Everyone told me the sun always shines on the Twelfth, but Belfast's Catholics always pray for rain. Irish Catholics harbour little love for the Orange Order and their annual marches. Few can deny the Order's overt anti-Catholic dogma. The Order bars Catholics from membership and forbids its members from marrying Catholic or even attending a Catholic Mass. For Nationalists in Northern Ireland, the Orange Order represents Protestant and Unionist supremacy over Ireland and is therefore despised. Animosity towards the Order reaches an apex on the Twelfth. Loyalists maintain that the parades celebrate Protestant culture; Nationalists argue that the marches are blunt displays of vindictive strength. Not unlike the Turkish flag that lights up over Nicosia, the Orange parade pokes a triumphalist stick in the eye of Belfast's Catholics, especially when the marchers pass through Nationalist neighbourhoods. The Orange Lodges insist they have the right to march along their "traditional routes," even if they pass through Catholic areas where they are not wanted. The British-run Parades Commission imposes restrictions on the Orangemen to keep them from parading through most Nationalist neighborhoods, but not all, and the Twelfth always ends in ugliness and riots.

The impact of the annual parades on the city's shattered psyche cannot be dismissed. Belfast's peace activists, especially those who work on the Nationalist side, dread July. Negotiations with the Parades Commission invariably fail to reach resolutions, cross-community dialogue falters, and the resulting violence nullifies gains made during the rest of the year. "In July, the people who used to talk to you suddenly don't talk to you anymore," one activist told me. At no other time of the year do the walls seem as thick or as high or as necessary.

A cold morning rain was falling on the city when I woke on the Twelfth, but true to tradition, the sky cleared by nine-thirty. I walked to the Red Barn Gallery to rendezvous with photographer Frankie Quinn. Frankie planned to

shoot the Orange parades for a new photography book and had invited me
to join him. John, a photographer friend of Frankie's, came along with us.

Frankie and I had walls in common. He'd recently travelled to Palestine
and Israel to photograph the Wall there and had produced two books of peaceline photography images in Belfast. He released his first book, titled simply
Interface Images, in 1994, during the time of the first ceasefires between the
paramilitary groups. In 2002, Frankie brought his camera back to the walls.
He marvelled that none of the peacelines had come down — if anything, they'd
been extended and strengthened — and nine new interface barriers had gone
up. Frankie wanted to show the evolution of the walls to "capture them in that
period of time." The new book, *Streets Apart*, came out in 2008. Comparing his
two books revealed that the walls in Belfast were hardly inanimate structures.
They had lives. The barricades in Nicosia degraded and died. The wood rotted,
barbed wire rusted, and sandbags split and leaked. Belfast, though, fathered
its barriers to a muscular maturity. They grew tall and strong. Only in Belfast
did I see the walls reach a kind of manhood.

Earlier that morning, Orangemen from various chapters around Belfast
and from abroad had marched from their lodges and converged on City
Hall, along with their accompanying marching bands. Frankie, John, and I
watched the parade stream through the downtown en route to the parade
grounds south of the city. Loyalist spectators lined the route to cheer on the
Orangemen and the bands. The marching Orangemen all hung V-shaped
orange sashes around their necks emblazoned with badges that suggested
their ranks and their home lodges. Some also wore black bowler hats and
white gloves that made them look like archetypal British butlers. Nearly every
short-sleeved shirt exposed tattooed arms, many inscribed with images of
King Billy astride his horse. The Orangemen varied in age, though most were
old enough for grey hair.

The marching bands, known as "kick-the-Pope" bands for their repertoire
of anti-Catholic songs, accompanied the Orangemen on their long walk. Most
were flute bands whose members whistled and trilled as they marched, filling
the streets with military birdsong. Baton twirlers led some of the bands. The
crowd favoured one young and muscled man in particular. He wielded his
baton like nunchaku, flinging the steel rod behind his neck, under his arms,

and into the air with the speed and force of a martial artist. I'd never seen a baton so resemble a weapon.

The bass drummers impressed me the most, though. Nearly every band had one, great bears of men with drums lashed to their chests and armed with a mallet in each hand. While the other members of the bands marched in formation, the bass drummers freely broke ranks and weaved and lumbered through the marchers, their elbows high, pummelling their drums until the centre of each skin resembled an immunization scar. Like the tattooed baton twirler, the big drum men seemed more warriors than musicians. I suppose this suited a parade meant to recognize a military victory, but the musical warfare lent the event a sense of menace and potential violence. Perhaps the images of the hateful bonfires still lingered, or maybe I simply dislike parades, but I shuddered each time I saw a bass drummer pound his drumskin into paste.

The Orangemen smiled and waved at the crowds lining the parade route. Many of the spectators wore red, white, and blue hats or held British flags. One woman, on seeing John's and Frankie's cameras, ran up to them and opened her eyes to show off her Union Jack contact lenses. Another woman, clearly drunk, rushed forward to lift the kilts on the marchers from Scotland. Dozens of people raised beer cans to the passing marchers and swigged toasts in King Billy's honour. Public drinking, though illegal, was part of the ritual. A police van bore the comically mild warning: "Alcohol *may* be confiscated." By the time the marchers reached the parade grounds, many of the spectators who'd been drinking all morning were pacing red-eyed and aggressive. "People are getting tanked up," Frankie said. "We should go."

We returned to the gallery and boiled water for coffee. I asked Frankie what drew him to the walls as a photographer. "I grew up in the Short Strand," he said, speaking of the tiny Nationalist enclave in east Belfast. Frankie's family had lived in "the Strand" for generations; his ancestors appeared on the 1811 census. The Quinns were there when the Northern Ireland government laid down the first barricade to separate Catholics from Protestants, in the early 1920s. At the time, the neighbourhood's Catholics suffered regular attacks from workers in the nearby shipyards, nearly all Protestants, who were easily roused by Unionist politicians to lay siege to the Strand. "All a politician had to do was go down and give a gay speech,"

Frankie said. The workers came up from the yards and pelted the Catholics with metal bolts and rivets used on ship hulls. The thrown shrapnel gave rise to the ironic term "Belfast confetti," which became both the title and the subject of a 1987 poem by Ciaran Carson that reads:

> Suddenly as the riot squad moved in, it was raining exclamation marks,
> Nuts, bolts and car-keys. A fount of broken type.[18]

The clashes escalated in 1921 when IRA gunmen shot into a mob of marauding shipworkers and killed two men. The British, fearing revolving vengeance, erected Belfast's first interface barrier. Frankie had a *Belfast Telegraph* article from 1922 that compared this barricade to Hadrian's Wall. "The language is striking," Frankie said. "To keep the warring tribes apart, we have to put up a wall like Hadrian did."

This first wall no longer exists. The Short Strand shrank over the years and the street where the Wall stood is gone. The Northern Ireland Office built new brick barriers around the Strand in the early years of the Troubles. Since then, the NIO has extended the walls with steel slatting or wire mesh. Sometimes both. They added metal spikes and barbed wire as well, but only on the Nationalist side — an insinuation, Frankie believes, that Catholics are the aggressors. Most of the walls around the Strand now stand more than seven metres high, and only the western edge of the Strand, where the neighbourhood meets the Lagan River, remains unwalled. "We're fucking surrounded," Frankie said.

I thought of Qalqilya, the Palestinian city almost completely enclosed by the West Bank Wall. "Why do you stay there?" I asked.

"Comfort," he said. All his friends and family still lived in the Strand. And the walls, for all their imposing sins, inspired a sense of kinship in those whom they surrounded. Unable to look outwards, the neighbours looked out for each other. Frankie never locked his car or the front door of his house. He believed the Strand's sense of community came from its "total isolation." The neighbourhood was peaceful most of the time. "The shit only happens at certain times of the year," Frankie said. "During the summer madness."

And there was at least one other reason to remain in the Strand. Frankie spoke with affection of a neighbourhood pub where it didn't matter what religion you were, "you always get treated like shit."

John knew the place. "They check you for weapons at the door. And if you don't have a gun, they give you one."

John planned on going to Ardoyne to photograph the Orangemen from Loyalist "upper" Ardoyne returning to their home lodge. The intersection of the Crumlin and Ardoyne roads became a flashpoint every year as marchers came through and passed about a dozen Nationalist homes. The parade angered residents and their supporters, who wanted the marchers rerouted away from their neighbourhood. John wanted to shoot the inevitable clashes between protesters and police. Frankie, bored with photographing riots, opted out.

John and I arrived at the Ardoyne junction an hour before the parade was expected to come through, and the police presence was already massive. Rows of armoured police vans lined both sides of the street, and police wearing full riot gear took positions on every corner. Water cannon trucks, looking like brawny, post-apocalyptic RVs, were parked at the ready. The community, too, had turned out in numbers. Families grilled burgers in their front gardens. Teenage girls in half shirts and too much makeup pranced in front of tough-looking boys. Only the army of body-armoured police officers and their vehicles suggested something other than a block party was going on. No one knew exactly what would happen, but nobody wanted to miss whatever did. Especially not the young. For Belfast teens, the night of the Twelfth meant gathering your mates to watch the riots. The clashes always provided a bit of *craic*, the Irish word for fun.

Before the Orange marchers appeared, a group of noisy protesters advanced up a side street, Brompton Park, towards the intersection. A phalanx of riot police and armoured vans rushed to block them. The protesters held signs identifying themselves as the Greater Ardoyne Residents Collective. Some had placards reading "No Parades = No Violence" or "End Sectarian Marches." One sign said "FARUC" — Fuck All Royal Ulster Constabulary, the former name of the Police Service of Northern Ireland. (My ability to decipher Belfast-acronymed loathing had sharpened. FA always stood for Fuck All, just as FT was Fuck The and KA was Kill All.) I stood immediately behind the line of police officers. Black body armour covered almost their entire bodies.

Their shins, shoulders, and necks were all plated against attack. They carried pistols and riot batons at their sides and hooked handcuffs to the small of their backs. Black balaclavas beneath their helmets ensured only their eyes and noses were visible. They resembled science fiction soldiers.

Despite the impressive gear, the police garnered little respect. I watched a photographer push his way past one of the officers and stand in front of him to get a clear shot of the protesters. The officer shouted at him to step aside. The photographer turned, glared at the policeman, and told him to fuck off.

"I said get outta the way," the officer shouted and pushed the man from behind with his riot baton.

"And *I* said fuck off!"

The officer jabbed the man again. "I'll put it up your arse!"

The photographer turned to the officer, glared at him through his bullet-proof visor, and sneered, "You're no police force!"

"I'll put it up your arse!"

"Yeah? Fuck you!" The photographer pushed past and walked ahead. The police officer did not respond.

The demonstrators quieted to allow a spokesman to make a speech through a megaphone. First, he assured the police officers that their protest was peaceful. He complained that the Parades Commission and the police service were treating the Nationalist residents of Ardoyne as second-class citizens while allowing the Loyal Order to pass unhindered through their neighbourhood. Then he demanded the demonstrators be allowed to proceed to the roadside to protest the marchers. The police held their line. The action lay at the heart of the Nationalist community's grievance over the parades. Not only does the government, represented by the Parades Commission, allow Loyalist marchers to proceed through neighbourhoods where they are not wanted, but the police service forbids the local residents from demonstrating against them. The citizens of Ardoyne were banished from their own streets to allow outsiders to march through. For the Nationalist residents of Ardoyne, the action proved the Loyalist bias of the police service.

In the end, the police did allow a different group of demonstrators to reach the roadside. About a dozen men and women silently held placards with messages such as "Respect Residents' Rights," "There is an Alternative Route," and "Shame on You." As these quiet protesters lined up along

Crumlin Road to wait for the Orange marchers, I saw Breandán storming up the sidewalk. He was scowling and barely stopped long enough to shake my hand. "I'm tired. I'm pissed off. And I'm fed up," he said and stomped away.

Farther up Crumlin Road, beyond the protesters and police lines, about a hundred Unionist supporters stood behind a banner reading LOYALIST ARDOYNE. The crowd resembled the start of a marathon, but this was more of a finish line. The group marked the end of the march for the local Orange Order, and they waved Ulster flags and Union Jacks and were ready to grant the marchers a hero's welcome. John wanted to photograph this homecoming. We rushed to the top of Crumlin Road just before the marchers appeared. The Parades Commission dictated that the parades must walk silently when they passed through Nationalist areas. Bands were forbidden to play and the marchers couldn't sing. The procession, then, resembled a military funeral: unnaturally quiet aside from a single drummer who tapped out a steady cadence for the marchers on his snare drum.

When the Order came within a few metres of their welcome party at the top of the road, the snare drummer offered a little drum roll. On cue, the parade burst into music like a bomb going off. The musicians started playing, the marchers started to sing, and the crowd threw up their hands and cheered. Then they all moved aside to allow the marchers to pass through.

The end of the march signalled the beginning of whatever was to follow. Everyone's attention moved from the parade on Crumlin to the young men who'd quickly taken the place of the peaceful demonstrators on Brompton Park. Most wore track suits and hoodies that they pulled up tight over their heads and zipped up over their mouths and noses. Others concealed their faces with scarves or bandanas. One man wore a black balaclava and a camouflage jacket and looked as if he'd stepped down from a paramilitary mural. Some also wore gloves to conceal wrist tattoos. Every hand, gloved or not, carried a stone or piece of brick. Teenage girls milled around among the masked men and smoked cigarettes. The residents of the neighbourhood — men, women, families with small children — watched from sidewalks and street corners. The police, in the meantime, parked armoured vans in two tight lines on Crumlin Road to flank the entry to Brompton Park. They had resigned themselves to a war and wanted to shrink the battlefield.

Once the masked men assembled, they started to hurl rocks and bottles at the police lines. The officers took cover behind the vans. One by one, the projectiles sailed overhead. Onlookers applauded when a stone bounced off the roof of a van or landed on the protective steel mesh over the windshields, but the rioters rarely hit anything at all. Many of them threw blindly over the roof of the betting salon on the corner of Brompton Park, their stones clattering onto the asphalt. One boy's sloppy throw earned giggles from the smoking girls and a rebuke from the gathered crowd. "Get that rubber arm outta there!" the man next to me shouted. Another onlooker carried his three-year-old daughter on his shoulders. She was crying. The man reached up, pinched her cheek, and told her not to worry. He continued to watch the show as she trembled above him.

The melee escalated as the rioters multiplied and their boldness increased. Steady volleys of stones and bottles sailed from Brompton Park onto the street. A pair of rioters lit a Roman candle and pointed it around the corner at the police line. The flares shot randomly into the street and scattered a group of spectators who scolded the rioters' clumsiness. Nothing hit the police. Once the Roman candles were spent, the rioters moved on to petrol bombs. They lit cloth wicks stuffed into Budweiser bottles filled with gasoline and hurled them at the police. The first mis-thrown petrol bomb hit an overhanging roof just above the thrower's head and exploded against the cinder-block wall. The neighbours laughed and jeered. Better arms threw the next bombs, which crashed in front of the police lines, smearing orange flames over the pavement. Another exploded on a police officer's riot helmet and set it briefly on fire. The officer, though, appeared unhurt.

The riot police rumbled the water cannon truck to the edge of Brompton Park and blasted rioters who dared come within range. Then the rioters ramped up their assault. Two men in balaclavas sped a stolen car out of Brompton Park and spun it onto Crumlin Road. The drivers barely controlled the car, and I feared they would barrel into the crowd of onlookers. They managed to stop the car in the middle of the road, a few metres in front of the police line. The men stepped out, poured petrol onto the seats, and lit the car on fire. The water cannon fired a single ambivalent blast of water at the car, but the police seemed content to let it burn.

I'd never witnessed a car on fire before; the speed of its destruction impressed me. The smell of burning vinyl upholstery filled the street. Then the gas tank exploded with a blast far less dramatic than in the movies I'd seen. The car horn went off and the sustained honk added a strange comedy to the violence. As the tires burned and melted, the car seemed to sink into the pavement. Black smoke shaded the street and granted better light for the photographers, whose shutters went off like machine guns. The water cannon–wet streets sharpened the stench of smoke and gasoline the way everything smells more intensely after it rains.

The riot continued with a randomness that made me nervous. This was not like the action I'd witnessed in Jayyous. There was no cadence to this battle. No apparent choreography. I tried to remain in a neutral space on the side of the action and out of range of the rioters. At one point, though, everything shifted. The police surged one way, the rioters scattered in the other direction, and as I scrambled to avoid standing between the two factions, I ended up among the rioters themselves. Nobody paid any attention to me, but I didn't feel safe. Returning to the other side of the street, though, would have meant crossing in front of the police line. So I hung back, watched a group of boys pour gasoline from a white jug into beer bottles and waited for a break in the fighting.

Instead of a lull, the rioters launched a surprise frontal assault. A battalion of about ten masked men burst out of a side street onto Crumlin Road and charged the police line of armoured vans. Using rocks, fence posts torn from nearby gardens, and their bare fists, the boys pounced on the police vehicles and forced them back several metres. The move was fierce. The police retreat, though slight and brief, emboldened the rioters. Being near them, I could feel them crackle with savage joy. "We need more weapons!" one of them screamed, and the rioters started to tear apart the neighbourhood like a pack of wild dogs. They ripped gates from their hinges and downspouts from the sides of houses. Broke paving stones into throwable chunks. Pulled street signs out of the ground. Kicked bricks loose from garden walls. Smashed anything they could find into things they could throw. They destroyed without hesitation, as if the neighbourhood were sacrificing itself, piece by piece, to be hurled at policemen in the name of some unclear cause. Hours earlier, protesters had gathered to demand respect for their community. Now the rioters seemed intent on breaking it into pieces.

I thought of the clashes in Jayyous and of the shabaab. They too were young men throwing stones at armoured enemies. But the shabaab never seemed like thugs. They possessed a grace that these rioting teens lacked. Even when their weekly battle against the IDF resembled sport, the action was born out of ideals. They fought for something, and there was dignity in those slung stones. The shabaab would never destroy their own village. There was no such honour on these wet Belfast streets. The balaclava boys showed no sense of cause. No righteousness born of injustice. Water from the cannon streamed like black fingers over the road and into the sewers. The car, still smoking, was now a shell of hot metal. Shattered glass, rocks, beer cans, and broken bricks were spread over the pavement like a pox. No wonder so few people in Belfast want the walls to come down.

While the rioters armed themselves, and the police waited for the next assault, I slipped across to the safer side of the street and behind the police line, where I rejoined John. "This is so fucking stupid," I said. My time among Belfast's colourful profanity had loosened my own curse-valve, and the vandalism I'd just witnessed made me angry. "What's the point of any of this?" John didn't answer. He just looked at me as if I could never understand. "If I asked one of those boys why he was rioting, would he even know? What would he say?"

"He would tell you to fuck off," John said. "And you would risk getting punched."

The riot settled into a comfortable standoff. The police regained the short section of street they'd lost and effectively hemmed the rioters in at Brompton Park with vans and the water cannon. The officers seemed content to absorb the stones and bottles from their positions and wait until the violence burned itself out. When rioters tried to advance onto Crumlin Road, the officers fired flash bombs and 37-millimetre "baton rounds"—hollow-nosed plastic bullets—from their riot guns to punch the youths back. The photographers gathered the empty shells as souvenirs. John handed one to me.

I felt my cellphone vibrate in my pocket. It was Ian. "I am on the other side of the street," he said. "I can see you from where I am standing. I just want to make sure that you are all right."

"I'm staying close to the journalists. They seem to know how to stay out of danger."

"Well, keep your wits about you." He hung up. His call surprised me and eased a little of my anger.

John and I stood behind the police line for half an hour longer. By ten o'clock, the police officers were starting to lean, bored and weary, against their vans. Aside from the occasional stone rattling onto the street, nothing much was happening, and John figured we wouldn't miss anything if we left. Before we walked back up the road to his car, I saw two young boys, about ten years old, standing nearby on the sidewalk. One casually kicked at a loose chunk of cracked sidewalk. He nudged his friend and pointed to the concrete. "Help me get that out," he said. He wanted to hurl it at the police. His friend glanced down at the pavement, then both boys looked at me. When they saw me listening, they walked away.

███

Breandán fell in love with Joanne when he was ten years old, but he needed six years to muster the nerve to ask her out. Not that there was anything shy about Breandán; there was just something about Joanne. One night, when they were teenagers and walking home from a date, Breandán got into a fight with four Protestant boys. "My father always told me that if you are ganged up on, make sure you give at least one guy the same as you're getting," he told me. Joanne watched as the boys brawled from one end of Ardoyne to the other. They hit each other with fists and stones and bottles.

After the fight, as Breandán stood hunched and bleeding, Joanne told him they would have to break up. Breandán asked her why. "Because I enjoyed that too much," she said.

"I'm glad you had fun, because I sure didn't."

"Yes you did," she said.

Breandán told me this story in his kitchen as he stirred a pot of spaghetti sauce. He may have been an Irish Republican, but Breandán was part Sicilian and put together a fine sauce. He and Joanne reunited in their twenties and got married. Now they had three beautiful, clever daughters. "Are you going to talk about that sauce all night?" the eldest, Aoife, asked him as he extolled the recipe. I didn't suspect Breandán's girls let him get away with much. Like Ian, Breandán doted on his daughters.

After dinner, Breandán and I had a Bushmills and water before Joanne drove us, along with Aoife, to the Gaelic football match at Clarmont Park. "*This* is football," Breandán said. "That other game is soccer." Despite his enthusiasm for the sport itself, the squad from Down soundly trounced Breandán's team, the Antrim Saffrons. Afterwards, Joanne came to pick up Aoife. Breandán and I walked downtown to a pub where he planned to meet friends. It was a long way to walk, though, so we stopped to rest at a pub on Springfield Road. Then again at a pub on the Falls. Then another before finally reaching Madden's.

As we walked, I told Breandán what Ian had told me, that members of the UDA never really leave the UDA. Breandán said the same was not true for the Republican groups. He pre-empted my next question by saying, "I've always been active in Republicanism." The phrase was akin to Ian's "allegedly": his way of letting me know, without telling me outright, that he volunteered for the IRA.

Breandán told me Bobby Sands and the hunger strikers inspired him towards "active Republicanism" when he was a young man. In 1981, a group of IRA prisoners in British jails demanded to be treated as political prisoners rather than common criminals. They staged a staggered hunger strike. First one prisoner would refuse food. Then, a week later, another prisoner would join the strike. Then another. A new prisoner began a hunger strike each week. The strikers knew that if their demands were not met, their eventual deaths would roll out one after the other. The strategy was brilliant. Bobby Sands was the first prisoner to refuse food. During his hunger strike, Republicans entered him as a candidate in the U.K. election to bring more attention to their cause. Sands won his seat by a tiny margin but starved to death less than a month later. The next hunger striker died a week after Sands, followed by two more prisoners the week after that. Over the summer of 1981, ten hunger strikers starved to death in prison. Nationalists refer to them as "The Ten." "The men were giants to me," Breandán said. He compared them to suicide bombers—those who, when deprived of all else, turn their bodies into weapons.

We spoke about the riot I'd witnessed in Ardoyne. Breandán insisted none of the rioters were from Ardoyne at all and certainly none of his Draw Down the Walls kids were involved. We spoke about art and books. When I asked him what novel I should read that best describes the conflict in Northern Ireland, he replied, "The *Iliad*." He told me about a woman he was with before he married Joanne and the daughter they had together. He told me that his nine-year-old daughter once asked him if he knew anyone in the IRA. He told her, "Yes, of course."

"I suspect her next question was whether you were in the IRA," I said.

"No. She never asked. And I never told her."

Breandán's honesty and openness reminded me of my conversations with Martin, Billy and Violet, Ian and Teena. Each offered me, a stranger with a notebook, glimpses into their pasts and personal lives that I had done nothing to deserve. Perhaps this is part of the generous Irish character or their quickness to friendship, I don't know. I was grateful, though, that I found very little standing in the way of the people I met. I don't know if it is ironic or apt that those most divided by physical walls, most mutilated by barriers, were also the most willing to let me in past their own.

Breandán and I rang the bell at Madden's and stared up at the closed-circuit camera. The bartender buzzed us in. No other pub I visited in Belfast — and I visited plenty — had such a security measure. I never knew if the security door at Madden's was just a relic of more violent times or if there was actually something to fear. We went upstairs and found Breandán's friends already crammed into a booth too small for them. About a dozen "session" musicians sat around the table next to us playing their instruments and downing their pints. The bar only paid one or two of the musicians. The rest showed up with their instruments — flutes and guitars, pipes in black cases, bodhran frame drums — and squeezed into empty seats to play just for the *craic*. Men in plaid shirts, blazers, and blue denim. Women in pretty dresses. They creaked the wooden chairs as they battered their drums and bowed their fiddles.

A few more beers with Breandán's crew and the night started to slip away. I remember, though, hugging Breandán when we said goodbye. And I remember a moment in the men's room. I stood at the long communal urinal next to an older gentleman while Breandán used the toilet in the stall. When

4

the man finished and walked out, Breandán tapped me on the shoulder. "The man you were pissin' with bombed the Brighton hotel. Tried to kill Margaret Thatcher." Then he put a finger to his lips. "Shhh."

In 1994, a three-metre corrugated wall went up in Alexandra Park, splitting a public green space into sectarian halves. The Wall divided Catholic trees from Protestant trees. Nationalist monkey bars from Unionist monkey bars. The barrier severed a pathway and even crossed the river — a wall built where a bridge should be. Authorities erected the barrier because gangs of youths used the parkland as a battleground. The Wall didn't stop the brawls at first; rival gangs used to tunnel underneath. Eventually, though, the combatants found more convenient places to fight.

In September 2011, the Alexandra Park Wall became the first barrier ever to open in Belfast. Thanks to the efforts of Breandán, Ian, and the community associations they represented, along with like-minded activists and city politicians, the two sides of the park reunited. Prior to the opening, a gate had been installed in the Wall. Then an artist with Draw Down the Walls "disappeared" the gate just as he'd done with the barrier on Flax Street, by fixing high-resolution photographs over both sides that depicted the view if the gate didn't exist. Finally, before a gathering of dignitaries and media, the gate swung open. Two primary school girls — one Catholic, the other Protestant, and both too young to remember the park without the Wall — met at the line as the ribbon was cut. David Ford, the local justice minister, said it was an "important day for Northern Ireland."

I had returned to Canada by that time and was disappointed the opening hadn't occurred while I was in Belfast. Then again, the hate-filled days of summer hardly stirred acts of reconciliation, even symbolic ones; the parties involved had to wait until the flames died down. The news from Alexandra Park failed to hearten me, though, especially after I'd witnessed the fangs of July. The terms of the opening were not inspiring either. For a three-month trial period, the park gate would open on weekdays between nine in the morning and three in the afternoon. At night, and all weekend long, the gate would be locked shut, so children could pass through the new gate only during the times they would normally be in school. Even the symbolism of the gesture felt thin. Unlike most of the interface barriers, the Alexandra Park Wall does not stand in a residential area. The barrier never offered protection to people's homes in the same way as, say, the Wall at Springfield or in nearby Tiger's Bay. The barrier hadn't accomplished anything for nearly twenty years. I couldn't help but feel that this wall was relatively easy to open. I doubted that this was, in fact, an important day for Northern Ireland.

I recalled my visit to Belfast City Cemetery, a burial ground dating back, like Alexandra Park, to the late 1800s. Following a map I'd copied from a city website, I walked among the old graves on the southern edge of the cemetery. The plots were overgrown and unkempt. Plastic bags and empty cans of Harp littered some of the sites. Some gravestones had broken or the carved names of the interred had nearly eroded away to anonymity. Others were marked by ornate metal bars that reminded me of bed frames. The graves were not lined up in neat rows but scattered haphazardly over the grounds. In the southwest corner, though, I found what I'd been looking for: a narrow path of grass extending between gravestones in a straight line. Buried beneath this line was a wall built to separate dead Catholics from dead Protestants.

When William Gay of Bradford, England, first designed the cemetery in 1867, he instructed his masons to build a nine-foot underground wall of black stone between the Catholic and Protestant sections of the cemetery. The division turned out to be unnecessary; a dispute between the Catholic bishop and Belfast officials meant no Catholics were ever buried on either side of the line. Still, the Wall remains. I walked back and forth overtop the buried barricade. Clover and white wildflowers grew out of the grass. Perhaps I was imagining it, but the ground felt firmer beneath my feet.

The underground wall provides a cheap and easy metaphor. I understand the idea of consecrated ground, and I know the cemetery's founders built the Wall long before the Troubles sowed the peacelines I'd come to Belfast to see. Still, the buried wall speaks to the permanence of Belfast's barriers. They rise between the living and follow the dead into the ground. The walls stand not just as architecture but as archaeology. Fossilized artifacts of enduring division. I found the deep scar tissue of an underground wall to be a more relevant symbol of the mutilated city than the image of little girls frolicking through a gate that opens every once in a while.

The Great Wall of Montreal
The l'Acadie Fence

Canada defines itself by openness, both in geographical terms — aside from Russia, no nation boasts such a span — and by our perceived tolerance. Canadians think of themselves as broad-minded. Friendly and welcoming and polite to an almost comic fault. There is space for everyone within our vast borders. Canada is a nation without declared enemies and thus above the fearful loathing of the wall builders elsewhere. "We don't even lock our front doors," Canadians claim, though this an exaggeration if not an outright lie. Canadian patriotism manifests most often as smugness. I'd travelled around the world to see the barricades built by less enlightened nations, and as I stood next to each, I told myself that this could never happen where I am from. Canadians don't build walls. Except, of course, when they do.

A wall built of chain links and steel posts separates the Town of Mount Royal, one of Montreal's most affluent areas, from Parc-Extension, the second-poorest urban neighbourhood in Canada. I had heard the barrier called the Fence of Shame and the Wall of Shame — the same term used for the berm in the Western Sahara. I had read writers who referred to the barrier as "segregation fencing" or an "apartheid barrier." When the Town of Mount Royal, known locally as TMR, erected their wall fifty years ago, one of Montreal's French daily newspapers compared the stretch of chain links to a concentration camp enclosure. The fence might not possess the infamy of the other walls I'd seen — even most Montrealers have never heard of it — but I couldn't resist visiting a barrier slathered with such hyperbole, particularly in my own country.

The l'Acadie Wall runs less than two kilometres along the west side of Boulevard de l'Acadie. For most of its length, the barrier stands about two metres high, a little shorter than the shrubbery planted alongside it. I arrived in Montreal in the early fall of 2011 after a wet summer. The rain-thickened hedge and delicate pink blossoms almost concealed the barrier entirely. Only the occasional gap in the foliage revealed the chain links and fence posts. The wire sagged. Green paint flaked off the poles, and rust scabbed the chain links. Five pedestrian gates on squeaky spring hinges, the only openings in the barrier, had been recently reinstalled. The silver metal still shone. The rest of the structure, though, betrayed its fifty years. The l'Acadie fence was the oldest wall I had visited, and it wasn't aging well.

There were no checkpoints along this wall. No coils of barbed wire. No security cameras or motion sensors or bored young men with guns. No teenage toughs waiting on the other side to lay beatings on trespassers. No groomed sand betrayed my footsteps as I passed through. No posted notices warned me of *Mortal Danger* or to *Keep Out*. Instead, bright bilingual signs on the gates read *Welcome* on one side and *Be Careful* on the other. For an alleged tool of apartheid, the Wall appeared rather gentle. Politely Canadian. Especially after the other walls I'd seen.

After three years of travel, all I had seen weighed heavily on me. If Mauer-krankheit meant "Wall Disease," by the time I reached Montreal I was suffering from *mauermelancholia* — a word I invented to describe the gloom born of too much time along the walls. I had started seeing barbed wire in my dreams. I avoided speaking about my project because, each time I did, someone quoted Robert Frost's "Good fences make good neighbours," which made me want to scream. More than the aesthetics of the walls, I grew weary of the tragedies the walls represented. I greeted every news story about Israeli-Palestinian peace talks with bitterness and regarded even pro-Palestinian activists with cynicism. I ignored the Cypriot elections and scoffed at every report about the looming reunification of the island. I cringed each time Republican Party leadership candidates in America debated the U.S.–Mexico border wall. (Herman Cain said he wanted an electric fence on the border. Then he said he was joking. Then he said he wasn't. Then he was gone.) The U.S. Customs and Border Protection crowed that a reduction of migrant apprehensions and dead bodies along the border proved their wall was working. *Only* 340,252 detentions and 310 corpses, the wall builders grimly boasted. Skeptics knew that a stronger wall was proving less a deterrent than America's failing economy. Migrants were not going to risk crossing the line if there were no jobs on the other side.

The Arab Spring had sprung, revolutions rattled, and newspapers reported on those who "took to the streets." But no one took to the walls. Those conflicts hardly budged, as if they'd been cast in the same concrete and steel as the barriers themselves. When I visited the Saharawi refugee camps, Mustapha Said Bashir predicted war within the year. He turned out to be wrong, and I was disappointed. I felt ashamed for wanting war, but at least a war would prove something was moving along the walls.

The world had not seen a significant barrier fall since the Berlin Wall tumbled more than twenty years earlier. Berlin marked the anniversary in 2009 with noisy pomp and celebration. Dancers dressed as angels descended from rooftops. A thousand giant foam dominoes knocked each other down along the Wall's route while fireworks exploded overhead. Rock band U2 gave away ten thousand free tickets to their show in front of Berlin's Brandenburg Gate, but the irony-blind organizers built a two-metre wall around the venue to keep non-ticketholders out. World leaders, past and present, made hopeful speeches about liberation and freedom, words that suggested the fall of the Berlin Wall ought to inspire us to tear down our own.

The buoyant rhetoric, though, disregarded the difference between the Berlin Wall and the walls I'd travelled to see. East Germany brought down their wall in 1989 as a sign of surrender. The Soviet experiment had failed, and the Eastern bloc realized they couldn't win the Cold War. The falling Berlin Wall was their white flag. The walls I'd visited, though, expressed the opposite. The *rising* of these walls was the surrender. The walls stood as evidence that their conflicts were unwinnable and permanent. When diplomacy and negotiation crumbles, when the motivation to find solutions wanes and dies, when governments resign themselves to failure, the walls go up. Instead of trying to solve the Israeli-Palestinian conflict, we build a wall. Instead of finding a way for Catholics and Protestants to live together in Belfast, we build a wall. Instead of addressing the despair that leads migrants across our borders, we build a wall. The walls admit our defeat. We throw up a wall right after we throw up our hands.

And our walls remain standing because we've allowed their fictions to win us over. I found it difficult not to blame September 11 for this. The attacks made us gullible and convinced us that there is something to fear on the other side of wherever we are. Something we are unable, or unwilling, to confront. Even the walls that predated 9/11 — Belfast's interface barriers, the fortified line on Cyprus, the Western Sahara berm, the embryonic barricades along America's border with Mexico and India's border with Bangladesh — saw their value surge after the attacks. For the old walls, September 11 was an act of renovation. We sat rapt and fearful in the walls' freshened shadows and started to believe the invasion dramas they staged for us. We celebrated the Berlin Wall's fall because we knew the bogeyman on the other side had lost his fangs. But we have new bogeymen now.

▓▓▓

In the late 1950s, the City of Montreal widened Boulevard de l'Acadie, then called McEachran Avenue, and converted what was a dirt track into a busy urban thoroughfare. McEachran formed the eastern boundary of the Town of Mount Royal, a civic entity surrounded by Montreal but municipally autonomous. (Not just a neighbourhood and not exactly a town, TMR stands as a geopolitical anomaly — yet another place that does not quite exist.) The new highway caused Town residents to worry for their children's safety, and they petitioned the town council to build a barrier along the Town's eastern edge. According to council meeting minutes from May 1960, the Town contracted builders to erect a two-metre-high chain-link fence with a single pedestrian opening and "an appropriate hedge." With an efficiency rarely seen in civic government projects, the Town's builders finished the fence in a few weeks.

The new fence faced Parc-Extension, a low-income Montreal neighbour-hood crowded, then as now, with new immigrants. Montrealers around the city saw the fence as a class barrier, a structure built by the rich to separate themselves from the poor across the Boulevard. They saw the fence as a wall. It was the sixties, after all; sensitivities to class prejudice, real or imagined, bloomed. In a letter to TMR's town council, the City of Montreal conceded that while they had no authority to remove the barrier, Montrealers "have been greatly offended by the unsightly fence." A former president of the TMR landlord association admitted the barrier was a terrible political symbol and said "everywhere we go in Montreal they want to talk about the fence."

The Town of Mount Royal did not want to talk about the fence anymore. At least not to me. I sent several emails to the Town hoping to arrange meetings with members of the municipality. Ava Couch, the Town Manager, wrote: "Good morning. Thank you for your e-mail, however the Town does not wish to be involved in this project. Have a nice day." The cheery missive was my only correspondence with Town officials. I imagined the Town did not want their already vilified fence associated with the world's big bad barriers. I suspected, too, that they found the juxtaposition absurd. I couldn't blame them. The rusty fence hardly cast the same contentious shadow as, say, the West Bank Wall, Belfast's interface walls, or the Wall along the U.S.–Mexico border. But I wanted to know what, if anything, those Great Walls and TMR's tiny fence had in common.

Figuratively walled out by TMR, I spent most of my time in Parc-Extension, where anger over the l'Acadie Wall seethed the hottest, at least in the 1960s. Residents in Parc-X believed the Town erected the barrier to keep them out. "I was quite mad at the fence. A lot of people were incensed," Nick Semeniuk told me. "The people in TMR were always like that back then. They wanted to keep out the riff-raff." I met Nick in his home on the east side of Boulevard de l'Acadie, the same house where he lived when the Wall first rose across the street. "There was never a barrier here. And suddenly they put this barrier up to keep us out, and that's really what it was."

Nick looked much younger than his seventy-seven years. He was born in Parc-Extension in a building on nearby rue Jean-Talon that has since been torn down. "We used to call it the Millionaire Block because we were all poor. No one had any money. We were there to feed the cockroaches and the mice, and there were plenty of them, let me tell you." For Nick, the Wall across the street expressed in galvanized mesh a rivalry that had always smouldered between the Parc-Xers and the Townies on the other side. Not outright warfare—Montreal is no Cyprus—but the rather more benign enmity of teenagers from opposite sides of an economic line. Parc-X was a poor and immigrant neighbourhood; TMR was a rich, white, and anglophone one. Neighbourhood toughs from TMR hung out at the corner store near Nick's mother's house and picked fights with the local boys, and Parc-X kids felt unwelcome in TMR. "You couldn't go to their parks. They would chase you out and say, 'You're from Parc-X and you don't belong here,'" Nick said. "So we beat them up."

He told me about an afternoon confrontation when he and a group of his Parc-X mates came upon one of their cross-boulevard rivals, a boy who'd chased him out of TMR in the past. "He was scared because there were four of us and only one of him," Nick said. "So we told him, 'We won't beat you up. We won't do anything. But you have to sit in the poison ivy.'" Nick laughed so hard at the memory he nearly choked. "That was mean! That was really mean!"

I thought of Breandán's epic four-on-one fist fight in Ardoyne. Lucky for Nick, he and his friends only tussled with soft Townie boys and didn't have to contend with the teenaged brawlers of Belfast. In both places, though, one's rivals were defined entirely by which side of the Wall their families lived on. The interface barriers in Belfast and the fence along l'Acadie dispensed with the need for personal vendettas. Geography alone bred rivalry. All you needed for an enemy was a kid from the other side. Stepping through the walls was no mere trespass, but an invasion to be repelled.

Nick saw the Wall go up and he saw it, briefly, come down. Months after the Wall was first erected, fifty carloads of students from the Université de Montréal celebrated their winter carnival by driving to l'Acadie Boulevard and laying siege to the Wall. They jumped out of their cars and, clad in wool toques and mittens, wrenched the wire back and forth until they uprooted the posts. Two twelve-metre sections of chain links collapsed onto the snow. The students chanted slogans declaring the Wall an affront to national unity. They likened Quebec to Cuba, though I suspect they would've chosen East Germany for their comparison had the Berlin Wall been erected then.

They were still trampling on the wreckage when police came and chased them away. Nick felt solidarity with the students and joy at watching them tear the Wall down. "It wasn't a riot, but it was a lot of noise," he said. "And

I was here watching the fun." Their act of civil defiance was short-lived. TMR resurrected the Wall by the end of the day.

The student attack was the only physical assault on the Wall, but local politicians from both communities repeatedly assailed the barrier in the press and in their respective council chambers. Only two years after the Wall went up, Reginald Dawson, the sitting mayor of TMR when the barrier was first approved, already regretted the decision and said that the Wall was in bad taste. Sofoklis Rasoulis, the Montreal city councillor for Parc-Extension, vowed to destroy the Wall in 1988 but was voted out of office before he had the chance. Town residents, though, continued to express their fidelity to the Wall. Montreal mayor Pierre Bourque, who served from 1994 to 2001, observed "the people of TMR seem to have some sort of psychological need for it."[19] Perhaps TMR's insistence on their fence reveals another strain of the Wall Disease, one suffered by those who demand the walls rather than those enclosed by them. Mauerkrankheit expressed as an addiction. A psychological need.

Since the City of Montreal founded Parc-Extension as a community in 1910, the neighbourhood has been a draw for those born elsewhere. The British bought the first houses here. Then, after the Second World War, the neighbourhood swelled with arrivals from Italy and Eastern Europe. Nick's Ukrainian family was among them. Few Eastern Europeans remain in Parc-Extension. Since his mother's passing in 2009, Nick considers himself the last "Ukie" in Parc-X. Greeks moved in en masse in the 1970s, and by 1976 Greek was the neighbourhood 's prevalent mother tongue.

The Greek community remains strong in Parc-Extension, and white-haired Greek men still crowd the entrances to their cafés, but the majority of today's immigrants to Parc-X come from south Asia, Latin America, the Caribbean, Africa, and the Middle East — almost everywhere but Europe. Many restaurant kitchens that once served Greek-style pizza, souvlaki, and roast lamb now offer up cheap lunchtime thalis and tikka kebab. The Europeans who stayed, and who can't bear the tongue-scorching spices, remain loyal to the few remaining Greek tavernas. Nearly every Parc-X *dépanneur* deals in pirated Bollywood videos. West African grocery stores import palm oil and cocoyams and advertise "outdooring" ceremonies for local Ghanaian children. Today, only a third of Parc-X residents were born in Canada. Eighty-six percent of their parents were born somewhere else.

Nick misses the Mediterranean sense of community the Greeks brought to Parc-X, but he appreciates the diversity and colour bestowed by the new arrivals. "There are eighty-seven different languages spoken here," he told me with some pride. On weekends, Montrealers from elsewhere in the city line up for tables in the Indian and Pakistani restaurants. Residents sit and gossip on the street corners until late at night, something Nick never saw even as a young man. "The Greeks still have their independence parade here. And we have the Indian independence parade. The Pakistani independence. The Bangladeshi independence. Everyone is independent, but they all come here to be independent. They don't stay there," he said.

███

The Town of Mount Royal has a more orderly history than Parc-Extension. Officials incorporated TMR in the final days of 1912. Urban planners designed it as a "model city," a sort of urban utopia featuring a central green space bisected by a pair of major roads. What was a small farming community known for its melons quickly became one of Greater Montreal's most desired addresses, especially among wealthy white anglophones. Today's Town is more ethnically and linguistically diverse and its aristocratic gleam has dulled, but the neighbourhood remains homogeneously affluent. Large single-family homes have tidy front lawns and backyard swimming pools. Unlike the littered roadways of Parc-X, Town streets are swept clean and their large park spaces are groomed. The grass is greener, literally, on the other side of the fence.

Jill Moroz lived in TMR, but she'd spent her childhood on the "wrong side" of l'Acadie. Her family home, the only single-family dwelling on the Boulevard, still stands. Her father built the house at an angle to the street so the front window faced directly into every sunset. The slightly askew house was one of the neighbourhood's quirks and countered the strict urban plan of the Town across the street and over the Wall. "I looked at the fence my whole life," Jill said. "Then I moved out and got married and moved to the other side of the fence."

I met Jill in the Little Shop, her store in Parc-X, which, like the neighbourhood itself, was an eccentric homage to disorder. The Little Shop overflowed with vintage clothing and antiques. Costume jewellery hung from the walls beneath shelves lined tight with hats befitting British weddings. In one corner, scraps of fur formed a pile resembling some headless, lumpy sasquatch. When I arrived, a bride-to-be searched for a vintage veil in the lace room, while Jill's university-aged daughter fiddled with an antique camera. I feared moving lest I knock something over with my bag and felt relieved when Jill asked me to sit.

Jill's mother, Ann Silverstone, opened the Little Shop in the 1950s. She filled it with old clothes and costumes and rented to Montreal's theatre and film companies. Ann never advertised and refused to have business cards printed. She felt the place would maintain a kind of cachet if it seemed like a secret. "People came from all around the world," Jill told me. "My mother was an inspiration." Jill took over the store in 2008 after her mother passed away. The Little Shop opens to the public for only three hours on Wednesday, Thursday, and Saturday afternoons. The store is less a secret these days. The Little Shop has business cards now. And a Twitter feed.

Although her mother never made much money with the shop, Jill's family was not poor. Her father worked as a dentist—one of the first in Montreal, she told me. In spite of their relative wealth, growing up in Parc-X implied a lower social standing. "The stigma was there," she said, "that you were on the wrong side of the fence. No question." Jill and her six siblings used to trick-or-treat in TMR when they were children. She always felt she had to "sneak around" there. Her father used to tell a story about crossing through the Wall into TMR to go for a walk. The Town police stopped him and asked if he lived in TMR and what he was doing there. "It really stuck out in his mind," Jill said.

My visit with Jill overlapped with afternoon tea. She respected a tradition begun by her mother decades earlier and served tea and cookies to her customers every day at three o'clock. More people visited the store to eat maple cookies and to chat than to buy anything. Because of my conversation with Jill, everyone talked about the Wall. Each of her customers sneered at the idea that TMR had erected the Wall to protect their children from traffic. They all agreed the barrier was built to keep out the "riff-raff." I heard this word over and over. Jill wasn't so sure. Growing up along l'Acadie, she knew the danger of the roadway. She'd lost a few cats beneath l'Acadie's speeding cars. But she also understood how Parc-Xers perceived the Wall. "It is impossible not to recognize the significance. This area is considered the poorest area in Montreal and it is stuck up against one of the wealthiest areas. So you can invent what you want."

Something else bothered Jill about the Wall, but I could tell she felt uncomfortable bringing it up. "Not that it is true or anything," she began cautiously, "but Parc-X was quite a Jewish area in those days. Jews came in the first wave of immigrants. My parents moved in. Now the community doesn't exist, but back then that was the first wave, before the ethnic communities came." She paused, then quietly added, "And there were no Jews in TMR."

"Are you suggesting the fence was anti-Semitic?" I asked.

Jill recoiled a little. "No. I am just exploring the idea. I don't want to be paranoid. People always say that people are paranoid about discrimination and everything. But look, it was the sixties."

Later, I met with Toby Gilsig at the Parc-X Tim Hortons. Like Jill, Toby grew up in Parc-X and eventually moved to TMR. His parents, too, were first-generation Jewish immigrants. But Toby was more explicit than Jill with the idea that TMR in the 1960s was unfriendly to Jews. After living in Parc-X for twelve years, Toby left Montreal and lived abroad. He returned to Montreal in 1968, when he was twenty-eight years old, with his then-pregnant wife and moved into an apartment in TMR. "My father was really pissed off about it," Toby said. "He told me TMR was a racist, anti-Semitic community. Apparently, not long before then, the Town had a regulation that no Jews could serve on the school commissions."

"Was that true?" I asked.

"I don't know. There were two schooling systems — one Protestant and one Catholic. I don't know if it was a bylaw or a de facto policy."

When Toby was a child in Parc-X, TMR seemed like a "fairyland," a place he would go on Christmas Eve to look at the Christmas decorations but not a place he ever gave much thought to. "You didn't worry about TMR. Those were other people. I would've had a hard time telling you what their faces looked like." When he crossed over the Wall and became one of those other people in 1968, he didn't fit the TMR mould. "It was a very old, anglo-

Britannic community, and we upset them. We were these kids from the sixties. One of my friends had Jesus hair and a Jesus beard. The neighbours got very upset with us. They wrote letters to the paper saying we were going to start growing corn in the front gardens."

Toby didn't give the Wall much thought. He understood the need for a barrier along l'Acadie the same way he understood a community wanting a sound wall to shut out traffic noise. "Does it put up human barriers? Is it a psychological barrier? Does it send a message about relative wealth? I don't know. You tell me. Psychologically, I can see people being pissed off. If my father lived there, he'd be pissed off." Toby paused. "We are conditioned by our upbringing. I can see if you are frustrated, and you feel trapped and hard done by, then this is one more symbol of how the world is keeping you down."

███

I first learned of the l'Acadie Wall through the work of Montreal artist Gisele Amantea. Gisele possesses a kindred fascination with walls and barriers. Before I travelled to Montreal, we spoke on the phone about the large-scale "barricade" work of artists Christo and Jeanne-Claude and discussed the books about barbed wire we'd both read. Finding someone with the same arcane interests was a comfort. None of my friends back home cared much about the aesthetics of chain-link fencing or the cultural history of razor wire.

I visited Gisele's sunlit apartment in Montreal's Mile End neighbourhood where she told me about four barrier-related installation pieces she included in an exhibition of her work in 2010. For a piece called *A Barbed Wire Typology*, Gisele covered a wall with brightly coloured squares of cloth embroidered with images of barbed wire taken from nineteenth-century patent catalogues. She labelled each with the name of the design: Delffs' Tattered Leaf, for example, and Woodruff–Hutchins' Kink. Including their folksy names and portraying each barb individually rather than as multiple pricks along a string of wire robbed the barbs of their cruelty. Gisele transformed them into oddly shaped flower blossoms rather than twists of metal designed to pierce flesh. Nothing of the images recalled the barbs that snagged Jeffrey James's shirts as he climbed into Ceuta. The embroideries would not have looked out of place on a child's bedroom wall. "I take something industrial and they become beautiful and seductive material objects," she said. "And kind of absurd."

Barbed wire featured in another of Gisele's works. Just like peacelines in Belfast and Nicosia's barricades, the fortified line dividing Berlin began as a stretch of barbed wire before it matured into the Berlin Wall. "When they set up the Berlin Wall, they first mapped it out in barbed wire, in the middle of the night, in August 1961," she said. "It was really huge. It went all the way up into the country, something like 160 kilometres long. And it was all erected in barbed wire."

Gisele found a 1961 photograph of East German soldiers standing in front of the barbed wire, the embryonic Wall, and reproduced the coils on a much larger scale with black textured wallpaper called flock. The barbed wire wallpaper covered an entire gallery wall. She called the piece simply *Barbed Wire (Berlin 1961)*. Again, the medium disarmed the image. Steel barbs are cold and sharp, but flock feels like velvet. And since flock wallpaper is always found indoors — Gisele's own childhood living room had red and gold flock — the piece uprooted the wire from its geopolitical line and transplanted it into the family home. Gisele tamed the Wall, domesticated it, and rendered it harmless.

Another flock piece, *The Great Hedge (British India, 19th Century)*, depicted an image of the "Great Hedge of India," perhaps the most bizarre wall I'd read about but had never seen. In the mid-1800s, British colonialists allegedly planted a line of thorny shrubs across India to act as a "customs barrier." The hedge aided the British collection of a salt tax from their Indian subjects. Gisele travelled to India to search for evidence of the hedge. She found none. No one she spoke to had even heard about it. "It was one of those weird things. It was two thousand kilometres [long] or some huge amount. It's believable — you could imagine people doing such idiotic things. Colonialism was bizarre. But it's also unbelievable that no one would know about it."

Gisele remained unconvinced the hedge ever existed, but the historical reality of the barrier interested her less than the image of a gigantic row of shrubs cutting across a nation in order to extract money from "the colonies." The vast vegetal farce appealed to Gisele's artistic sensibility. "It doesn't matter if it was real," she told me. For the work, Gisele researched the sorts of plants that might've made up the Great Hedge, drew her imagining of the barrier, then re-created the image as an eighteen-metre-long flock piece on a gallery wall.

Gisele's final exhibition piece featured the l'Acadie fence. For *The Fence of Shame (TMR<>Park Ex, Montréal)*, she photographed the Wall from both sides, in both winter and summer, and then printed the photographs as long horizontal strips of repeated images that spanned two gallery walls. By including the l'Acadie Wall alongside images of barbed wire, the Berlin Wall, and the colonial nonsense of a titanic hedge, Gisele suggested to her Montreal audience that their wall should not be ignored. "It is really important for the viewer to know that it is not just in some far-off country that we have divisions. It's actually in our own society. It's not just about the 'Other.' We have our own values and prejudices."

Gisele did not aim to subvert the Wall with *The Fence of Shame* as much as to create a consciousness of it. "When you are confronted by those works, I hope you see the repetition and the sense of monumentality. The scale is really important. The works are big, and they kind of immerse you in them. For me, it was more like trying to get people to note that the walls are here, part of our day-to-day life in Montreal, whether you pay attention or not. Look at this. Look at this big line. Think about it."

■■■

Perhaps no one has thought more about the l'Acadie Wall and all it stands for than newspaper columnist Mike Boone. "Growing up in Parc-Extension during the 1950s and '60s, I nurtured a passionate hatred of that fence," Boone wrote in 2005. "It was a divider between Us, apartment and cold-water flat dwellers playing ball hockey in the street, and Them, rich people living in large houses and walking exotic dogs across lush, underused green spaces."[20]

I called Boone to ask him about his childhood across the Wall from the Town of Mount Royal. "TMR was this foreign territory," he said. He didn't remember the Wall going up, only that suddenly it was there, standing between him and his friends and the forbidden green fields where they liked to play football. "It's really hard to play on the narrow urban streets in Parc-X. You fake towards the Chevy and cut towards the Buick. And stop every time a car went by."

So Boone and his mates crossed l'Acadie to play on the Town's athletic fields. Between passing plays, they always looked out for officers of the Town's private police force, who chased them out of TMR and confiscated their footballs. "Occasionally you would see them coming from several blocks away and the game would end. You'd run like hell to get back to Parc-X, football in hand. We were very much made to feel that we were not welcome in the park. And the fence became the physical manifestation of that unwelcome-ness, which isn't a word, but you know what I'm trying to say."

I knew exactly what Boone was saying, because I'd seen it before. Walls everywhere stood as the physical form of prejudices that, though perhaps unspoken, were long held. The walls around Ceuta and Melilla functioned in the same way. They clarified the distinction between the civilized Spanish "Us" and the savage Arab "Them." The l'Acadie Wall discriminated the Townies from the "riff-raff" across the Boulevard. In both cases, the relation-ship between the divided parties was complex. The Spaniards and the Moors shared a long narrative of conflict layered with race and religion, colonialism and servitude, victory and slaughter. Parc-Extension and TMR lacked such historical bloodshed, but notions of exclusivity, relative wealth, culture, and ethnicity likewise blurred the border between them. In the Spanish enclaves as in Montreal, the Wall confronted an intricate relationship with a ham-fisted expanse of steel. The builders of Ceuta's and Melilla's walls opted for a futuristic and motion-sensing barrier, but they needn't have bothered. The plain chain links along l'Acadie achieved the same end. I was struck by how such a simple construction — a few posts, a roll of linked wire — could "disappear" such complexity.

███

In French, the word enclave is also a verb, and Parc-Extension is enclavé. The l'Acadie Wall hems in Parc-X on the west, and railways, themselves guarded by fences, border the neighbourhood on the east and south. Highway 40 forms the northern boundary. The four "walls" enclave Parc-Extension and create one of Montreal's most crowded communities. Thirty-three thousand people press into an area about a kilometre long and half as wide with few official routes in or out. The residents, of course, make their own ways through. Fences fail in Parc-X as they do everywhere else. Employees of businesses on the other side of the railway tracks ignore signs warning DO NOT CROSS UNDER PENALTY OF PROSECUTION and break openings in the fence. Farther north, children used to cut through the same fence to reach the baseball diamonds on the other side of the rail line until the borough opened the fence and added a level crossing over the tracks.

This opening has its own saint. She is painted three storeys tall on an apartment building wall facing the crossing. Her ethnic origins are ambiguous. Borderless. Her dark skin could come from almost anywhere — Pakistan, Barbados, the Ivory Coast. The orange golf shirt she wears gives nothing away. Afternoon swimmers emerging from the public pool below pause to look up at her with chlorine-reddened eyes. So do the hijab-clad mothers on the benches that edge the playground who dare to glance away from their swinging, sliding children. The woman, though, does not return their gaze. She looks, instead, at the fabric in her hands. An embroidered tablecloth from Hungary, lined with lace. A flower-printed bolt of Haitian cloth. Chinese sequins glinting gold against blue. Around her hang fabrics from India, Pakistan, Greece, and Sri Lanka. Canada's "two solitudes," a binary rendered old-fashioned by the multiple ethnicities of Parc-X, plays out with Québécois quilting and English lace.

Parc-Extension commissioned the mural, titled *Cent Motifs, Un Paysage* — "A Hundred Patterns, One Landscape" — for the neighbourhood's centennial celebrations in 2010. Annie Hamel painted the mural and MU, an organization supporting public art in Montreal, coordinated the project. I met MU's Emmanuelle Hébert in front of the mural, and she told me about transforming the wall into a canvas.

"An eighty-year-old Greek lady was the landlord," Emmanuelle said. "She still lives on the third floor. She doesn't go out often because it is hard for her legs. And she only speaks Greek."

The woman's grandson made introductions and translated for Emmanuelle, and the woman granted MU permission to use her wall. Then a team of five artists worked on the mural twelve hours a day for ninety days. The project excited the entire community of Parc-X. Children visited the site every day to mark the artists' progress. During cold mornings in October, a Bangladeshi family who lived in the building, and who spoke no French or English, leaned out of their third-floor window to pass hot coffee and pancakes to the artists. Emmanuelle has seen this sort of engagement with all of MU's projects. "It is amazing the dynamic that murals create," she said.

The dynamic is a sort of insurrection. Murals everywhere subvert the walls they adorn. Walls exclude, but murals invite. During my travels, I'd seen how the walls could be physically defeated. Jeffrey James climbed over. Patricia tunnelled under. Rocky Ghotra was smuggled through. But the artists defeated the walls by transforming them into art. In Arizona, Glenn hammered and bowed the Wall and morphed the vertical steel into music. He revealed that the barrier, instead of dividing two nations, resonates with sounds from both sides at the same time. Breandán Clarke's Draw Down the Walls artists disappeared the walls with photography to imagine an unmutilated city. The Send A Message writers in Ramallah undermined their wall by turning a barrier built to divide into a message board meant to connect. Even the clumsy and clichéd messages of peace hand-scrawled on Belfast's "peacelines" chip away at the barrier by recasting the Wall as a site for shallow tourism. Since anyone with a felt marker, a spray can, or a pair of drumsticks could make art on the walls — and since anyone can then view the art — the barriers became expressions of democracy in spite of themselves.

I asked Emmanuelle if she knew about the Wall along l'Acadie. She scowled. "People of my generation, my friends from Outremont, we all knew about it." Emmanuelle first noticed the barrier when she was in elementary school. "I remember asking my dad, 'Why is there a fence?' and my dad telling me, 'Because TMR people don't want the Parc-Extension people to go there.' I was outraged." Emmanuelle went on to study political science. She advocated for women's rights and trained women to enter politics. She felt that the Wall somehow inspired her to this work. "It was one of the fundamental events when I said, 'Are you fucking kidding me? That's unfair and gross. Who do they think they are?'"

Emmanuelle had a twelve-year-old son, Antoine, who asked her about the Wall a few weeks before my visit. Antoine did not possess his mother's trained eye for social injustice and he was not politically active, or at least not yet, but he knew that something about the Wall looked wrong. When Emmanuelle told him why TMR put up the barrier, Antoine said, "Well, that's stupid."

Antoine's pre-teen comment lacked eloquence but revealed something about the human defiance of barriers. Even though we seem predestined to build walls and fences, once they are up, they simply look wrong. I was a little older than Antoine when the Berlin Wall came down. I was a teenager and too busy ogling the girls to care much about the world beyond the brick walls of my high school. I didn't understand Cold War politics, but I understood, in a most superficial way, that the fall of the Berlin Wall was a good thing. I knew that the Wall was wrong and that its collapse should be celebrated. Like Antoine, I could intuit the Wall's malice in dividing people from one another.

Humanity yearns for open space — space to throw our footballs or grow our olives or graze our camels — and we regard any striation of the land as an affront to our genetic urge to move. We can find joy and comfort in stillness, surely, but only on our terms and only with the certainty that we can stand and walk without obstruction. We are a species of claustrophobic travellers. Walls may define our borders, but they defy our nature. Even a child can see this.

███

TMR's town council may well have erected the Wall to keep their children from chasing errant soccer balls onto the roadway. I had no reason to believe otherwise. But fifty years on, those original intentions no longer mattered. The l'Acadie Wall had mutated into an enduring symbol of the divide between Montreal's moneyed class and immigrant poor. Fairly or otherwise, the Wall labelled TMR a bastion of economic bigotry. Since one side of the Wall is predominantly white and the other predominantly not, the barrier also stirred accusations of racism. Elsewhere in the world, the barrier builders used walls to brand those on the other side as dangerous or devious. The walls cast Bangladeshis, Mexicans, and Palestinians as bogeymen. TMR's wall, though, made a villain of the Town itself. "I've always hated TMR ever since the first time I saw the fence," Emmanuelle told me.

I'd learned that the walls everywhere acted as theatre. Some portrayed a sense of security and exclusion they failed to deliver on. The Wall in Arizona did not keep out Mexicans, but Bill Odle's "lard-ass in Dubuque" thought the steel bars looked pretty secure on television. Other walls, like the barricades in Cyprus, created an illusion of danger that did not exist. The Town of Mount Royal, by contrast, did not use the l'Acadie Wall as theatre—their opponents did. In 2011, when a social housing activist group called FRAPRU wanted to demonstrate the disparity between Montreal's rich and poor and campaign for affordable housing, they marched from Parc-Extension, through the Wall, and into the Town. FRAPRU's coordinator, François Saillant, told me, "TMR is where the money is. They want to hide it and protect it behind their fence. The fence is a strong illustration of how the wealthy are protective of their wealth." Certainly, there were wealthier communities in Montreal than TMR, but those neighbourhoods lacked the convenient symbol of a hated fence.

FRAPRU had used the l'Acadie Wall as a theatre to stage their own drama of inequality and greed. This hardly seemed fair, and I felt sorry for TMR. In spite of the convenient symbolism, I didn't believe the Town deserved the reputation their rusty fence imposed on them. My sympathy waned, though, when I learned that the Town locked the gates on Halloween.

Halloween was the only day of the year that residents of Parc-Extension had a compelling reason to visit TMR. Many Parc-X parents took their children into the town to trick-or-treat. Children would rather ring doorbells at TMR houses than get buzzed into Parc-X apartment buildings and spend the night hiking steep stairwells. Besides, many new immigrants were unfamiliar with the concept of Halloween. I imagined the confusion of a Bangladeshi answering the door to find a little girl dressed as a witch and demanding candy. More importantly, Parc-X children knew the wealthy Townies doled out top-shelf sweets, the bags of chips and full-sized chocolate bars that stood as Halloween's Holy Grails. Each year, the costumed pilgrims from Parc-X migrated across l'Acadie to pass through the Wall into the promised candy land of TMR. Patricia and Rocky crossed their walls in search of better lives; Parc-X kids crossed their Wall in search of better candy.

Mary Deros, the long-serving city councillor for Parc-Extension, used to bring her own children into TMR on Halloween. When I met with Deros in her constituency office, she told me about the difficulty her kids had amassing a "big stash of candy and chocolate" in Parc-X and the "quality candies" given out by residents on the other side of the Wall. Even parents scored in TMR on Halloween night. "There was one lady who made cosmetics and had the habit of giving out samples for the mothers to try out," Deros said.

Starting sometime in the 1990s, however, the costumed kids who crossed l'Acadie for their annual Halloween pilgrimage through the Wall found padlocks on the gates. The Town of Mount Royal had shut them out. Town officials claimed to be protecting the Town against Halloween vandals. The locked gates insinuated that youths from Parc-X were criminals and assumed TMR kids were not.

"We found that demeaning," Deros told me. She pressed TMR's council to stop the annual blockades. TMR refused. The local press covered the story almost every Halloween, but the momentum of outrage peaked in the fall of 2001 when the Quebec secretary of state for immigration issues called the practice of locking the gates a "gesture of racism and visible intolerance."[21] In Ottawa, Member of Parliament Claude Bachand rose in the House of Commons and said: "This means that children from low-income families will not be able to knock on doors of the homes of the wealthy in Mount Royal. This is unacceptable."[22] Even the mayor of the Town of Mount Royal at the time, Ricardo Hrtschan, railed against the locked gates. "It's disgusting," he told the press. "I asked that the gates be left open, but I was overruled."[23] (While the politicians raved, the costumed children of Parc-X shrugged and walked around the fence. They would not be deterred from TMR's high-end chocolate, gate or no gate.)

The Halloween blockades further soured the reputation of the l'Acadie Wall and of the neighbourhood that erected it. One Town resident, wisely remaining anonymous, told the Montreal Gazette, "We have a fence to differentiate us, and we want to keep it that way." The comment revealed that at least some residents of the Town valued the l'Acadie Wall as a symbol of difference. Just like the Wall along India's border with Bangladesh, the l'Acadie Wall imposed an identity on residents of either side whether they liked it or not. Saints on our side of the Wall; sinners on the other. "It would be best not to have relations with the Bangladeshis," Fasluhak had told me along the fence in Tripura, though he could not explain why. The same sentiment existed in TMR. To compare the rusted chain links along l'Acadie with floodlit triple-layer barbed wire may seem ridiculous, but the same desire erected these walls: to clearly distinguish Us from Them.

In the wake of the annual bad press, TMR stopped locking the gates on Halloween in 2002. The gesture did not soften Mike Boone, though, who wrote: "A squad of emergency proctologists should be on standby to help those benevolent Town people extricate toffee apples from where they ought to shove them."[24] After Halloween, the new mayor of TMR, Suzanne Caron, removed the gates completely. When Caron lost her re-election bid in 2005, the new mayor promptly put the gates back in. Residents had stood up in town council meetings and demanded them.

"It would be nice, just for respect, to remove the gates again," Deros said. "Just to indicate there is an openness. To show that we are welcome. If truly in their hearts they feel like we are welcome, that we can come and go without restrictions, then redesign the entrance."

"There are people who call the fence the Berlin Wall or the Fence of Shame," I said. "Do you?"

Deros exhaled, as if frustrated by the hyperbole. "You have to understand that there are some people who will take things out of context. I grew up here. I brought up my three children here. I never thought of the fence as the Berlin Wall. I was always allowed to go across." She repeated to me that she would like to see the gates come out again, but fighting the barrier was hardly a priority for her office. "I have more pressing issues than the fence at this point."

▮▮▮

In Parc-Extension, a dollar buys three cucumbers, five oranges, or a pound of tomatoes. Five dollars buys a box of mangoes sold out of the back of a van on Jean-Talon or a phone card to talk to your family overseas. High weeds along the roadside trap the discarded cards—the detritus of the poor and newly arrived. Cars declare allegiances to gods or homelands. Tiny flags of Greece or India or Ghana are bumper-stickered beneath brake lights or suctioned to dashboards. Plastic Virgins peer over steering wheels. Rosaries, Hindu *malas*, and Muslim *misbahas* hang from rear-view mirrors and divulge with strings of beads the faith of their drivers.

The homes of Parc-Extension reveal nothing of the neighbourhood. At least not in the view from the street. Parc-Extension's flat-fronted row houses and apartment blocks draw the neighbourhood in only two dimensions. One must walk behind the buildings to find any depth of field. Parc-X expresses itself in the back lanes. Here, women clip their wash to clotheslines that run to lampposts and back through squeaking metal wheels. Saris and bedsheets hang like flags. Sequins on *shalwars* flash with sunlight. The women — brown and black, clad in hijabs or the bold prints of Africa — chat across this canyon of brick and laundry on balconies linked by iron stairwells that coil upwards like strands of DNA. Below, squares of lawn — some trim, others surrendered to dandelions — lay littered with plastic toys and bicycles. Foil plates dangle from bits of ribbon to frighten birds away from tiny gardens. Satellite dishes snatch foreign football and cricket games out of the air. These images of Parc-Extension fed poet Carmine Starnino, who lived for a while in the neighbourhood and wrote:

> It suits me down to the ground, this place
> Of sodium-lit nowheres between
> Jean-Talon and St. Roch. Its eighteen-
> Nineteenths of a toehold on the world.
> Flattops beside flattops, planted
> In acres of concrete — ungentrified
> Eden at the brink of the sticks: Parc Ex,
> God said, and up sprang sidestreets of shoebox
> Flats (plus rats), chain link fences, plain-
> Penny bricks, and paint-splashed garages.
> After that, rust-odoured alleys
> Where balding towels and pink panties
> drip dry together like arranged marriages.[25]

Among the poetry of immigrant life in Parc-Extension were other things I'd seen before. The south Asians and Africans making a life in an enclosed space once the realm of Greeks and the multilingual masses at Catholic churches reminded me of Nicosia's Old City. I laughed out loud when I walked down Rue St-Roch and saw a Greek bakery and a Turkish bakery facing each other across the street — the Cypriot conflict played out in cookies and flaky pastry. Each Friday at the Al Sunnah Al Nabawiah Mosque across from the metro station, Bengali Muslims like those on the wrong side of the Wall in northeast India bent their prayers eastward alongside Arab immigrants from Palestine. Jeffrey James's and Rocky Ghotra's failed migrations trapped them behind Ceuta's wall, but their more successful brethren ended up in Parc-X, seeking familiar comforts in African groceries and Sikh gurdwaras while exploring the possibilities of the new country. Non-status immigrants reside in Parc-Extension just as they do in Tucson. They work lousy jobs to send money home, evade deportation, and wonder if Canada was really worth the trouble. Much of what I'd seen elsewhere was here in miniature — alongside a miniature wall. I felt an affinity for the Parc-Xers whose homelands I'd travelled to see and with whom I now share a country.

Parc-Extension represents the best of Canada. The neighbourhood stands as a symbol of the inclusivity and openness that Canadians take pride in. But seeing the Wall on l'Acadie made me think of my time with Bill Odle and the profane sadness he expressed with respect to his wall. On that November afternoon in Arizona, Bill recited the inscription on the Statue of Liberty that invited the tired, poor, and "tempest tost" masses to find a home in America, where Lady Liberty lifted her lamp "beside the golden door." The Wall betrayed Bill's belief in Liberty's promise. The Wall committed patriotic treason and tarnished his gilded idea of America. At the time, I couldn't understand Bill's grief. His country does not represent for me what it does for him. I do not love America. But I do love Canada, and as I walked along l'Acadie, I felt a kindred sadness with Bill. The l'Acadie Wall betrayed the vision of what *my* country stands for: equality, opportunity, and welcome. The two barriers could not compare in scale, but the Wall along l'Acadie seemed even more sinister because it defiled my sacred sense of home.

The immigrants themselves, however, didn't seem to care. I visited the cavernous Shree Ramji Temple on the edge of Parc-X to speak with Vijay Patel. So as not to disturb the Hindu worshippers in the prayer hall, Vijay and I spoke in the temple's quiet cloakroom. He told me that about 1,200 Hindu families held membership at the Temple, and most had immigrated to Montreal from villages within fifty kilometres of each other in Gujarat, India. "Some whole villages are here," Vijay said. "Not a single house is left." Vijay worked in a machine shop, making parts for a valve company. In Gujurat, though, Vijay had worked on the family farm. To keep his fingers in the soil, Vijay tended a small garden in his Parc-X backyard. "We do the chili, the eggplant, lady's fingers, and beans," he said.

When I asked him about the Wall, he seemed embarrassed for me. "I know there is a fence on l'Acadie, but I not notice about that," he said in imperfect English. "There is no time to fight, we are working so much." This was the common refrain of the immigrants I met in Parc-Extension. Like Mary Deros, they had more pressing issues than the Wall to deal with. They filled their days with the obligations of the New Country. Citizenship papers and school fees. Daycare and groceries and rent. Second-hand coats for their first cold winters, and money wired to families who've never known such cold. No one had the luxury of time to worry about a rusted old fence on the other side of the road. Perhaps the most effective way to bring down a wall is to disregard it. To simply not care. An ignored wall ceases to be a barrier at all.

After spending three years travelling along the barricades, though, I could not ignore the l'Acadie Wall. I'd fastened everything I'd seen, and all the stories I'd heard, on the scabbed chain links. Felani Khatun hung wedding-day dead from the fence, with shreds of Jeffrey James's shirts and flesh snagged around her like confetti. I watched a Moroccan soldier's lighter flash on the Boulevard and a Palestinian farmer peer through the fence at his starved olive trees. I could not look at the fence without seeing slung stones and petrol-filled beer bottles arc overhead from one side to the other, clattering beneath the cars on l'Acadie or spreading brief flame over TMR's tidy streets. The battered fence strained under the weight of all I laid upon it and leaned like the old fence posts on Imperial Beach. Most people I spoke to in Parc-Extension said the fence was "just a fence." Not to me.

███

About six kilometres east of the "Berlin Wall of Montreal" stands a section of the actual Berlin Wall. In 1992, on the occasion of Montreal's 350th birthday, the City of Berlin gave the city a rough sliver of concrete about three metres tall and a metre wide salvaged from the Wall's great fall in 1990. Vivid graffiti covers what was the western side of the slab. An orange sunburst. Swirls of green and blue. The letters "EAS," no doubt part of a longer word truncated when the Wall came down. There is no such decoration on the severe eastern side. Just a few numbers and initials. The lost acronyms of the Iron Curtain.

The slab used to form part of the "anti-fascist protection bulwark" near Berlin's Brandenburg Gate. Now it stands in a shopping mall on the first floor of Montreal's World Trade Centre, a name that sounded less ominous back in 1992. I considered a downtown shopping mall an undignified resting place for a fragment of the Berlin Wall. A mall is a place to find an Orange Julius, not an exalted remnant of the Cold War. Then again, all the walls I'd seen represented the trade and transfer of goods. Smugglers carried toilet paper through the walls in Morocco and lifted cattle over the fences in northeast India. Coyotes led migrant workers past the Wall, *narcos* pushed drugs through it, and kids from Parc-X walked around it in search of candy. Shoppers in Nicosia knew that prices were lower on the other side of the dead zone. Both the berm in the Western Sahara and the Wall in the West Bank hoarded valuable real estate. Sometimes the Wall itself became a commodity. In Ramallah, artist Basel Abbas complained how the Wall had become a simplified and easily digestible symbol for activists to consume. Tourists posed for photos in front of Belfast's barriers, paid Bethlehem taxi drivers to show them the graffiti on the West Bank Wall, and passed through the barricades in Nicosia for the thrill of crossing through forbidden space. Each wall symbolized commerce in one way or another.

The shard of the Berlin Wall reminds us that walling is a human impulse. The ancient emperors of Rome and China taught us this first and passed along a hereditary urge to harden our edges with bricks and mortar, barbs and steel. I'd travelled to see what happens after the Walls rise and to learn what it means to live alongside a wall. I discovered that the walls breed societies of resistance in their shadows. Resilient men and women such as Patricia, Malainin Lakhal, and Rocky Ghotra, who physically defeated their walls. Artists such as Glenn Weyant and Breandán Clarke, who drew down the walls by reimagining them. Activists such as Ian McLaughlin, Mohammad Othman, and Kat Rodriguez, who worked to dress the wounds the walls inflicted. Although I never found a wall about to fall, I did find a kind of optimism in the actions of the resisters—a faint glance to an imagined time when the walls stand disassembled in distant shopping malls. This is what I had wanted to find.

But I found more despair than hope. I found families shattered along the walls and bodies scarred. I learned of withered dead lying in deserts and saw hate boil hot and steady. Torn flesh and thrown stones did not stall the new Hadrians, nor did the tears of mothers and migrants and refugees dissuade them. The walls rise and grow and multiply. They are both human and inhumane. The walls are our compulsion. The walls are our chronic disease.

The cracked relic of the Berlin Wall stood in downtown Montreal because it revealed something else: the urge to tear down barriers is a stronger impulse than the urge to build them. We cannot help but subvert the walls. What eventually wins out is not the crude desire to wall but the impulse to break through. The piece of the Berlin Wall in Montreal was a gift to the city, a trophy, because it symbolized a fallen wall and a barrier that surrendered to a human compulsion greater than that which built it. The fragment reminds us of the inevitability of our better natures and in this the constant thrum of hope. The walls will continue to rise, and we will continue to tear them down.

Acknowledgements

I owe a great debt to the other "wall thinkers" out there, especially Bryon Finoki, whose work both inspired and informed this book; and Christine A. Leuenberger, who first introduced me to the concept of Mauerkrankheit. I would also like to thank Jayinta Ray, Wendy Brown, Colm Heatley, Elisabeth Vallet, Miguel Diaz-Barriga, Margaret Dorsey, and Ronald Rael for their work on the walls.

I am most grateful to those I met along the Walls who were so generous with their stories, their insights, and their time. This book is for them. They are:

In the Western Sahara: Malainin Lakhal, Abdulahe, Damaha Lahcen, Mustapha Said Bashir, Nasiri and Hamid in Smara, the two Saleks, and all the refugee families who welcomed me into their homes. Also John Thorne, Eve Coulon, Tom Pfeiffer, and Sadat in Tarfaya.

In Ceuta and Melilla: Rocky Ghotra, Benji Lopez, Mercedes Rubio, José Palazón, Linda Ebbers, Kevin O'Donovan, "Sha," and the staff at Centro UNESCO Melilla.

In India: James Perry, Kazu Ahmed, Xonzoi Barbora, Utpal Barman, Debunker, Dhanya Pilo, and Angad Chowdury.

In Cyprus: Stavros Stavrou Karayanni, Thodoris Tzalavras, Ioanna Mavrou, Stephanos Stephanides, Paul Stewart, Öncel Polili, Yiannis Papadakis, Captain Mike Solonynko, and Nilgün Güney.

In Israel: Ilene Prusher, David Elhrich, and Ir-Amim.

In Palestine: Mohammad Othman, Aidan Macdonald, Basel Abbas, Yusef Njim, Faris Arouri, and Mahmoud Abu Hashhash.

283

Along the U.S.–Mexico border: Bill Odle, Kat Rodriguez, Ofelia Rivas, Walter Collins, Glenn Weyant, Father Peter Neely and the KINO Border Initiative, Margaret Regan, Randy Serraglio, Steve Johnston, John Heid, No More Deaths, Patricia, Mark Adams, Ginny Jordan, John Fanestil, Alberto Rios, and Kinsee Morlan.

In Belfast: Teena Patrick, Breandán Clarke, Neil Jarman, Ian McLaughlin, Billy and Violet, Santos, Manpreet Singh, Frankie Quinn, Martin Adams, Andrew Johnston, Robin Wilson, Ruth Graham, Ursula Burke, and Zoë Murdoch. (Thank you, too, to Will Ferguson for the pile of books.)

In Montreal: Mary Deros, Giuliana Fumagalli, Mary McCutcheon, Tamara Atchman, Toby Gilsig, Jill Moroz, Nick Semeniuk, Gisele Amantea, Emmanuelle Hébert, Maria Di Giambattiste, Vijay Patel, and Carmine Starnino.

I would like to thank the Banff Centre and, especially, those who worked with me during the 2008 Literary Journalism Program: Ian Pearson, Marni Jackson, Moira Farr, Rich Poplak, Medeine Tribinevicius, Jeff Warren, Jeremy Klaszus, Megan Williams, Lynn Cunningham, and Ruth Lopez.

I completed much of this book during my residency with the Calgary Distinguished Writer Program at the University of Calgary. Thank you to the Steering Committee and, especially, Janice Lee and Jackie Flanagan.

Special thanks to Chris Koentges, Richard Harrison, and Peter Oliva, who offered feedback on messy fragments of early drafts.

I could not have survived this project without funding from the Canada Council for the Arts and the Alberta Foundation for the Arts. Thanks, too, to Shirley Dunn and the Dave Greber Freelance Writers Prize.

Special thanks to the editors of *Geist Magazine*, who published two excerpts from the work-in-progress. "Wall of Shame" appeared in *Geist*'s Fall 2009 issue, and "The Great Wall of Montreal" appeared in the Fall of 2011.

I owe a fantastic debt to my friend and editor, John Vigna, whose hard work helped transform a collection of travel journals into something that resembles a book. Thanks, too, to my agent Jackie Kaiser and to Susanne Alexander at Goose Lane—both of whom believed in this project long before they had any reason to do so.

Finally, thanks to Moonira Rampuri and Amedeo Ihsan Di Cintio. I cannot think of two people I'd rather share four walls with.

The Author gratefully acknowledges the permission to reproduce the following material. Every effort has been made to secure permission for excerpts reproduced in this book on the following pages:

p. 13 Excerpt from "Maginot Line" by Geoff Berner from *We Shall Not Flag or Fail, We Shall Go On to the End*, copyright © 2002 by Black Hen. Reprinted by permission.

pp. 13-14 Excerpt from *The Butter Battle Book* by Dr. Seuss, TM & Copyright by Dr. Seuss Enterprises, L.P. 1984. Used by permission of Random House Chidlren's Books, a division of Random House Inc.

p. 22 Excerpt from unpublished poem by Malainin Lakhal. Reprinted by permission.

pp. 23-24 Excerpt from "Living Next Door to Alice" by Nicky Chinn and Mike Chapman, from *Smokie*, copyright © 1978 by Universal Music Publishing Group. Reprinted by permission.

p. 74 Excerpt from "Partition" by W.H. Auden from *Atlantic*, copyright © 1966 by W.H. Auden. Reprinted by permission of Curtis Brown, Ltd.

pp. 184-186 *"La Ruta de las Mujeres"* ("The Women's Route"), written and translated by Reverend Delle McCormick. Reprinted by permission.

p. 245 Excerpt from "Belfast Confetti" by Ciaran Carson from *The Irish for No*, copyright © 1987 by Gallery Press/Wake Forest University Press. Reprinted by permission.

p. 277 Excerpt from "This Way Out" by Carmine Starnino from *This Way Out*, copyright © 2009 by Gaspereau Press. Reprinted by permission.

ENDNOTES

1. Hans-Joachim Maaz, *Der Gefühlsstarr: Psychogramm einer Gesellschaft* (Berlin: Argon Verlag, 1990), p. 152.

2. Geoff Berner, "Maginot Line," lyrics, *We Shall Not Flag or Fail, We Shall Go On to the End* (Vancouver: Black Hen Music, 2002).

3. Dr. Seuss, *The Butter Battle Book* (New York: Random House, 1984), pp. 4-6.

4. Malainin Lakhal, unpublished poem.

5. Nicky Chinn and Mike Chapman, "Living Next Door to Alice," lyrics, *Smokie* (London: Universal Music Publishing Group, 1978).

6. Michel Vieuchange, *Smara: The Forbidden City*, trans. Edgar Fletcher Allen (New York: W.W. Norton and Co., 1932. Reprinted New York: Ecco Press, 1997).

7. R.K. Prabhu, "Preface," in M.K. Gandhi, *India of My Dreams*, compiled by R.K. Prabhu (Ahmedabad, India: Navajivan Publishing House, 1947), p. 4.

8. W.H. Auden, "Partition," *Atlantic Monthly*, August 1966.

9. Sunil Khilnani, *The Idea of India* (London: Penguin, 1998), p. 80.

10. Jagdish N. Bhagwati, "US Immigration Policy: What Next?" *Essays on Legal and Illegal Immigration*, ed. Susan Pozo (Kalamazoo, MI: W.E. Upjohn Institute for Employment Research, 1986), p. 124.

11. Neşe Yaşın, Filiz Naldöven, Lily Michailidou, Fikret Demirağ, Elli Peonidou, Zeki Ali, Takis Hadjigeorgiou,Tamer Öncül, Feriha Altok,

Neriman Cahit, M. Kansu, Stephanos Stephanides, Gür Genç, Jenan Selçuk, Michalis Papadopoulos, and Aydın Mehmet Ali, "Yes, What a Joyful Word," *Bianet News*, April 5, 2004.

12. G.S. Geoghallides, "Cyprus and Winston Churchill's 1907 Visit," *Thetis* 3 (1995), p. 184.

13. Gloria Anzaldúa, *Borderlands La Frontera: The New Mestiza* (San Francisco, Aunt Lute Books, 2007), p. 25.

14. Reverend Delle McCormick, "La Ruta de las Mujeres" ("The Women's Route"), *Conspirando*, October 2008.

15. Alberto Alvero Rios, *Capirotada: A Nogales Memoir* (Albuquerque: University of New Mexico Press, 1999), p. 12.

16. Barack Obama, "A World That Stands as One" (Speech delivered in Berlin, July 24, 2008).

17. Thomas Harding, "The Security Wall on Our Doorstep," *Daily Telegraph*, February 25, 2004.

18. Ciaran Carson, "Belfast Confetti," *The Irish for No* (Winston-Salem, NC: Wake Forest University Press, 1987), p. 31.

19. *Montreal Mirror*, November 8, 2001.

20. Mike Boone, "Time to Rethink Symbolic Fence," *Montreal Gazette*, May 17, 2005.

21. *Le Devoir*, November 1, 2001.

22. Claude Bachand from 37th Parliament, 1st Session, *Hansard*, Number 106, Wednesday October 31, 2001.

23. *Montreal Gazette*, November 1, 2001.

24. Mike Boone, "Halloween Gesture Another Class Act," *Montreal Gazette*, October 11, 2002.

25. Carmine Starnino, "This Way Out," *This Way Out* (Kentville, NS: Gaspereau Press, 2009), p. 19.